PAINTING INTO
THE LIGHT

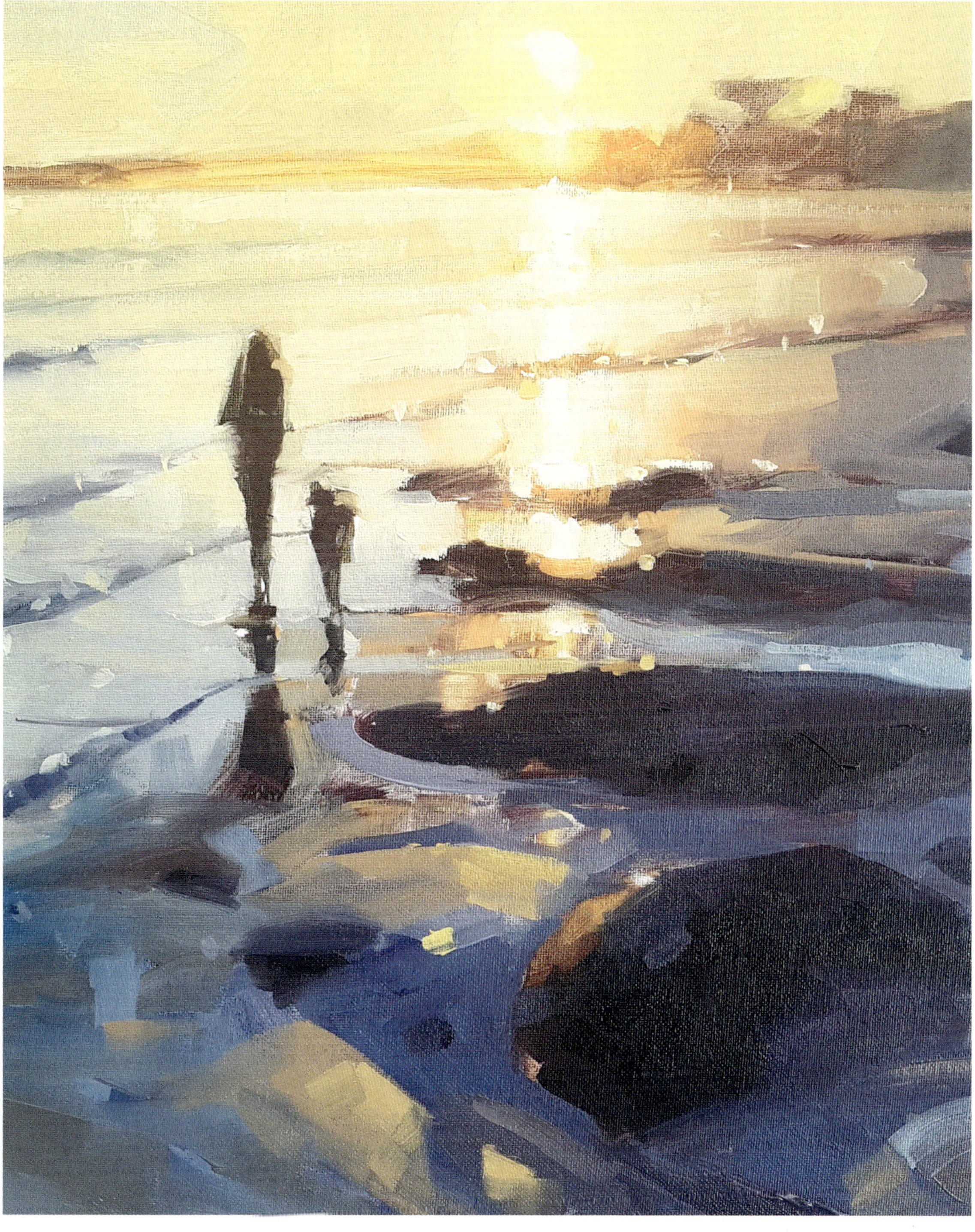

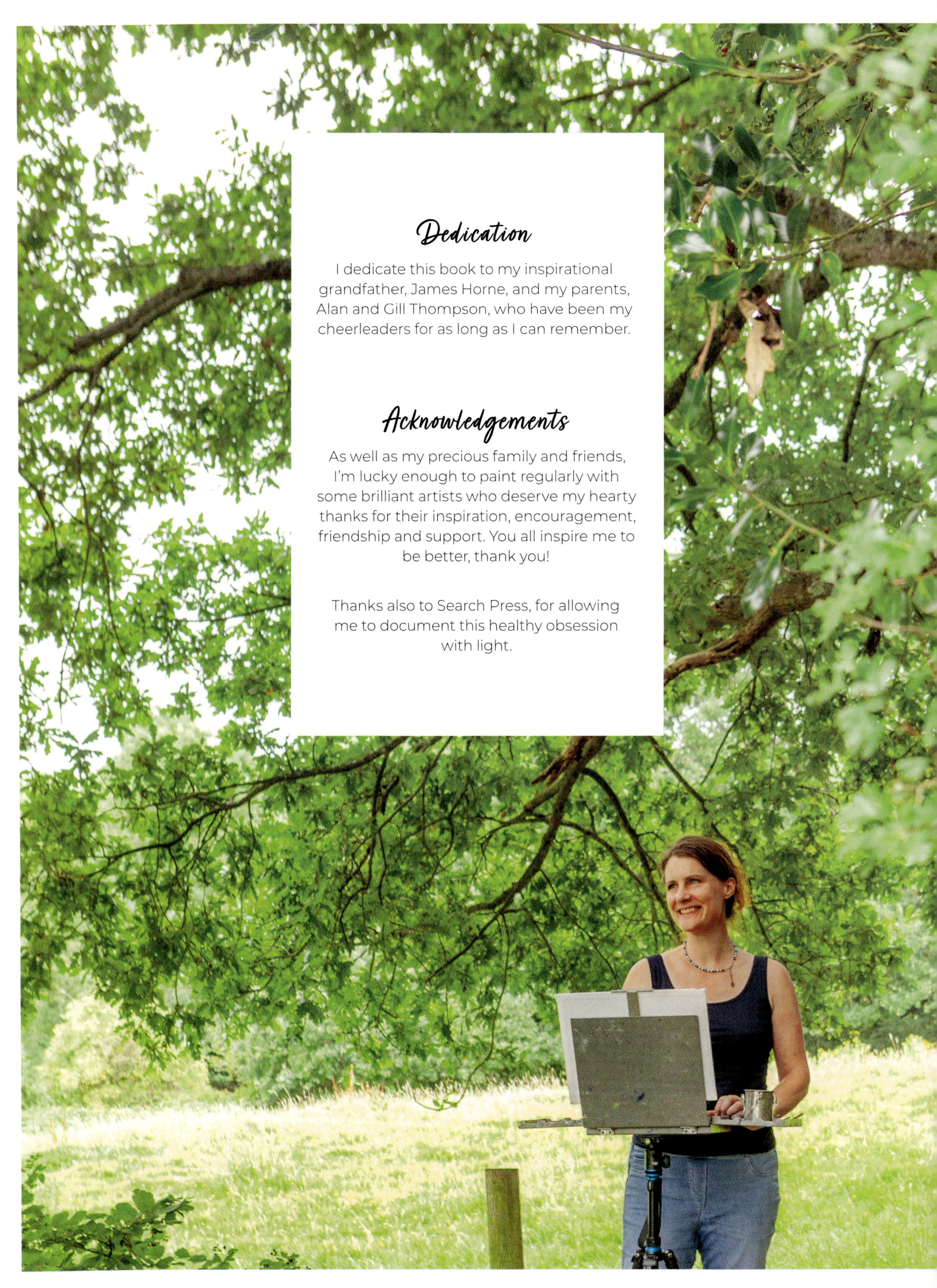

Dedication

I dedicate this book to my inspirational grandfather, James Horne, and my parents, Alan and Gill Thompson, who have been my cheerleaders for as long as I can remember.

Acknowledgements

As well as my precious family and friends, I'm lucky enough to paint regularly with some brilliant artists who deserve my hearty thanks for their inspiration, encouragement, friendship and support. You all inspire me to be better, thank you!

Thanks also to Search Press, for allowing me to document this healthy obsession with light.

PAINTING INTO THE LIGHT

HOW TO WORK ATMOSPHERIC MAGIC WITH YOUR OIL PAINTS

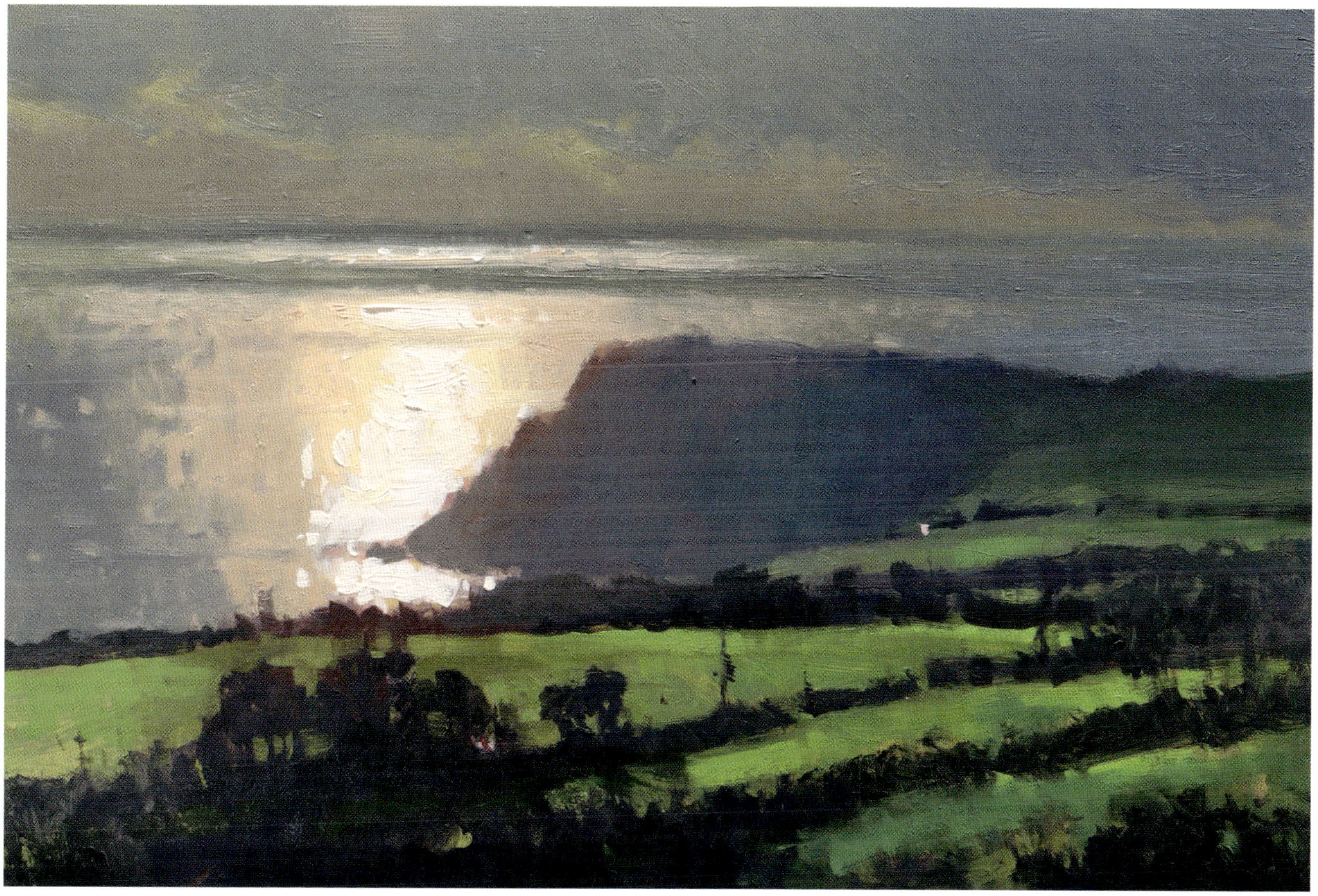

JENNY AITKEN

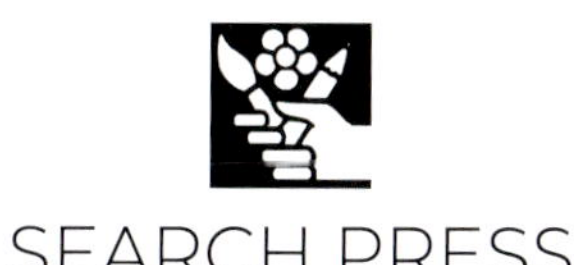

CONTENTS

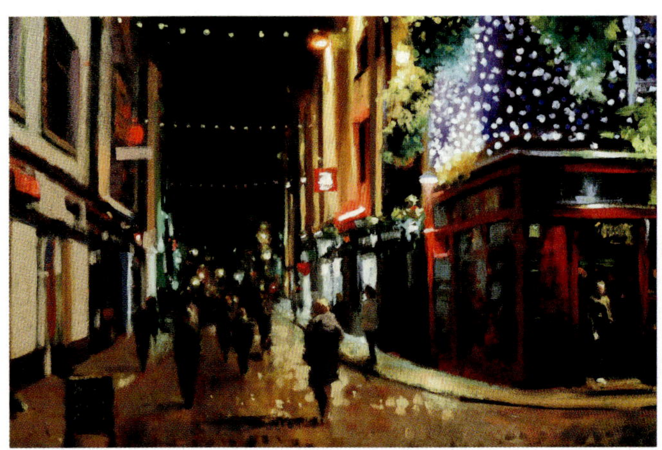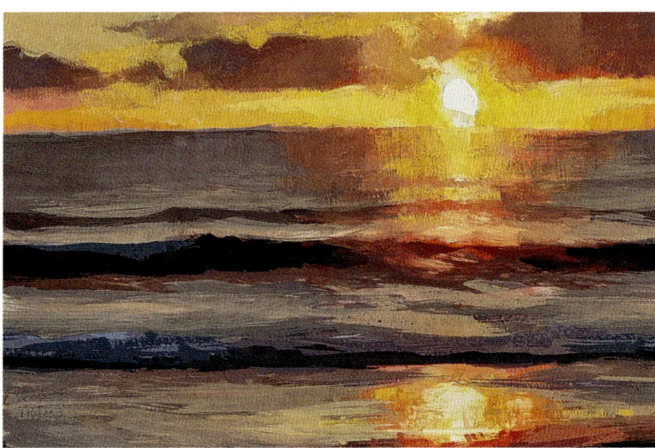

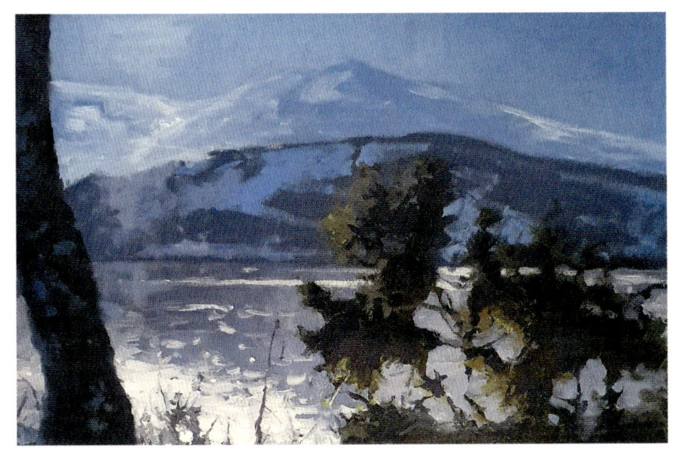 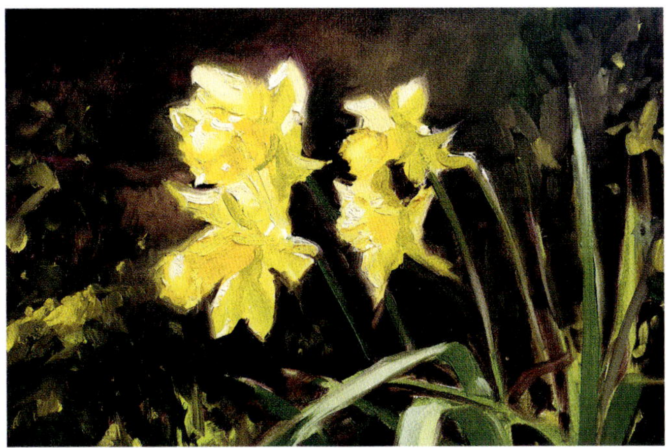

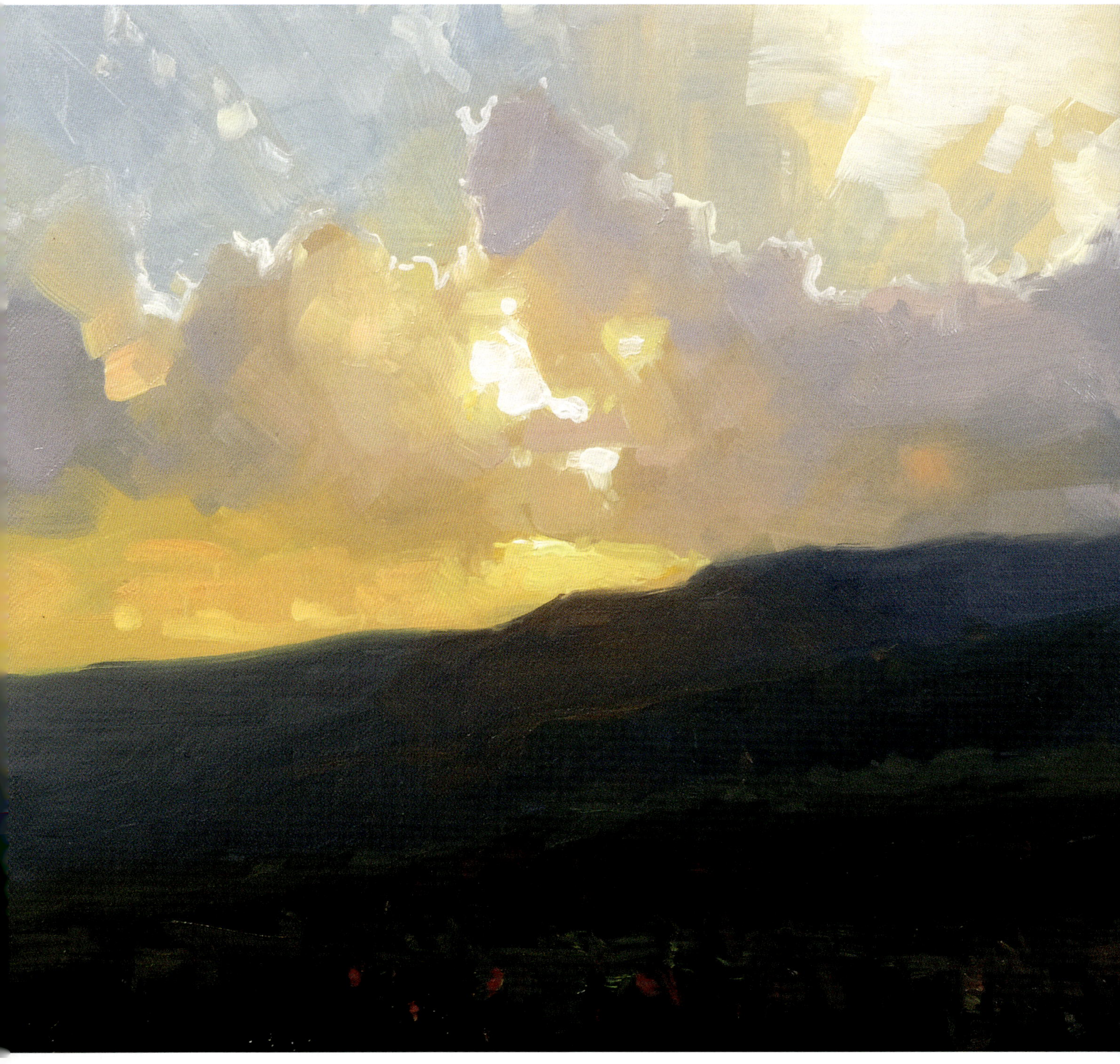

Owls and Clouds, Whernside

30 × 20cm (11¾ × 8in)

During the turbulence of 2020, wildlife seemed to take a big breath and thrive. This view, bereft of contrails, was a moment from a silent evening walk that brought me glimpses of tawny owls hunting, and a barn owl so close I could almost feel his wing beats.

The land looks dark, but if you look closer, you can see the warmth in the hill nearest the yellow sun, and some orange notes in the foreground for unity. I applied the paint with the face of a 12mm (½in) flat brush, looking for subtle blends and temperature contrasts. Any obvious angles are there to draw the eye in towards that focal point of brightest light.

FOREWORD

by David Curtis ROI, RSMA

This book is testament to Jenny's extraordinary energy in celebrating her love of painting into the light. She explores all the possible nuances that extreme light can play on the landscape and figures within her compositions.

My association with her is largely through outdoor painting venues with our group of like-minded and very experienced professional painters. Invariably the first to set up an easel, she will, on occasion, briefly leave the painting in progress, to speedily produce some delightful cameo of a fleeting backlit waterfowl, cow, horse or anything unmissable that has caught her sharp observant eye – then back to the original work on the easel.

Jenny is much admired by us all. We marvel at her dedication and determination to this most demanding of creative processes. She loves to be out in the open landscape of the Lake District and her native Derbyshire Peak District, producing stunning images of mountain, moorland, waterfalls and woodland scenes, invariably bathed in bright sunlight... all a joy to the eye.

The paintings in this book will delight all who celebrate subjects depicting dazzling light, and I am sure it will encourage readers to learn from the guidance and demonstrations presented within these pages.

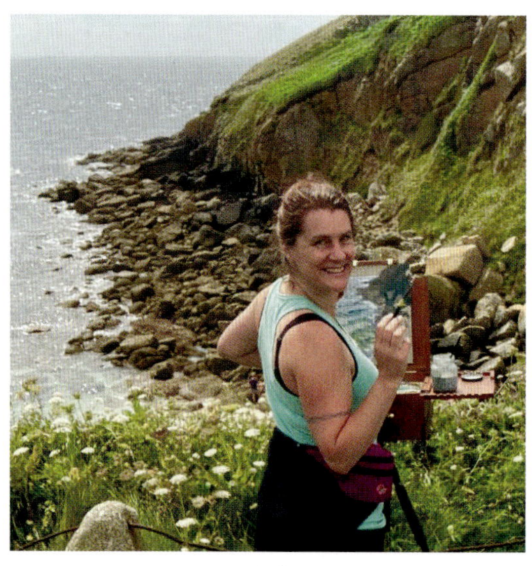

INTRODUCTION

I have spent most of my artistic life studying the magic of light. To gaze at a two-dimensional surface and consider how best to use paint to describe real depth, atmosphere and light upon it is a source of constant fascination to me.

Contre-jour painting – to paint looking into the source of light – takes this illusion to the next level. A successful result will cause the viewer to squint into the glow emerging from the canvas. With their hazy light and singing colour, such paintings can seem magical.

Magic, of course, is only ever achieved by method, and looseness achieved through discipline. With this book, I hope to demystify light and provide a practical guide to help you create the illusion with oil paint. Through stage-by-stage painting demonstrations and clear, illustrated methods of working, I will show you how to bring every painting to life with light.

Opposite:

Beach Dancing

50 × 76cm (19¾ × 30in)

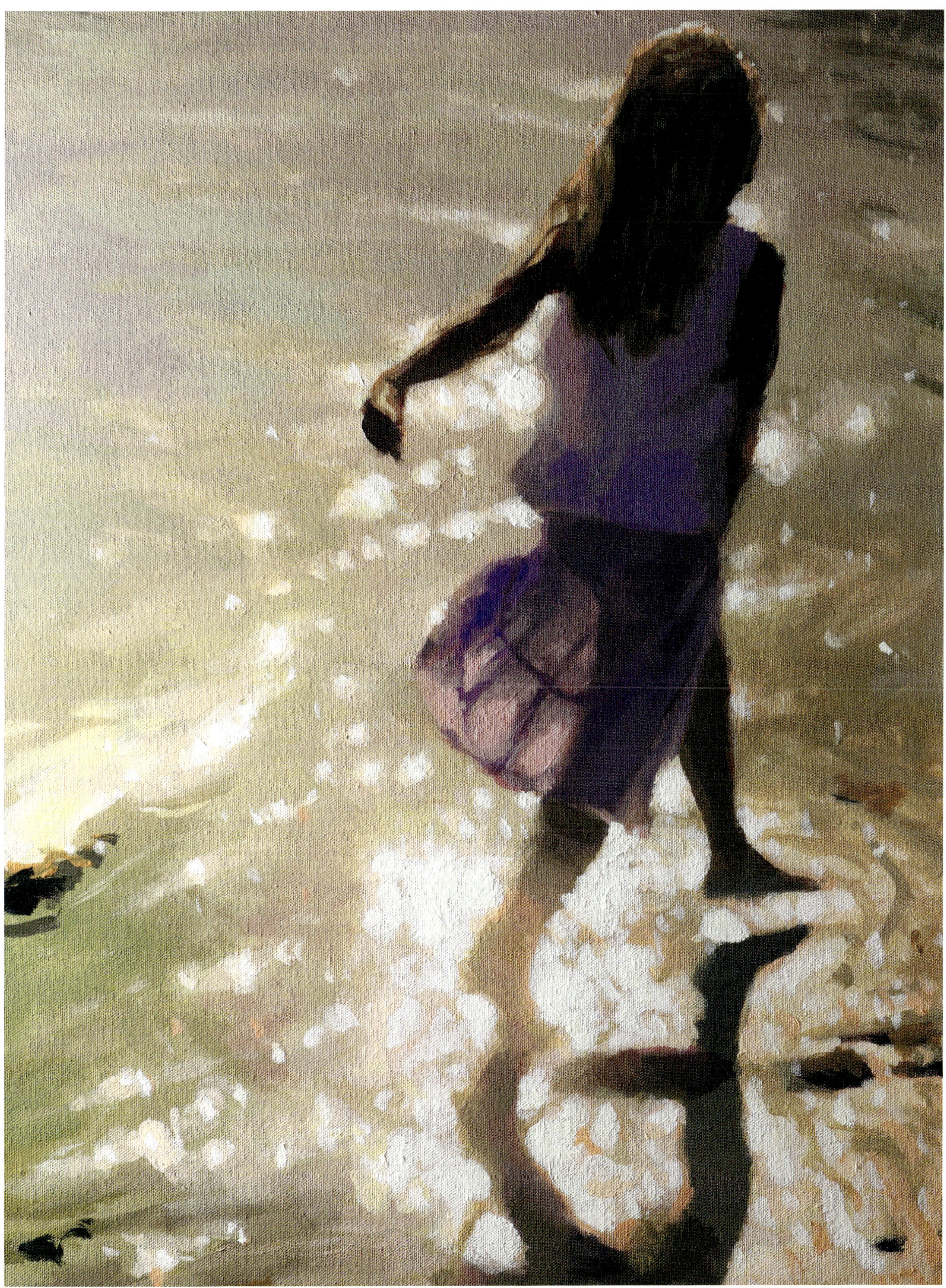

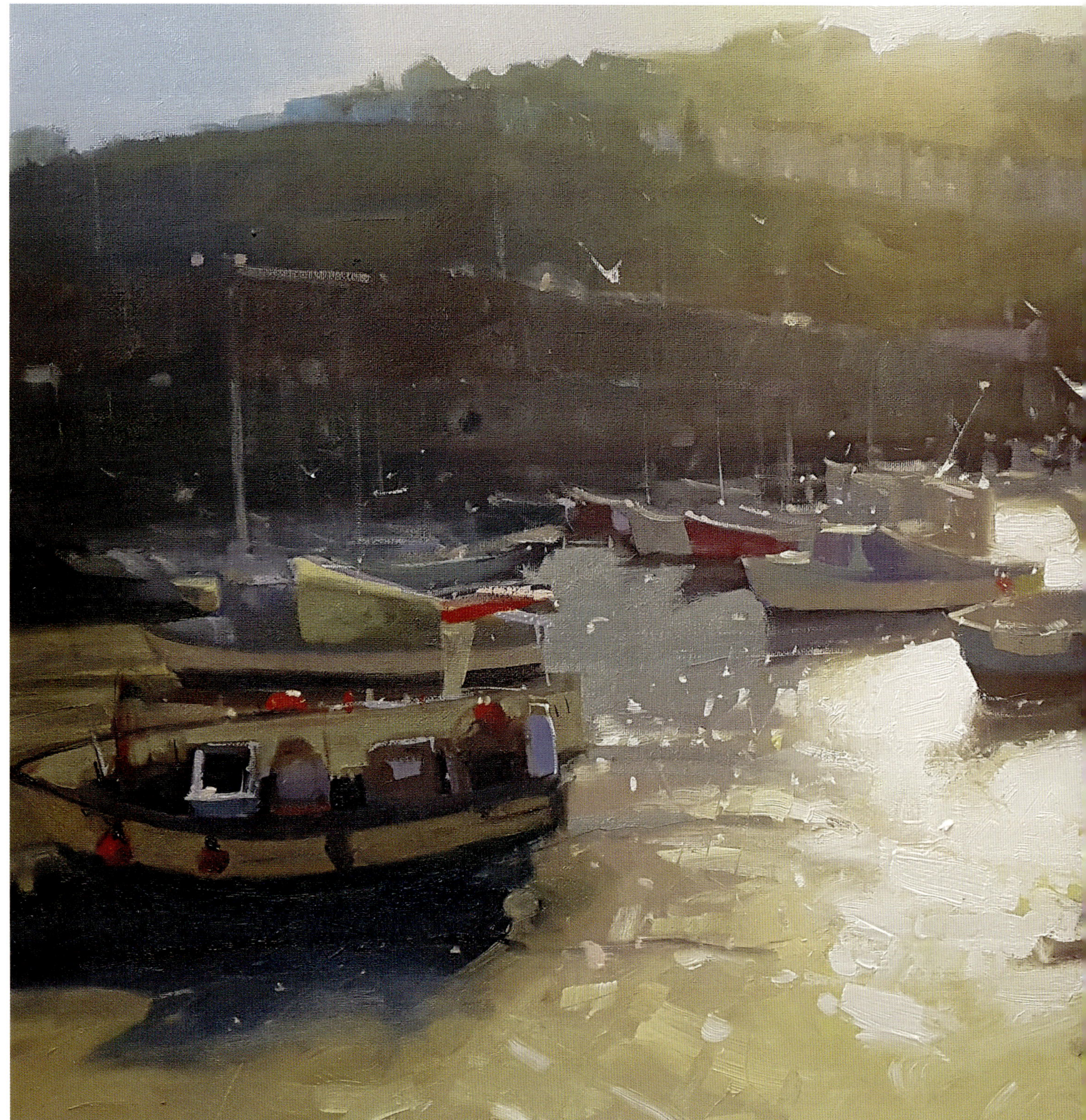

Mevagissey Light

76 × 50cm (30 × 19¾in)

Early evening by the harbour, as the sun heads round to the west. I love including dark backdrops in contre-jour work for the added drama.

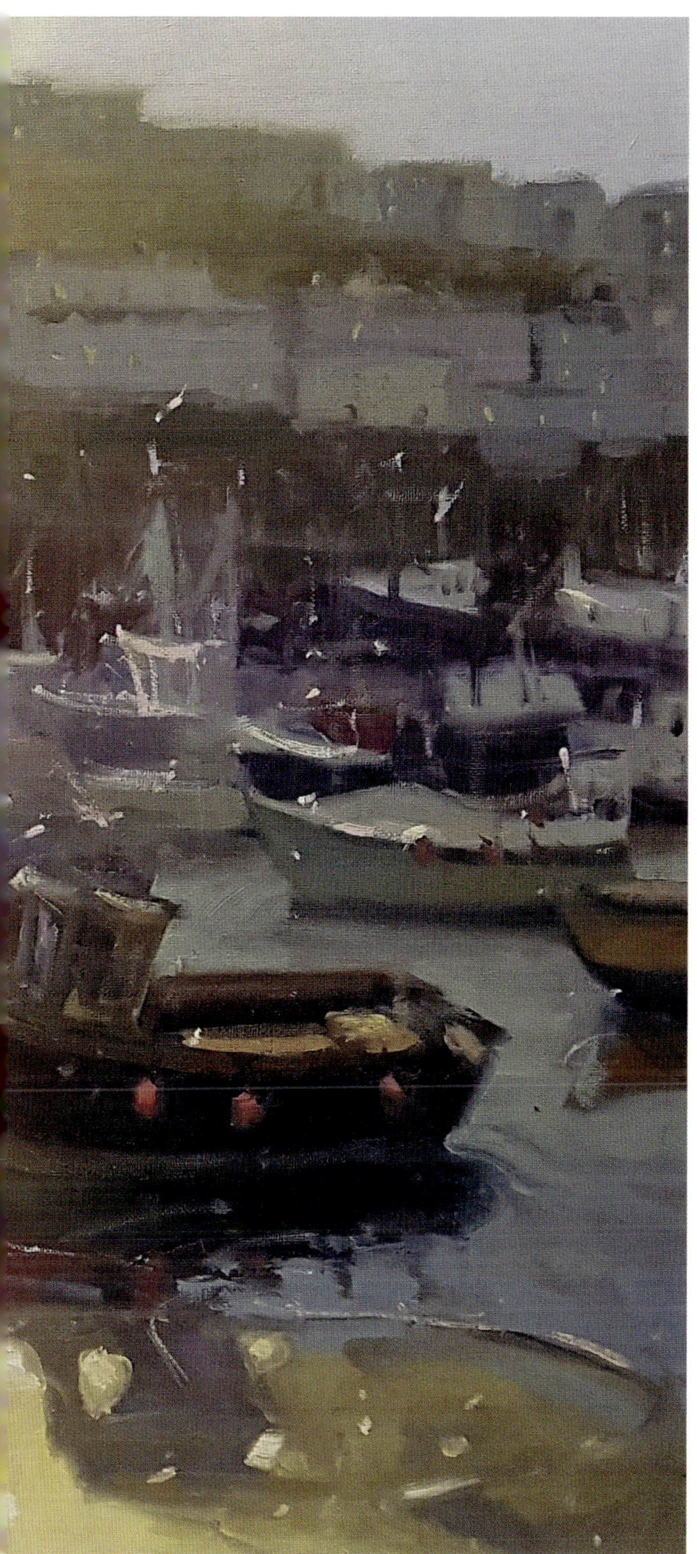

No matter the subject, the art of sparkling *contre-jour* begins with careful observation of colour values and temperature contrasts – but knowing and understanding what you are likely to be seeing is key.

Painting the light relies as much on noticing it in the first place as being able to evoke it on a canvas. John Singer Sargent (1856–1925), one of the most prominent painters of light, said this:

'Appreciation of value is merely training of the eye, which everyone ought to be able to acquire.'

As entranced by light as I have always been, I certainly couldn't always paint it – or even discern it – the way I do now. I trained my eye, and I continue to do so, by studying all aspects of this subject that I love. I take and pore over thousands of photographs, play with effects in the studio and spend a lot of time painting outside, *en plein air*. The more I learn, the more I see that there is to learn. The world of *contre-jour* painting is a treasury to discover and explore.

Perhaps the main message I would like you to take away from this book is to slow down and stare. Look, look more, then look again! We move so quickly through life, our experience of events so brief, that the beauty surrounding us can pass in a blur. There is so much to discover in even the simplest of subjects.

PREPARING TO CAPTURE LIGHT

Whether painting indoors or out, lighting must be your first and most important consideration. The light in which you are working needs to be as constant as possible for the duration.

Rushing into a painting without planning and forethought is never the best idea. It may sound obvious, but once you start, you want full focus on your subject – and as far as is possible, to be without distraction or interruptions. To help with this, read through this chapter, make sure everything you need is ready and accessible, and you have the right tools for the job.

The paints and brushes you need are explained in more detail in this chapter. Working *contre-jour* demands a lot of subtle greys that don't come straight out of the tube, so make sure you have a large enough palette for mixing colours. Besides these, you'll also need a surface to paint on – I recommend canvas boards, which are widely available in a range of sizes. Have rags or wet wipes to hand for cleaning, a bag for waste and a couple of jars of low-odour solvent for thinning paint and washing brushes.

An easel, whether a standing easel or one that sits on a table, is another key piece of equipment. Your neck and shoulders will thank you! I use both a studio easel and a pochade box when painting outside. Working this way encourages you to stand back often and evaluate your work.

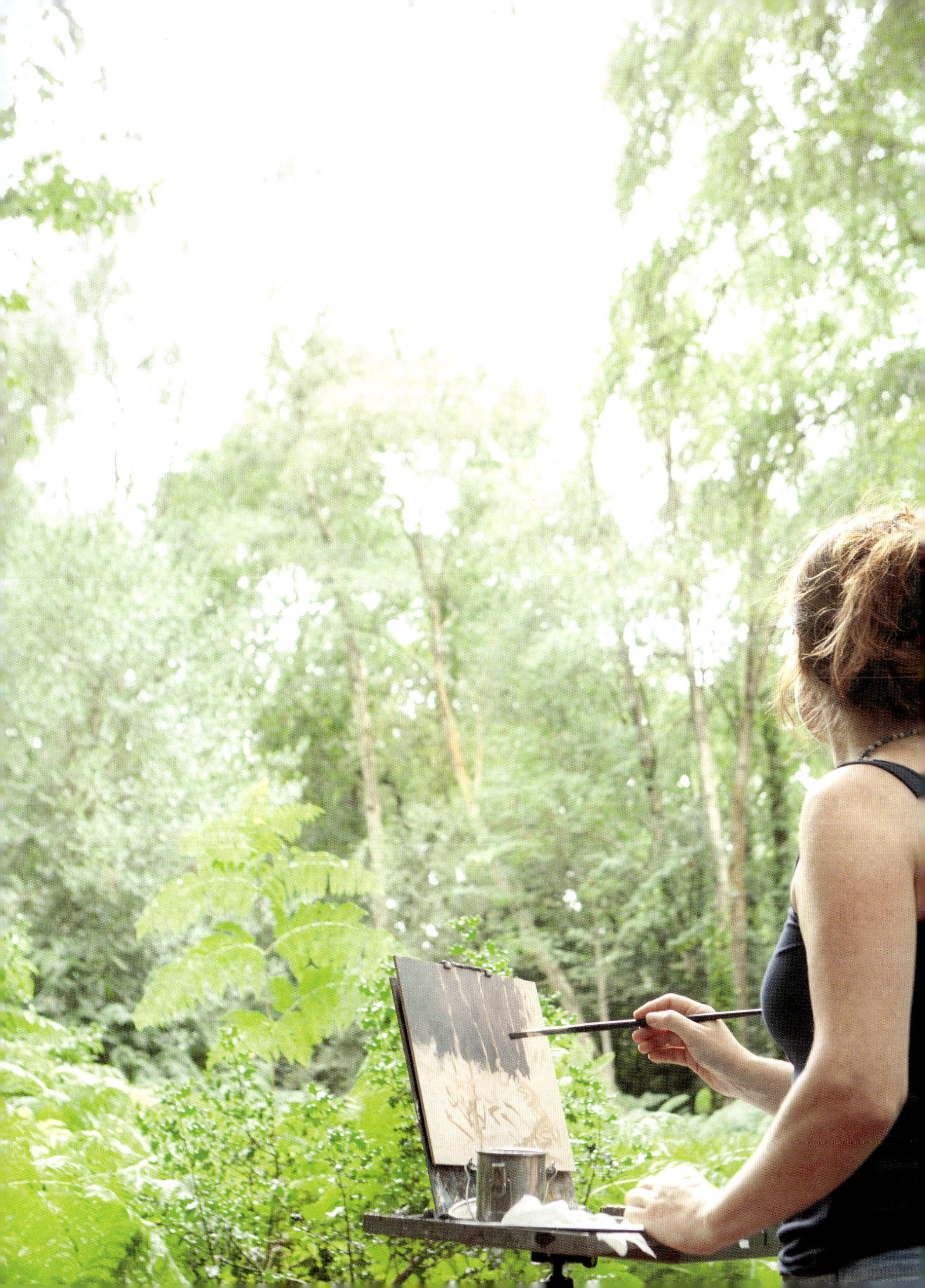

INDOORS: THE STUDIO

A good studio space does not have to be grand. It is just a dedicated space for painting; a place you can organize to suit your needs and leave set up permanently. Here is a glimpse into my studio, which is in my dormer loft. Each space will be entirely individual to you, and it should reflect how you work – I confess that mine is not usually this tidy!

My work area has a sturdy, height-adjustable easel (A) with dedicated lighting (B). If you paint for long stretches of time, change your painting position frequently to help prevent muscle tension in your back. When painting, I alternate between standing on an anti-fatigue mat (easier on your joints!) and sitting on an adjustable stool.

I have my laptop (C) next to my easel, as I prefer to work from digital images in the studio. I then place a table on either side (D and E), one for my working area and one for brushes, paint tubes and solvent. Furniture you can fold away is really useful for adjusting to individual project needs. Like most artists, sometimes I have to turn my studio into a more minimal space for photography, framing, or writing, so it is great to keep things flexible.

Try as I might, the studio is also a space for my cats, so it is great having high shelving (F) and cupboards (G). Beyond my painting area, there are several less photogenic cupboards rescued from an old kitchen, which I use for storage of paints, boards, frames and various artistic detritus. Shelving and plenty of work surface allows me space to store wet paintings and keep some areas paint-free for clean work, such as framing and writing.

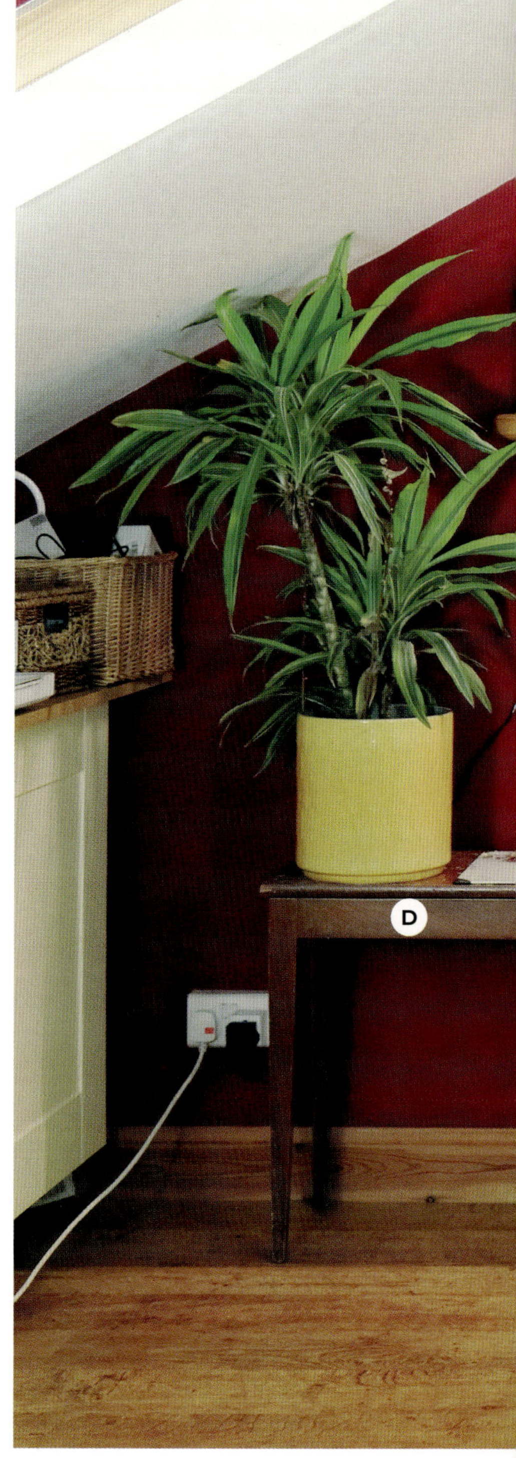

Above   *My studio in tidy mode!*

Opposite   *Bilbo the studio cat is usually around keeping me company somewhere. When I leave the studio, I make sure all my wet paint is stored safely away. Fortunately he hasn't figured out how to reach the shelf yet...*

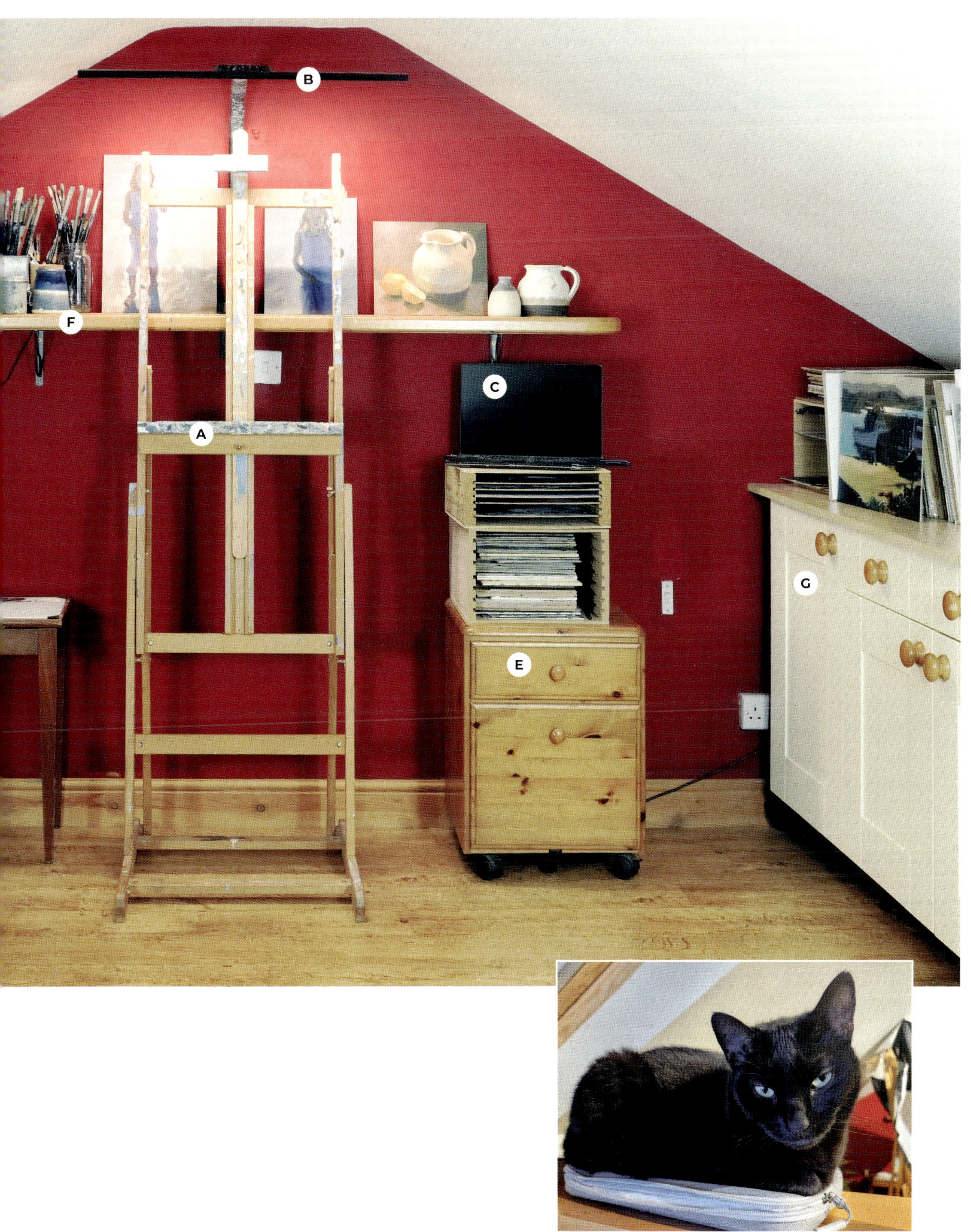

INDOORS: SET-UP FOR SMALLER SPACES

You don't have to have an airy studio to produce beautiful work – you can set up a temporary studio space anywhere. I worked for several years in kitchens of various sizes, making the best of the space I had. This certainly helped me to condense my kit to the essentials. It also encouraged me to move outside and paint from life, which is where the greatest painting lessons lie.

As a work area, anywhere in your home will serve if you have kit that's quick to set up and pack away. Here are the key considerations for choosing a smaller space to paint in.

Minimize kit Think about your own space and storage and go for the most practical options for kit. This may be a small desk easel, or you might like to invest in a pochade box. These combine easel, palette and secure storage for materials; some even have spaces for wet paintings. It's then safe, quick and easy to pack away.

Key tools and equipment There is no need to buy in lots of paint – you only need a basic array of colours. Likewise, canvas boards are light and take up much less room than box canvases.

Fresh air Ventilation is key in smaller spaces as you will be using solvents – make sure yours are low-odour and as environmentally friendly as you can find. Most art suppliers offer a large selection. I use low-odour solvent for both brush cleaning and thinning paint. Lidded jars are useful for quick storage (a jam jar will do, but make sure it is watertight if you are planning to transport it to paint outside).

Create distance Whatever the size of your space, it's important to step back from your painting as often as possible, even if this means taking it outside. It is much easier to judge the values and contrasts in your work from a distance.

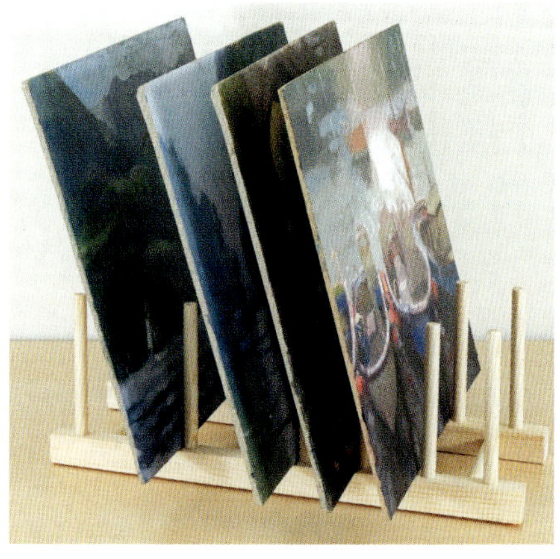

Storage One of the challenges is wet paint storage, and where to stack paintings when they're drying. You will find plenty of DIY ideas on the internet for wet painting carriers, which will protect your work from curious hands or paws! A basic wood dish drainer (above) works brilliantly for smaller wet painting storage. I found this low-cost option online, but get creative – there are many similar solutions out there.

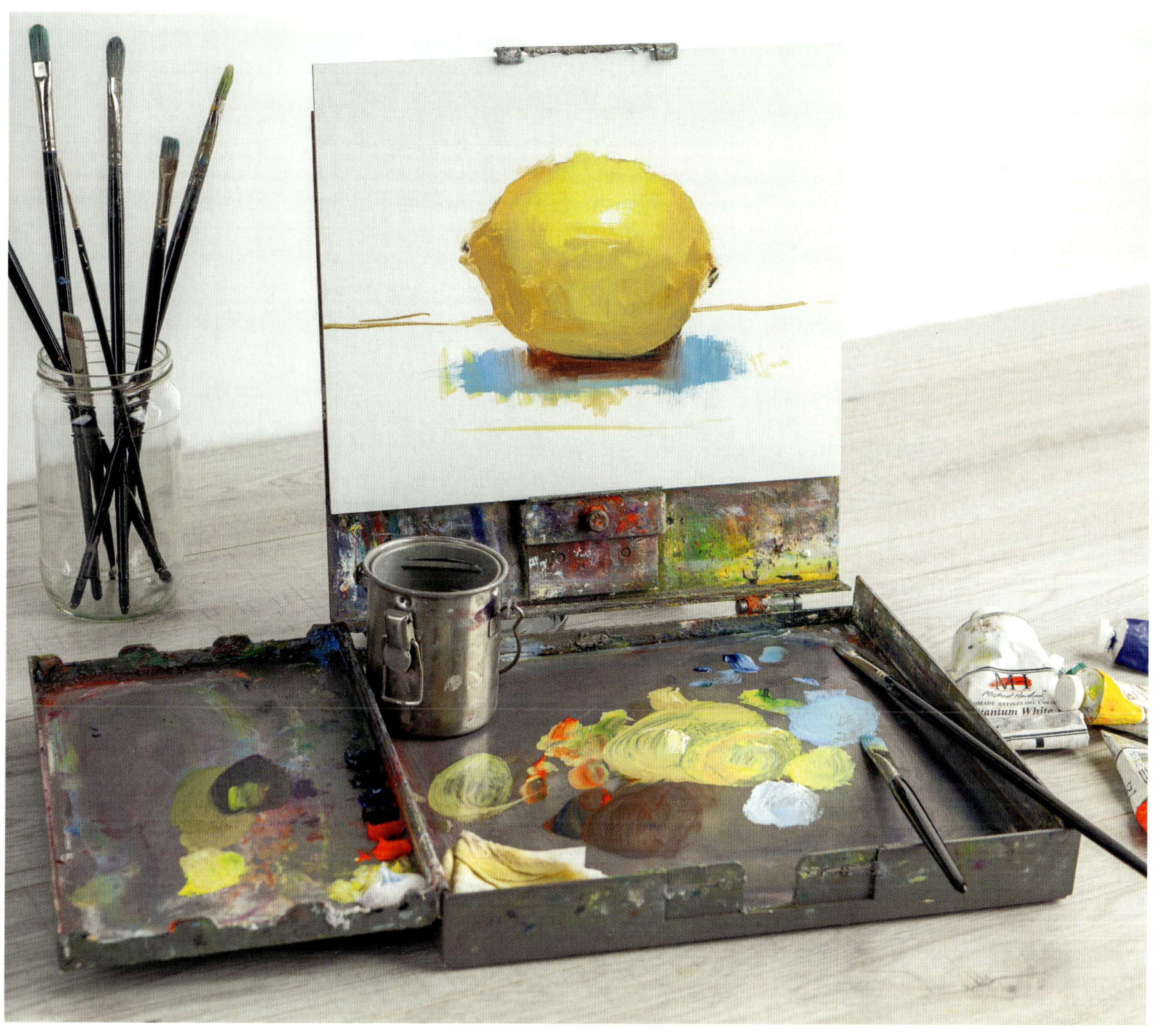

Combine to save space

Don't let lack of space get in the way of your painterly dreams. You really need very little to get going: just a table, constant light and the basic kit shown. A pochade box like the one shown above can provide you with palette, paint and brush storage. There are plenty of options to choose from.

INDOOR LIGHTING

Lighting is key to a good painting set-up, and in my view, key to good painting full stop. It influences everything – and there are many opinions on which is the best option. I would encourage you to have a look online, where plenty of artists share their own lighting methods. One size does not fit all.

Your light will determine your colour choices, so at the very least it is important to set up in a consistently-lit space. If the light changes as the sun comes through the windows, the colours you have mixed will look very different. If your light is too cold, you will overcompensate with warm colours; if too warm, you won't see the cooler colours and everything will turn out very blue.

Seeing colours accurately is very important to my process, so I want as natural a light as possible – and also to be able to work at any time of day. I have tried many different set-ups, including soft boxes, fluorescent strip lights, daylight bulbs and more – but the best solution I have found is both economical and practical for almost any space in a home or studio. It is a clip-on easel light (see below), which I fix to my shelf or another suitable edge wherever I am working. The lamp is about 5,500K on the CRI scale, which means it gives a neutral, bright light that results in natural colour choices. I always block the direct sun out for consistency, so the rest of my studio is quite dark.

Lighting from above avoids glare on the canvas as I paint, and also provides enough light for my mixing palette. Depending on your own space, you might find it better to install another lamp specifically for lighting your palette.

MEASURING LIGHT AND COLOUR

Colour temperature is measured by the Kelvin scale, with the optimum neutral light measuring between 5,000–6,000K.

The temperature can be read against the colour rendering index (CRI), which tells us how well the light source will mimic sunlight. Daylight ranges between 4,500–6,500K, and has a CRI of 100. Look for as high a value as possible on this scale – anything above 90 will be fine.

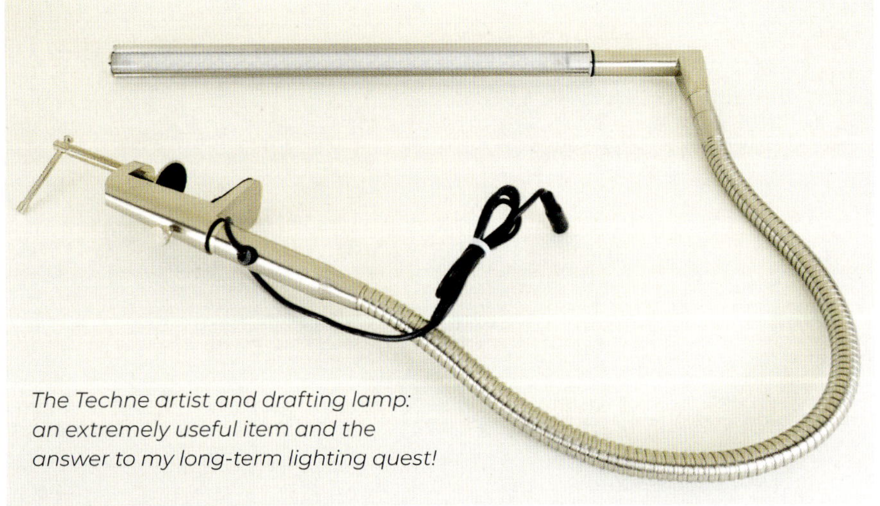

The Techne artist and drafting lamp: an extremely useful item and the answer to my long-term lighting quest!

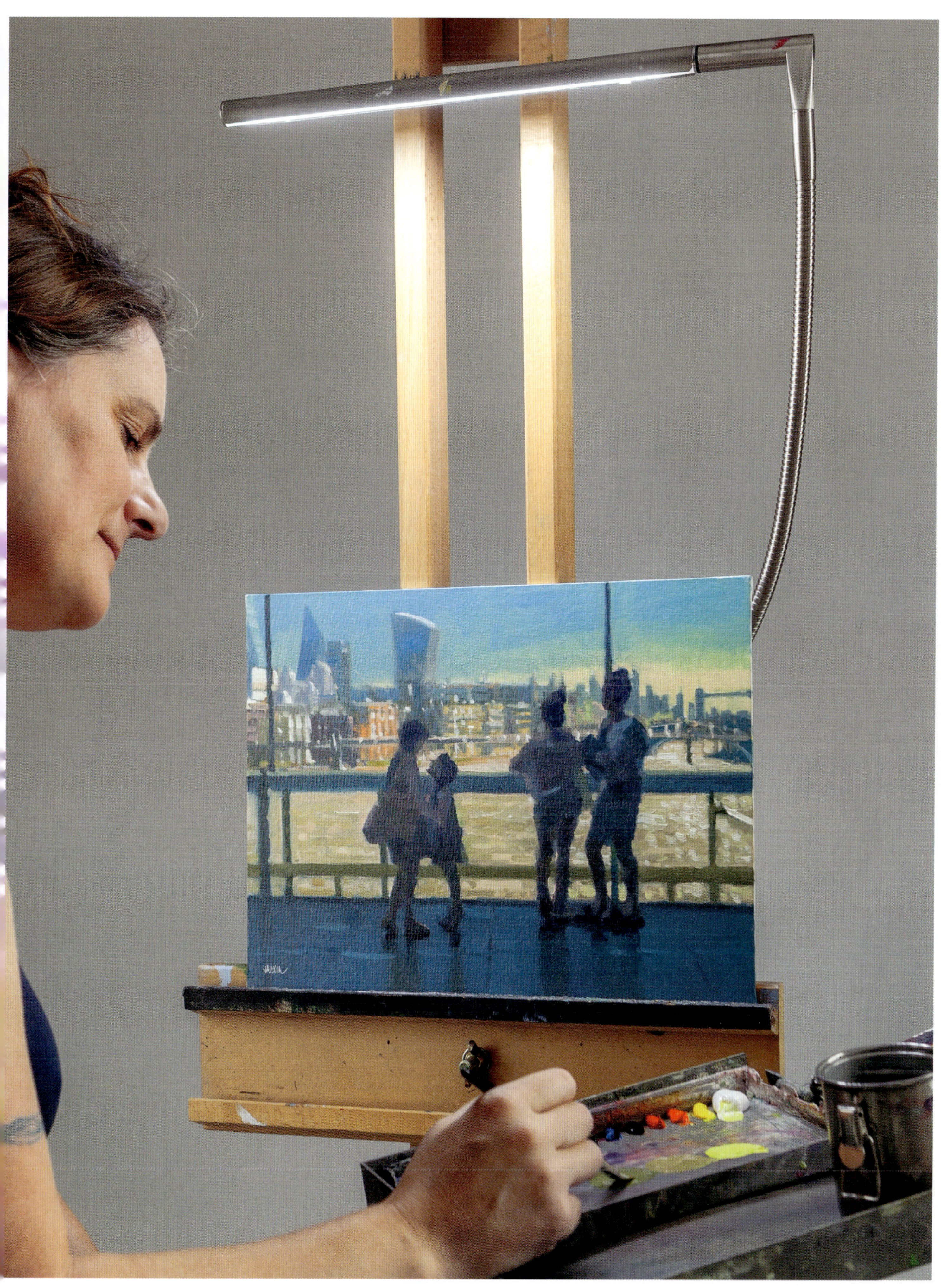

WORKING OUTDOORS

Working outside can be a much less predictable experience than working indoors! I've dedicated a whole chapter to painting *en plein air* (see pages 100– 113), but here are a few things I've learned over the years to help you prepare.

Clothing Check the weather and dress accordingly. I always have factor 50 sun cream on for *contre-jour* working, as I'm facing the sun. A peaked cap is likewise very useful for shading your eyes as you study lighting effects.

Kit There's a world of choice out there, but I recommend kit that goes happily into a single day-size backpack. I take a pochade box and a lightweight compact tripod, which all fit nicely into my daypack. I squeeze my paint out into the pochade box (see opposite) before setting out, so I don't have to carry all my heavy paints around. The board can also be safely carried inside. I take a small selection of four or five favourite brushes plus a painting knife, an airtight pot for solvent and wet wipes. I also have various wet panel carriers, though only in a couple of sizes as I tend to stick to the same 30 × 24cm (11¾ × 9½in) panels for *plein air* work.

Location If the option is there, station yourself in the shade to make the observational process easier on your eyes. You only need enough light to see your palette while you switch focus between the view and the easel.

AVOID DISTRACTIONS

Friendly chat with passers-by is great but sometimes it prevents a decent outcome when your concentration is broken too often.

If you are concerned about onlookers, stand with your back to a wall – apart from anything else, people appearing over your shoulder can be quite surprising when you're focusing on painting!

To discourage unwanted commentary, you could try popping headphones in.

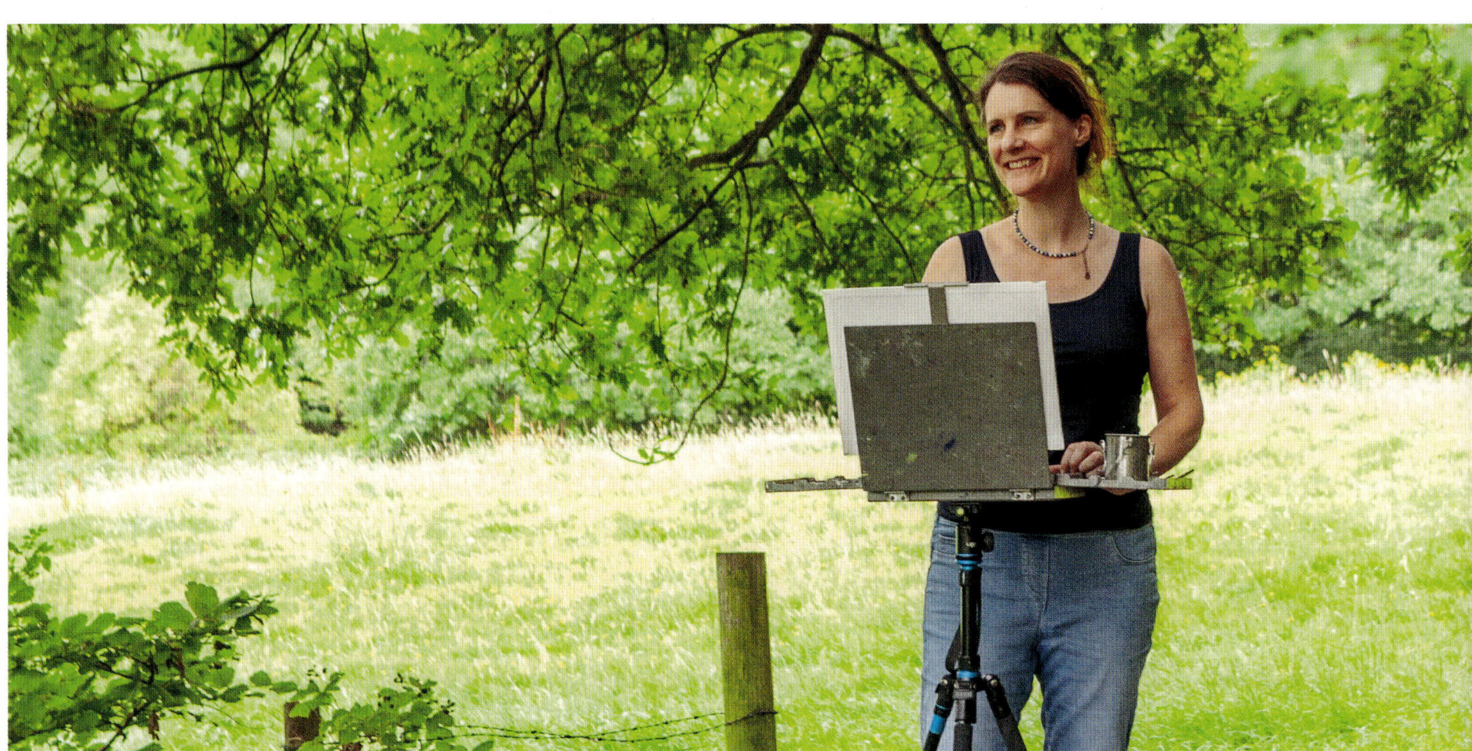

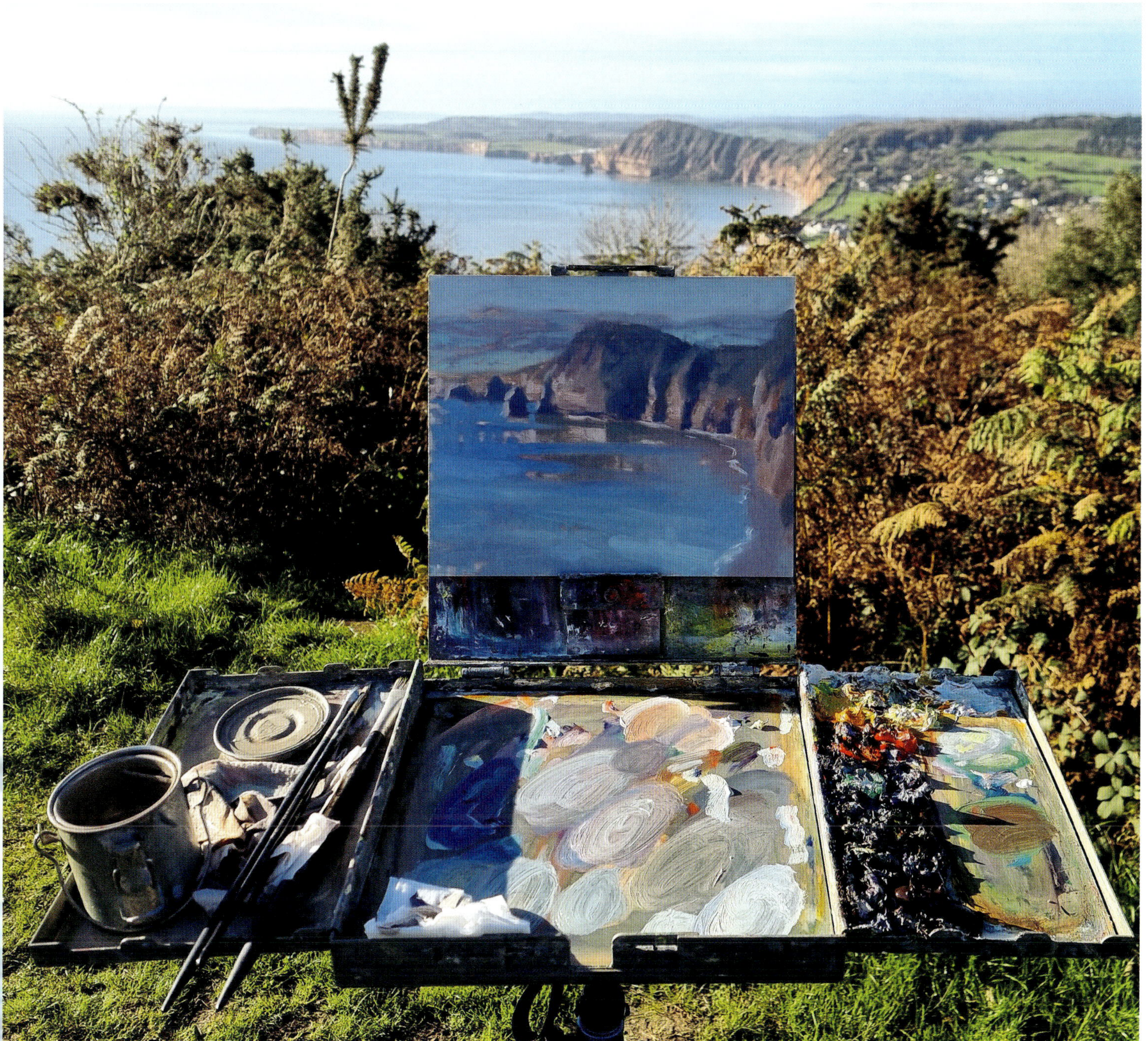

MY SET-UP

Here is an action shot of my set-up while out painting the Devonshire coast in autumn. Pictured is my Strada Midi pochade box. The side panels can be telescoped in for transport. My easel gives me plenty of mixing space – worth bearing in mind when choosing your own. I use it with a u.go Tripod LCS1 for support – and I have hung my backpack from the centre of the tripod to weigh it down in case of wind. Both tripod and pochade box are light to carry and brilliantly sturdy!

MAKE A CHECKLIST

As soon as you work out your ideal configuration of kit, make a checklist that you can go back to for each trip. Otherwise, like me, you'll always forget at least one essential item. (One day, I am sure, I will follow my own advice!)

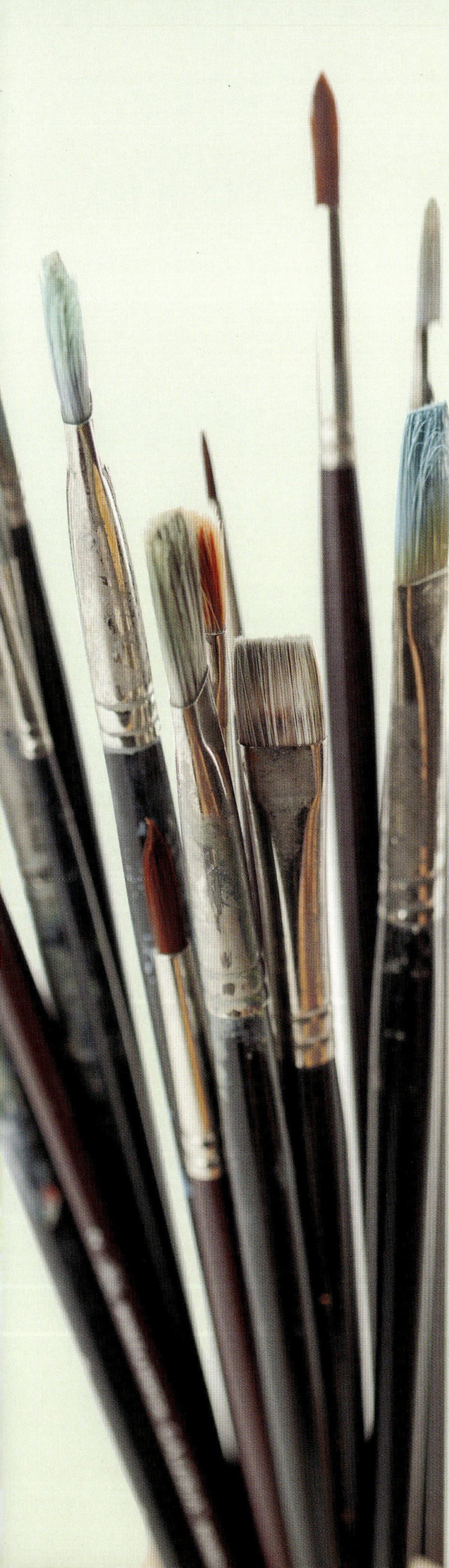

BRUSHES

I can't write a book on painting without including a little on brushes and brushcare! I have, unsurprisingly, used many different brushes from many different brands. Some have been on the cheaper end, others ridiculously pricey. My favourites, however, are cheap–middle range, and I've been loyal to them for many years. I paint every day and these little workhorses get used well! All that brushing, scrubbing, solvent and cleaning takes its toll, so I replace them every so often rather than try to make one set of expensive brushes last a lifetime.

I was lucky enough to be gifted a rather large amount of brushes by the manufacturer Rosemary & Co. a few years ago. This gave me the opportunity to work through lots of them and find those that suited me best. Consequently I have all the sizes of filbert and flat in the Ivory range, which I highly recommend as good value and excellent quality. My most-used brush sizes from this range are 2, 4, 6 and 8: 6mm (¼in), 10mm (⅜in), 12mm (½in) and 15mm (⅝in) respectively. If you choose a different range, then look for similar sizes.

The Daler-Rowney System3 12mm (½in) flat brush is also on my list of essential tools. It is a soft, synthetic brush, short handled, not too thick, has a nice edge (when it is new) and gives beautifully smooth application. It is relatively inexpensive and so I replace mine fairly often. I am sure other brands produce similar, this one just won my heart!

I always have a size 0 synthetic rigger to hand. These are great for the tiny dashes and noise at the end of a painting.

I have plenty of extras to play with – a nice fan brush, some beautiful Ivory range egberts and round brushes, and some synthetic hog bristle brushes for thicker placement of paint. I love to experiment and I encourage you to do the same, as that is always when the exciting things happen.

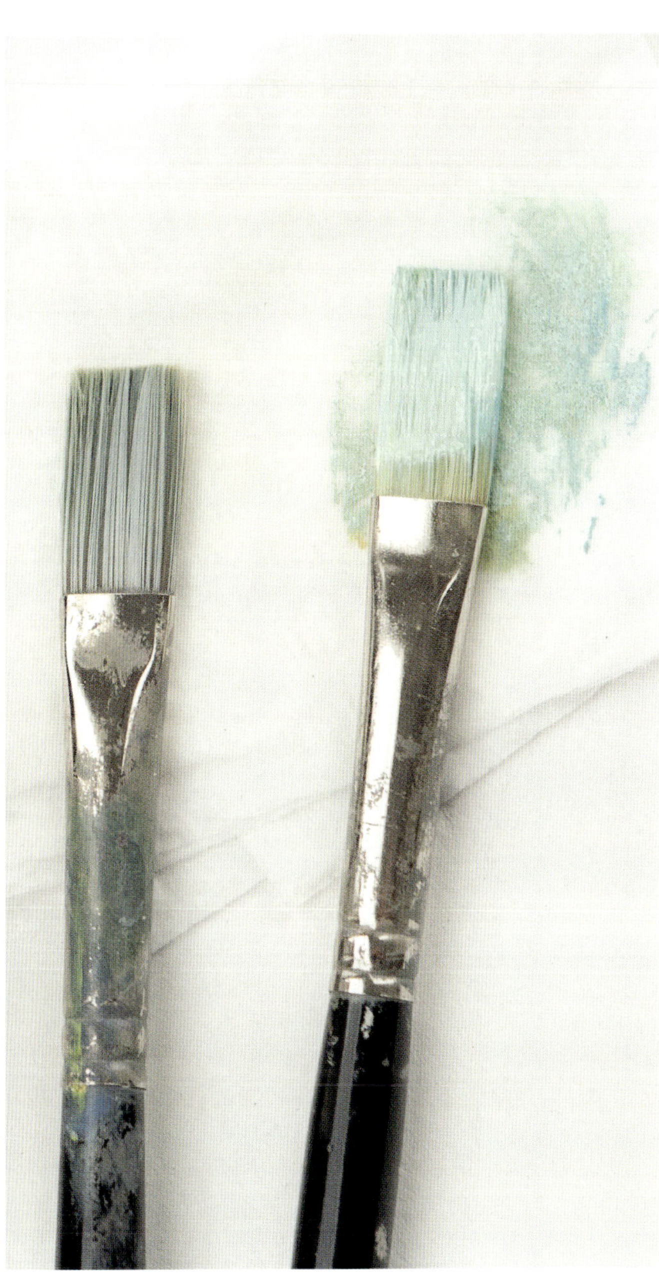

Brushcare

Oil is best for cleaning oil, as solvent is bad for brushes. However, while painting, solvent is often the only practical solution – it is this, or being very organized and using a number of brushes for each painting, sticking to similar colours for each brush. I simply get too lost in the act of painting, and often end up using just one brush all the way through!

Everyone out there has a special tip for cleaning brushes when you've finished for the day, and I think I have tried most of them. Here's my advice: during painting always wipe the brush before washing it gently in solvent. When you fully clean the brushes at the end of the day, remove as much paint as you can using a cloth or wipe, then wash them in a little vegetable oil or Murphy's oil soap. This draws out more paint. Next, use washing detergent and warm water to clean them further, lathering them softly. Finally, reshape them and leave them to dry.

Solvents

Whether painting indoors or outside, I use a low-odour solvent such as Roberson Studio Safe or Zest-it. If I am flying, I use a high flashpoint solvent safe for air travel.

Leave used solvent in a lidded jar for a few days until the paint and solvent separate. You can then decant the solvent off to a new jar and reuse it – never dispose of it down the drain.

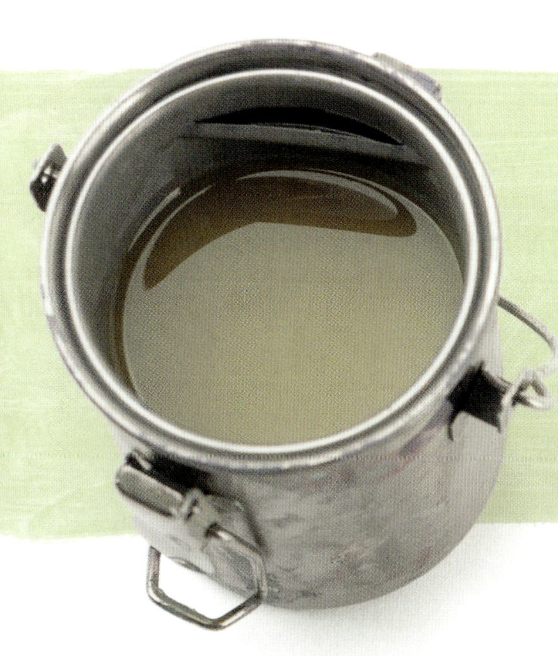

GREY PRIMER

Decanting off clean solvent into a new jar (see left) will leave the remainder behind. This doesn't need to go to waste!

After a few painting sessions, you will end up with a large amount of grey oil, which you can use as a colour ground for white canvases.

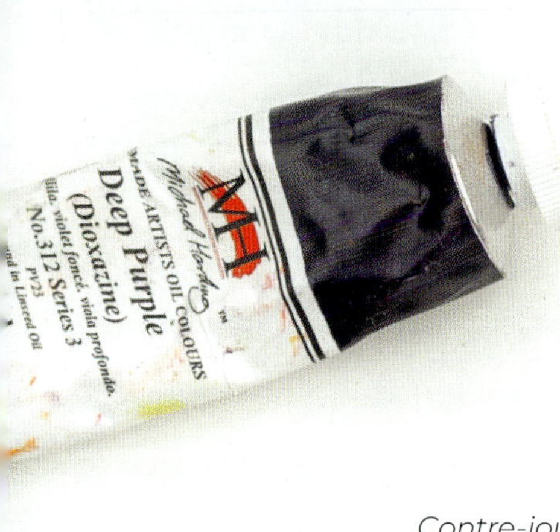

OIL PAINT

Contre-jour work can be powerful in any medium – but for me, the glossy, rich finish of oil paints produces the illusion of light most satisfactorily. Oils are a wonderful experience to use, albeit with an endless learning curve! They allow you to build up layers of paint to multi-dimensional effect – I love laying on buttery, tinted highlights over a wash of warm greys, with rich, cool darks occupying the corners, and saturated accents linking everything together. Oils are also the easiest option for mixing and blending subtle tones.

I usually work *alla prima*, which means finishing a painting in one sitting. With oils, there is no rush to beat the drying process or colour shift that have to be accounted for when working with watercolours or acrylics. There are ways to deal with these problems with these types of paint, but I find it quicker and less frustrating simply to use oil paint instead.

Whatever brand of paint you have, strength, consistency and even colours will vary. Regardless of make, there are some colours with tinting abilities that are notably strong (phthalo colours) or weak (bright yellow lake, for example). This doesn't have to be a problem, as through practice with mixing you will naturally adjust – but it is worth bearing in mind when you read my instructions on using a 'touch' of a colour!

Over the page, I'll show you how to get to know the power of your paints by painting your own colour wheel. You'll add the primary colours, mix the complementaries and gradually add white to see where the colours go. This exercise will help you to quickly find which are the strongest colours in your palette, and get to know your paint better.

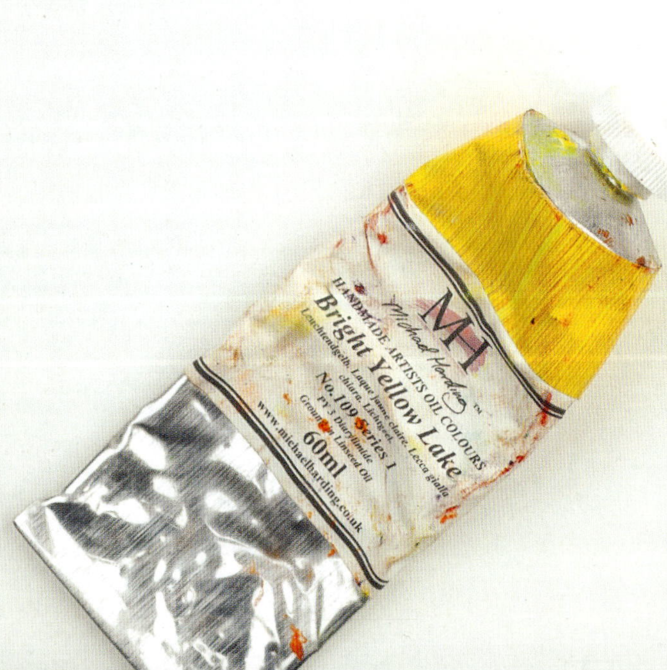

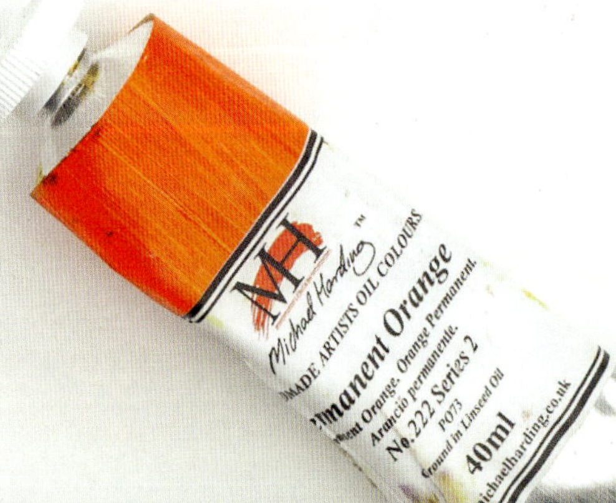

My choice of oil paints

My first oil colours were inherited from my grandfather and were in various states of freshness! For years I used whatever brand of oil paint was most affordable or accessible, as long as the colours were lightfast. Today I am a convert to Michael Harding colours, for their strength of colour and buttery consistency. They suit the way I work, and are a pleasure to use, but the effects achieved in my work are not reliant on a brand of paint. Any oil will work wonderfully – as long as it hasn't dried up in the tube.

Most colours are mixable using red, blue and yellow, so when choosing your colours, at the very minimum I recommend having these primaries to hand. I typically use scarlet lake, ultramarine blue and bright yellow lake.

In terms of colour usage, I find that I get through more yellow and white than anything else, so I keep in large tubes of those, and smaller tubes of everything else.

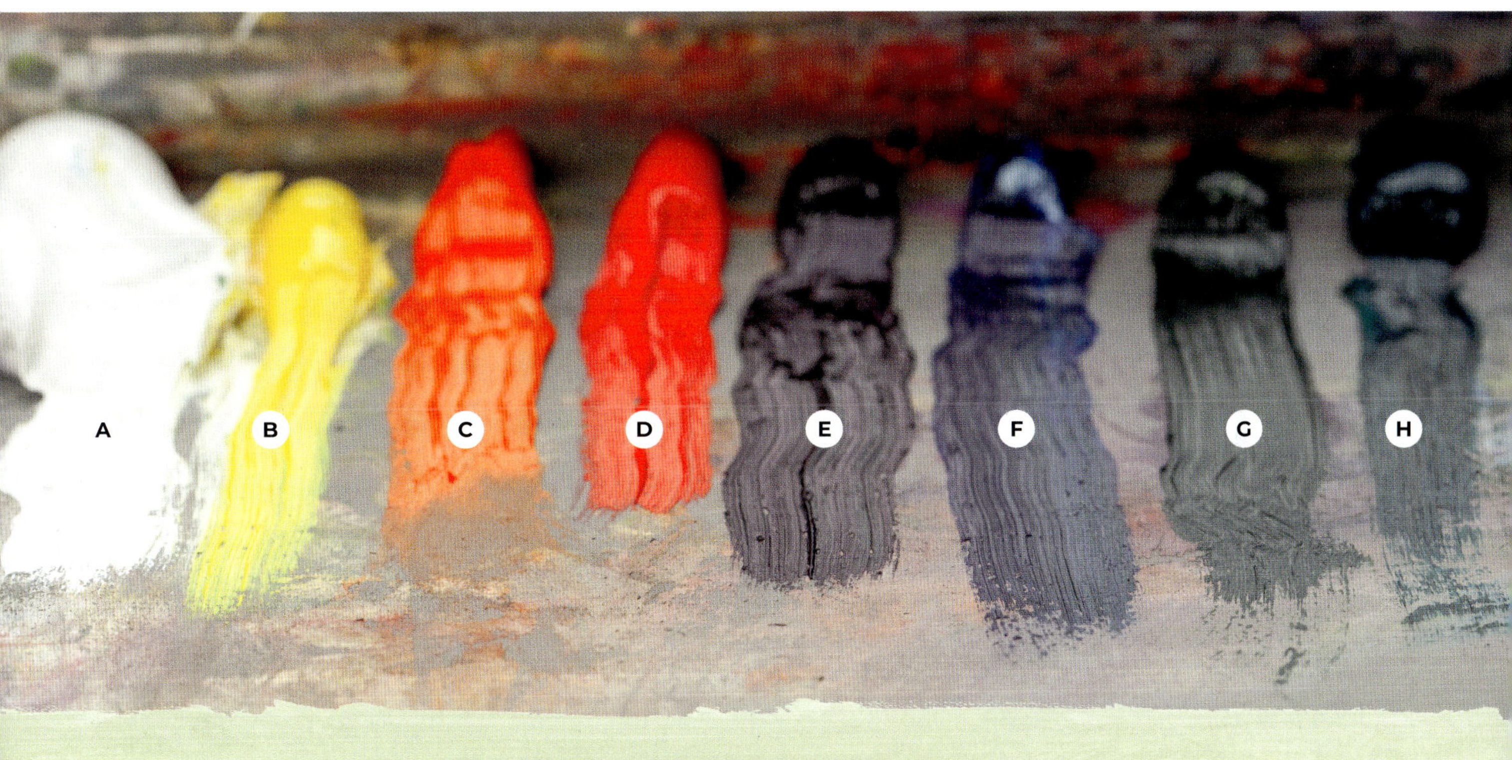

MY COLOUR PALETTE

My regular palette of colour, which suits the lighting and landscape of my UK home, consists of:

- Titanium white (A)
- Bright yellow lake (B)
- Permanent orange (C)
- Scarlet lake (D)
- Deep purple (E)
- Ultramarine blue (F)
- Phthalo green lake (G)
- Sap green (H)

I also make frequent use of burnt umber. Turquoise and cadmium yellow also make guest appearances for special occasions – such as when the seas sing and the daffodils bloom.

PAINT AND COLOUR

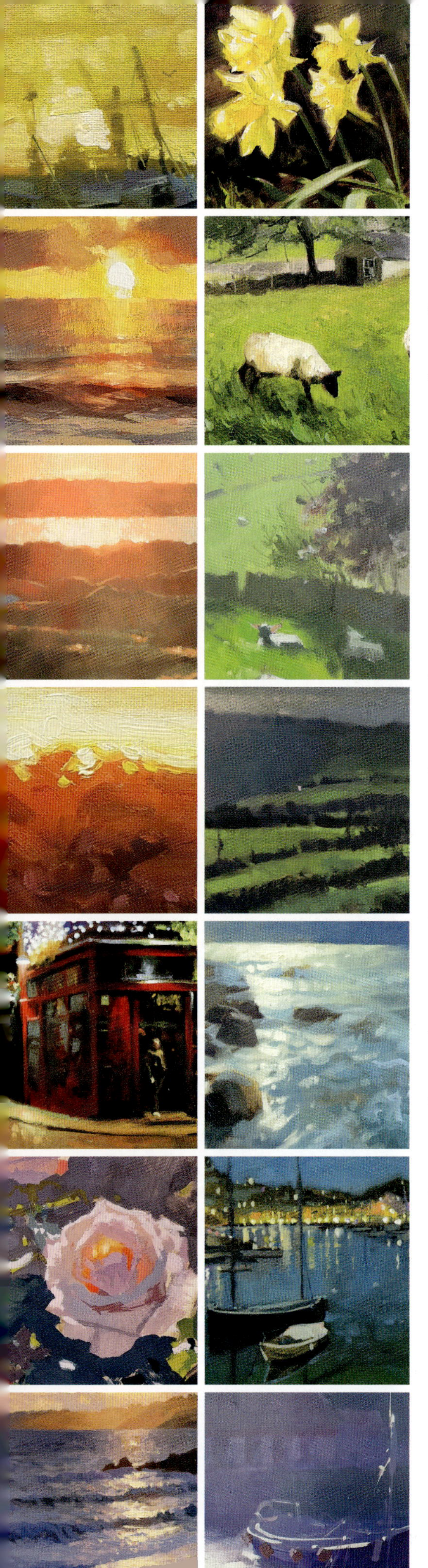

'Colour is my day-long obsession, joy, and torment.' **Claude Monet**

There is a world of colour theory and terminology out there which I will not delve into too deeply in this book. I am no scientist, but over the course of my painting journey I have found ways to make light in my practice: that is what I'll be sharing with you!

- This colour wheel shows us the three **primary colours**, red, yellow and blue, set out at equal points around the circle. The colours halfway between each pair of primaries are the three **secondary colours** – orange, purple and green – each a mix of the two nearest primaries. There are also the six blends between each: orange-yellow, red-orange, red-purple, purple-blue, blue-green and yellow-green.

- The wheel also demonstrates **colour temperature**: Half of the wheel, from primary yellow through to red/purple, has warm undertones, the other half cold.

- Opposite any colour on the wheel is its **complementary colour**. Pairs of complementaries are opposite each other in both hue and temperature: warm red is opposite cool green, for example. In painterly terms, each can be described as the balance, contrast or complement to its counterpart.

- **Shades** are a colour mixed with black. I do not use a black on my palette, as I prefer to use complementary colours to make my shadows. I have found that this is an easier way to keep every colour balancing and working together across the canvas .

- **Tints** are colours mixed with white. I use tints to strong effect in the brightest of highlights.

- **Saturation** refers to the purity of a colour. If a colour is fully saturated, it will have no white or grey within it. A colour low in saturation, or de-saturated, is a grey.

- **Greys**, at their most basic, are a mix of the three primaries, or a mix of a colour with its complementary. Greys have temperatures and opposites, and can create subtle and wonderful lighting effects. Mixing tonal greys is a huge part of my *contre-jour* process and will be covered throughout this book.

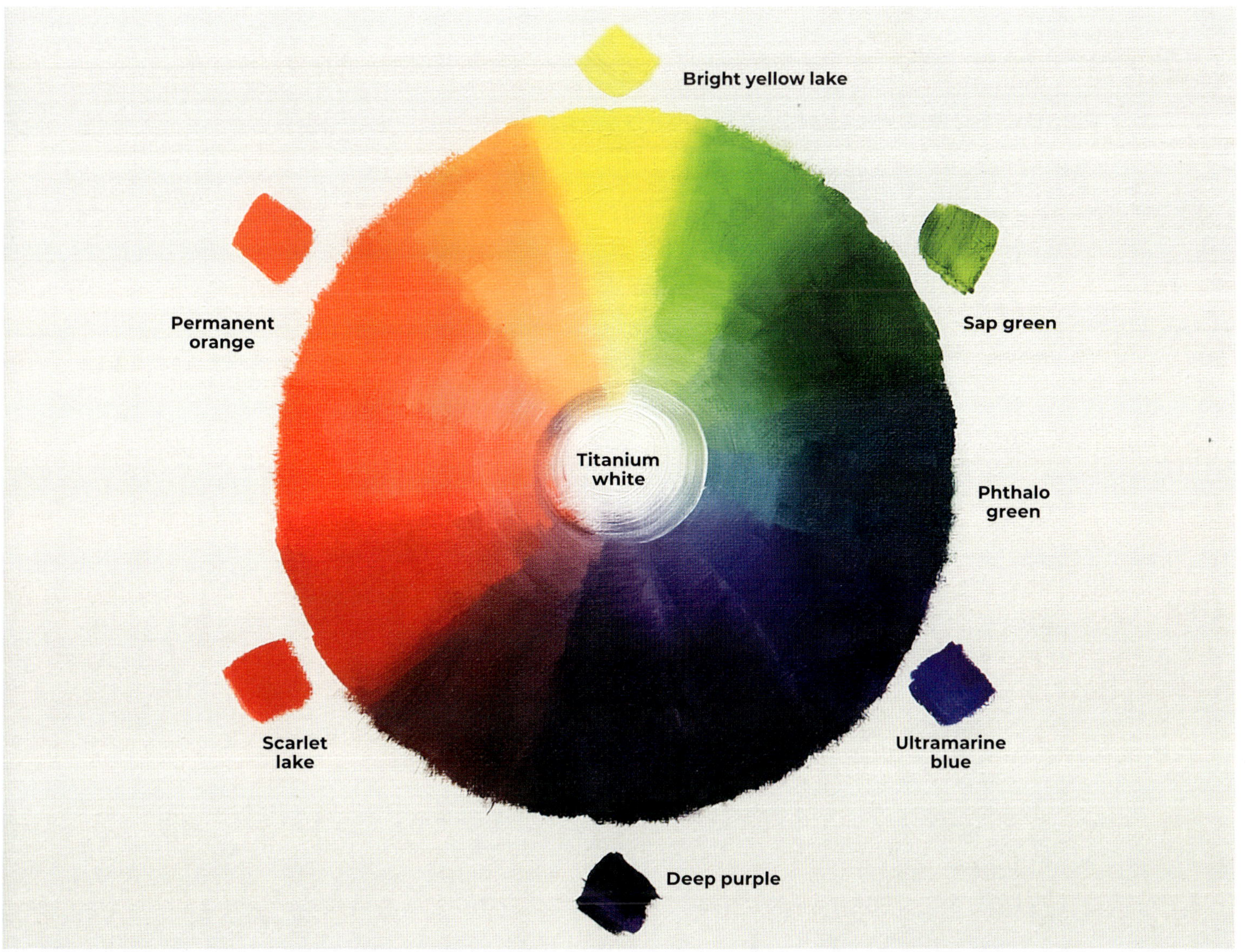

THE COLOUR WHEEL

I painted the colour wheel above using the essential colours from my palette. Look how dark the mix of scarlet and deep purple is above! A hint of green touches the yellow and *boom!* – a beautiful, glowing lime.

While a little fiddly, painting your own colour wheel is a great exercise. It requires a bit of careful brushwork and an awareness of the tinting strength of your colours. Start with the primaries, add the secondaries in between, then mix the border between each (see page 47 for more on how to mix these colours).

It's worth experimenting with adding pre-mixed colours, fitting them into the gaps – I've done just that with phthalo green, instead of mixing the adjacent paints into this area.

My two greens, warm-tinged sap green and cooler phthalo green, are so useful for mixing with their complementaries to make darks. I almost always keep them in my palette.

COLOUR RELATIONSHIPS

Complementary colours cause each other to stand out to the eye – look for these relationships in the world, they're everywhere: deep green holly leaves and their scarlet berries are a perfect example. I look for this balance in all my paintings of the illusion of light.

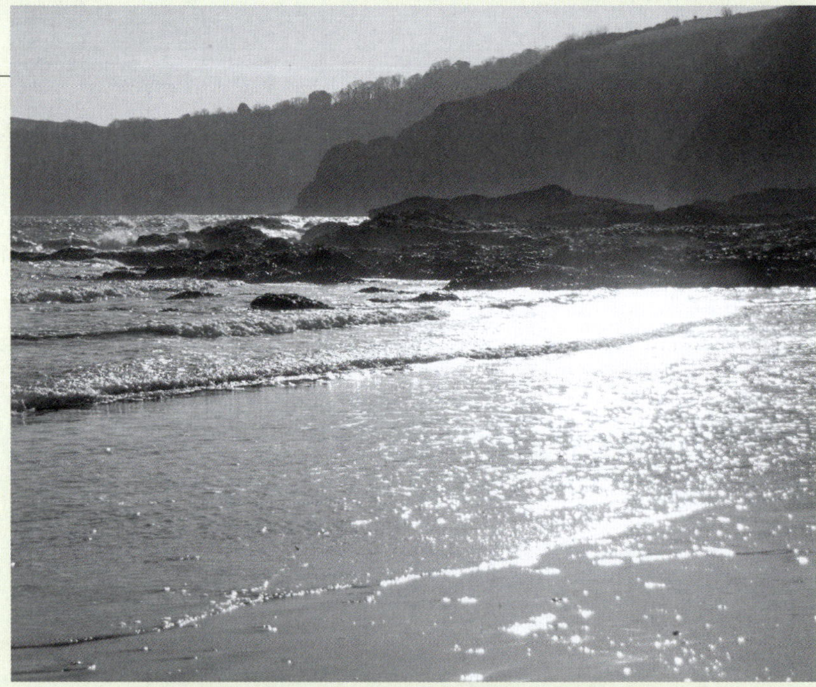

TONAL SEASCAPE

Before we start working with juicy colour, there is a great deal we can learn from monochrome tonal painting. If nothing else, it certainly simplifies the mixing process! I always look for a wide spread of tones in my work, with the darkest and lightest always present somewhere for contrast and the 'wow' effect. Learning how to represent lighting in black, white and a series of greys will help you to discern what is needed for the same effects when working in colour.

When painting monochrome *contre-jour*, you discover very quickly that the lightest value shouldn't touch the darkest value directly – not if you want the effect of illusory light. This is more easily shown in black and white photographs, without the distraction of colour – as you can see above.

There are two reasons for this guideline: first, we are trying to represent how our eyes and sight actually behave when we look into the sun. Think of having to squint when you look into brightness – what you see when you are squinting is what we are trying to paint. Equally, objects that stand directly between you and the light should never be painted a solid dark. Their edges will be lighter and hazy, as the light passes around them.

The second reason is that bright light will always have an effect on its immediate area. If sunlight is bouncing off a reflective sea onto a black rock, the rock must be a grey, hazy colour where it is directly affected by the light. In paint, this just means a softer, more gradual contrast between tones.

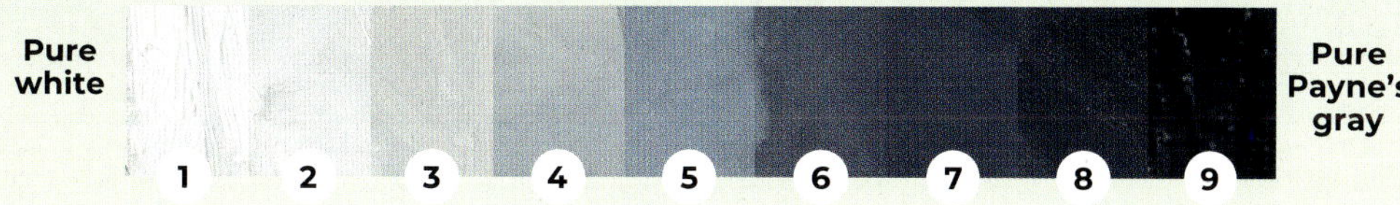

1 To begin, mix nine tones on your palette, starting with pure titanium white and increasing the proportion of Payne's gray paint in the mix until the last is pure Payne's gray.

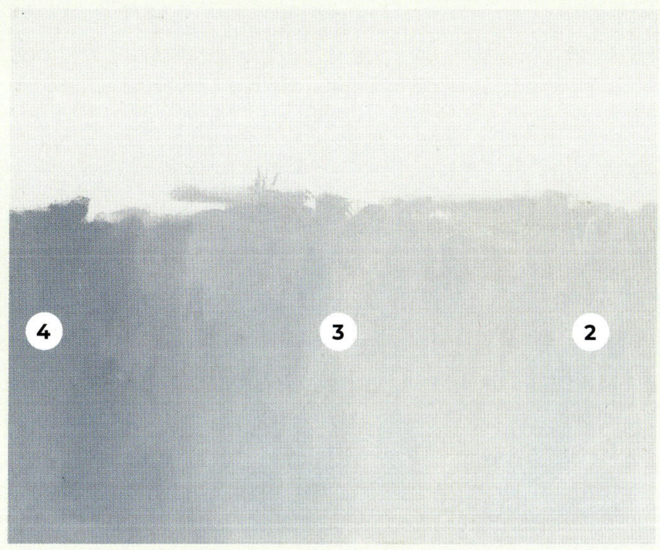

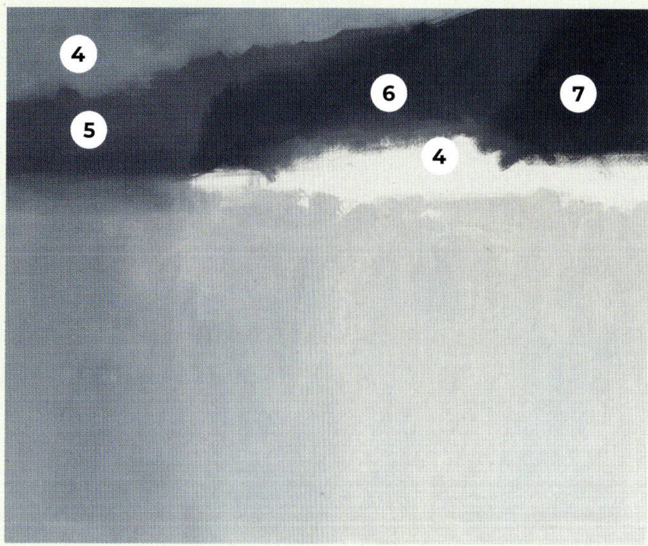

2 Dilute tone 2 with a touch of solvent and paint it onto the right-hand side of the canvas, with a 12mm (½in) flat brush. Blend in tone 3 in the centre, and tone 4 on the left. Use vertical brushstrokes, as this will make the water look reflective.

3 Continuing with the flat brush, but with less solvent, block in the distant headland with tone 5, followed by tone 6 then 7 for the nearest cliff. Lay in the sky with tone 4, blending it lightly into the headland for a soft, atmospheric effect. Brush tone 4 into the base of the cliffs on the right, too, for a glowing effect. Brushwork for these areas should be relatively texture-free, to keep it in the background.

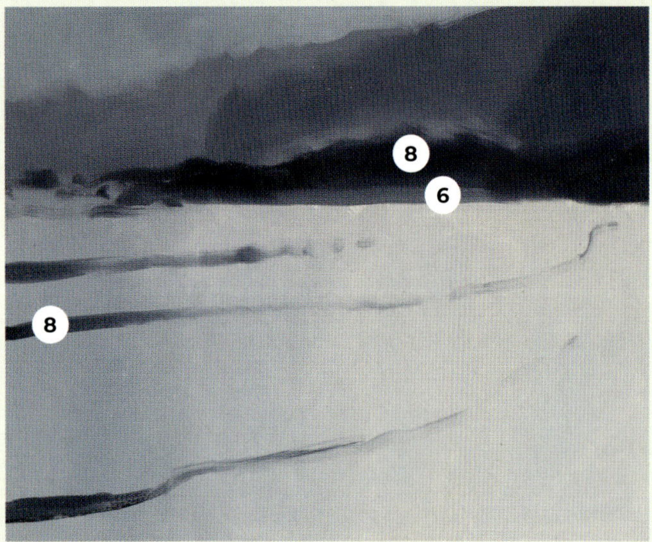

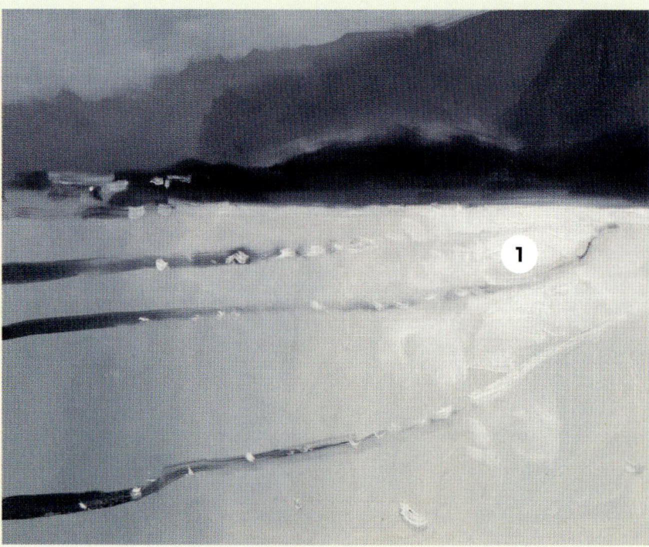

4 With the same brush, and adding only enough solvent for the paint to flow, use tone 8 for the rocks. This was also good for the wavelets, with a light brushing out in the brighter areas. Blend tone 6 in to the base of the rocks above the brightest sea. Before moving on, clean your brush – when you start on the tinted whites, brushes need to be clean!

5 Lay pure, thick white – tone 1 – on the area of brightest light. Use the face of the brush to deliberately place this thick highlight paint. If you brush it on with the tip of the brush, it will mix with the thinner colour underneath, and you won't get the same impact. Pop in some blobs along the wavelets with the corner of the brush, too.

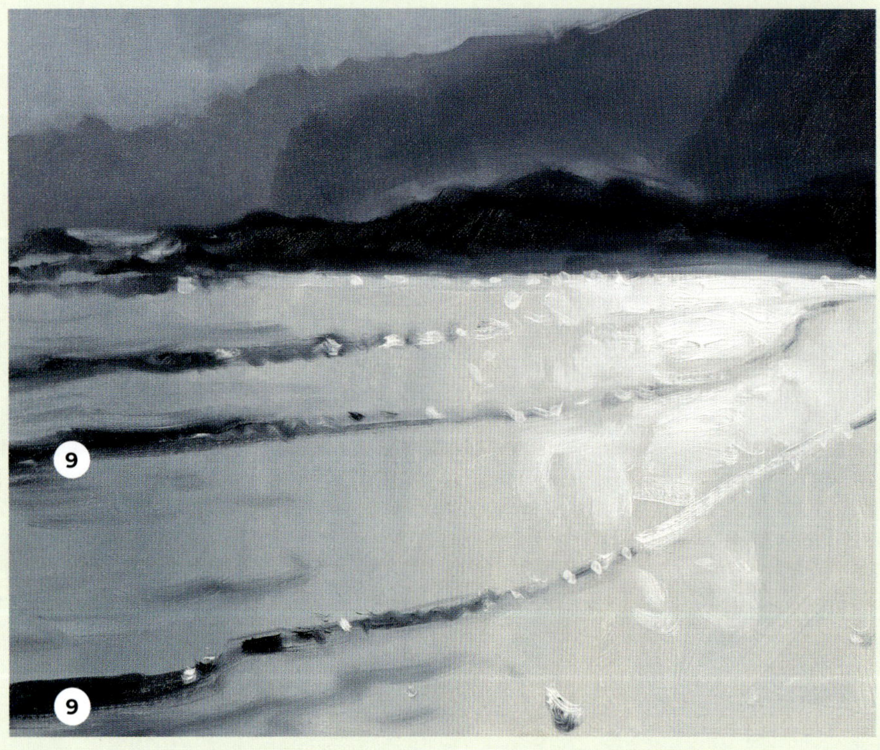

6 To finish, use pure Payne's gray (tone 9), to paint the faces of the two nearest waves on the left. Brush in some curving shapes to the water, too, in order to suggest surface movement between the waves.

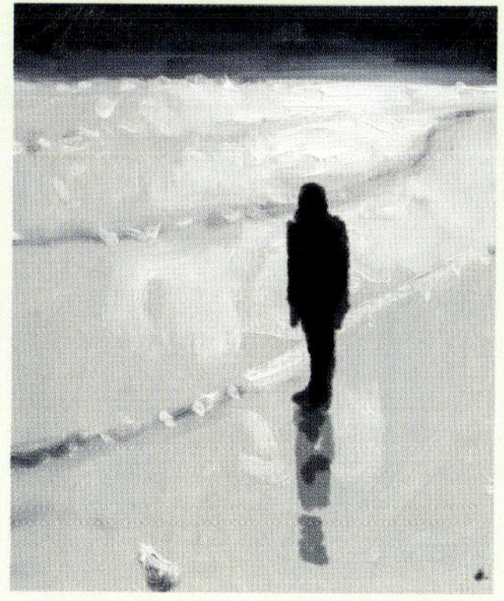 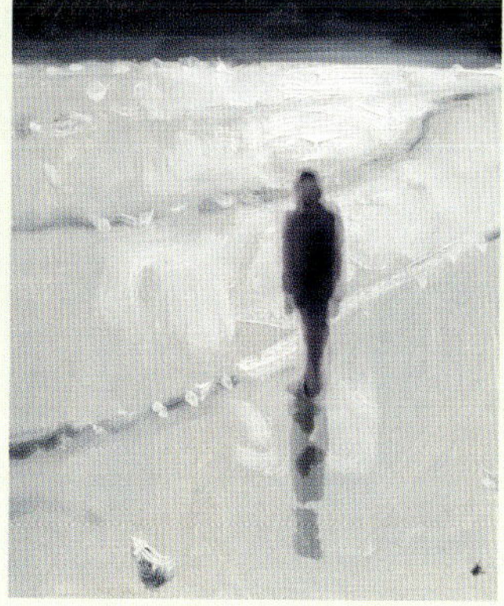

ADDING A FIGURE

Optionally, you can add a figure to your painting. It is tempting to make the figure black, a silhouette, like the left-hand image. See how this looks like a hole in the painting!

As an object between you and the sun, it needs to be showing the effect of the brightness. On the right, the figure is much lighter, with a central dark area and lighter tones around their edges.

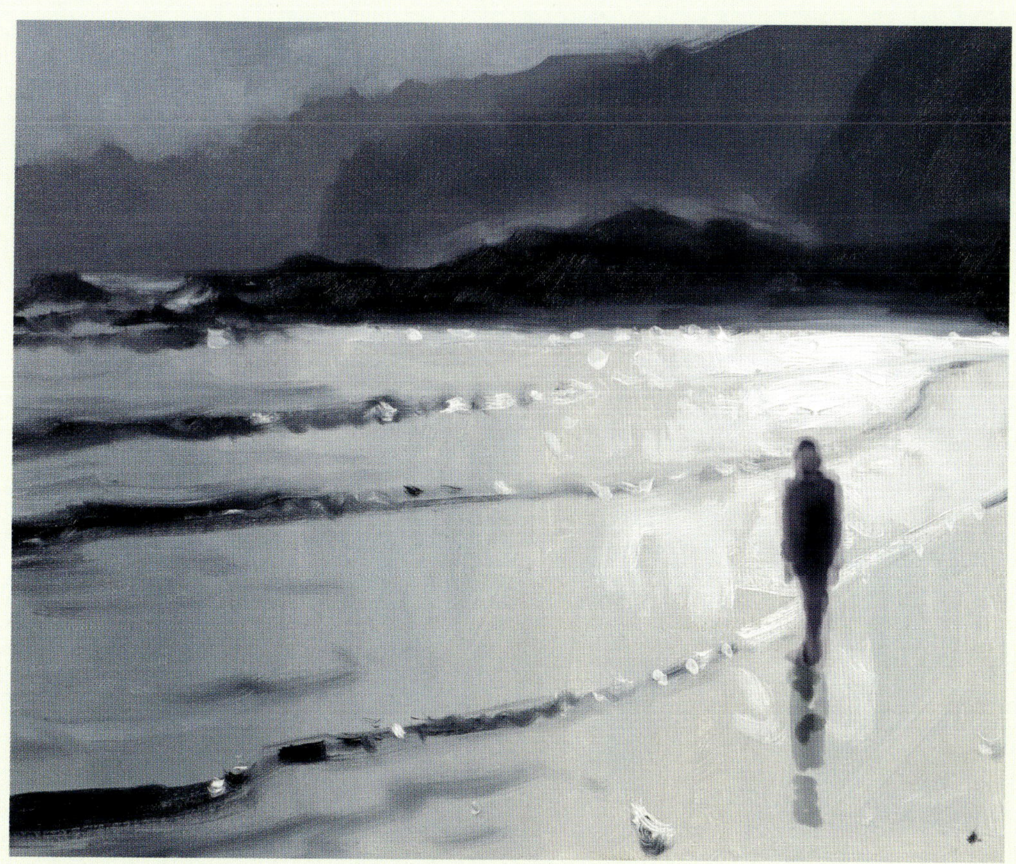

The finished exercise

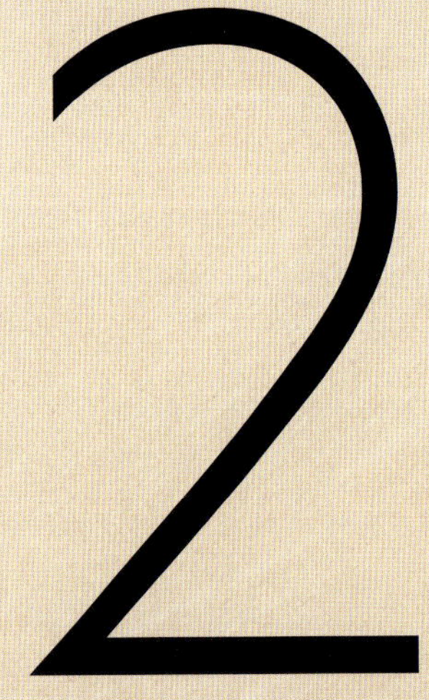

COMPOSITION, COLOUR AND CONTRAST

'Everyday I discover more and more beautiful things. It's enough to drive one mad. I have such a desire to do everything, my head is bursting with it.' **Claude Monet**

Understanding colour and recognizing tones are essential strings to your bow, along with communicative brushwork and focused lighting; but strong composition is the structure that holds it all together.

Revisit the work of your favourite artists with an eye for discerning exactly what it is that appeals to you. What makes those paintings work? What do you want to paint? How do you decide what to paint?

The answer is to paint what moves you. The view that lingers in your mind, or the subject that catches your eye. If the subject touched you, it will touch others too, and will work as inspiration for a painting. Trust your own interests and passions as starting points. And the good news is, pretty much anything looks great when it is dramatically back-lit! *Contre-jour* lighting turns the mundane into magic.

Once you have your idea, you can refine it by following the compositional rules that are explained in this chapter. You don't have to follow them rigidly; but once you're aware of them, you'll find them brilliantly reliable for the creation of successful paintings.

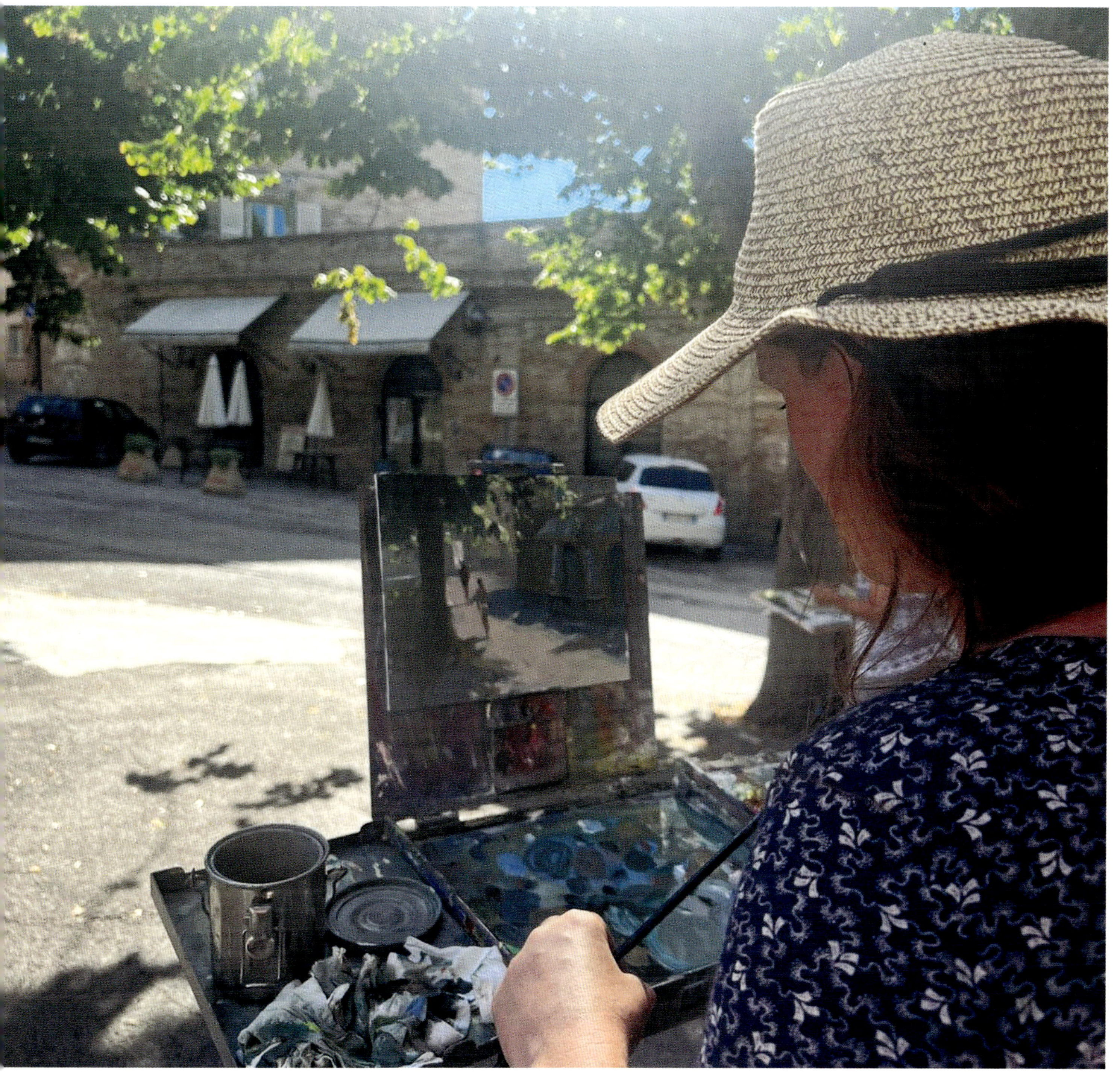

Painting in Italy

The more I learn what I like in my painting, the more I am inspired to paint. It is like a never-ending puzzle to be worked out throughout life. There are uncountable compositions out there – we spot them all the time. It is just being brave enough to jump in and go for it! Don't let the unfamiliar put you off – exploring new subjects is the way to learn what you love.

OUR AIM:
THE ILLUSION OF LIGHT

I think of each painting as an orchestral movement, a sum greater than its parts; where every element plays its part in the creation of magic.

The object of my *contre-jour* paintings is to convince the eye that it is directly facing the sun – enough to make you squint. I am not sure how I became obsessed with this effect, but I do find it fascinating that the effect is even possible in paint. I think what appeals to me most is that this moment is so often the one that stops me in my tracks.

Forest Light came about after a spring painting session in a nearby woodland. The weather relented and the mist burned off in the afternoon sun. I stood in the damp leaves and focused on the path ahead, where the mist obscured the bank in the light. It was a glorious moment that needed to be painted in a suitably large format!

The brightest whites in the painting through the canopy are tinted with red, both for warmth and to stand out against the surrounding cold green. Restricting my lightest whites to this one area draws the eye with blinding impact. The colours of the wood become desaturated nearer the sun, emphasizing the illusion. Where the trees block that light, their rich brownness also fades. The leafy greens are fully saturated in the foreground, cooler and lighter in the distance. The lush bank itself is desaturated and cooled a little, above the warm light of the path, to give the impression of misty light.

Special effects like this in paint are visual tricks, created through the use of complementary colours, greys and multiple contrasts – everything we've covered so far. Let's learn more about how to apply these in practice.

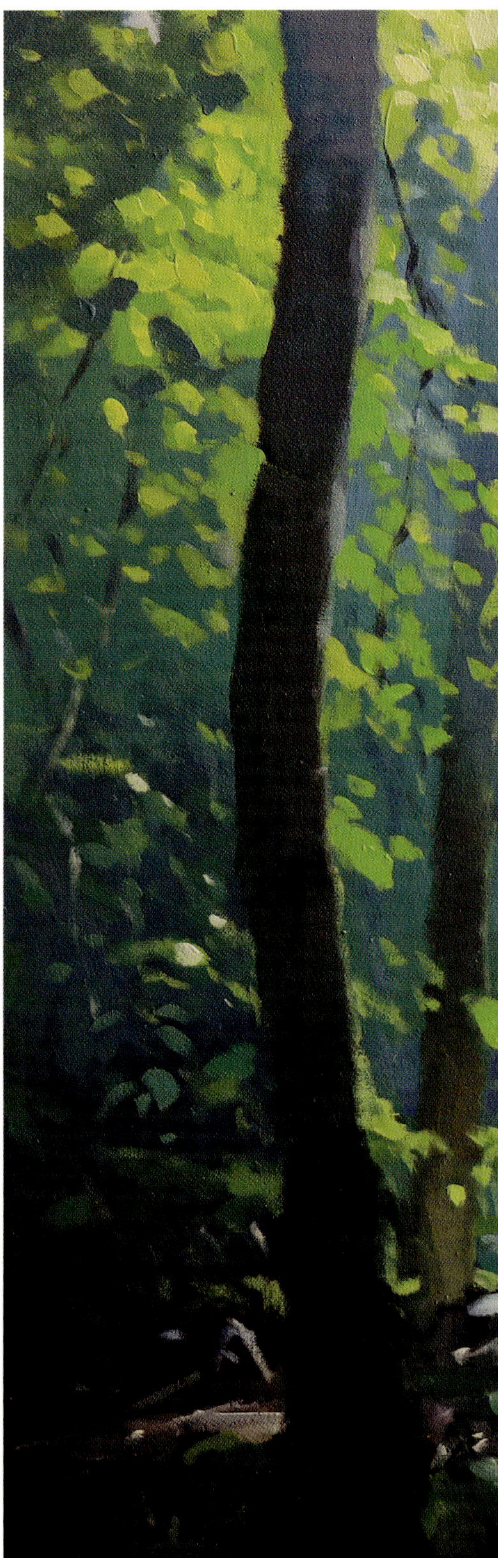

Forest Light
100 × 80cm (39½ × 31½in)

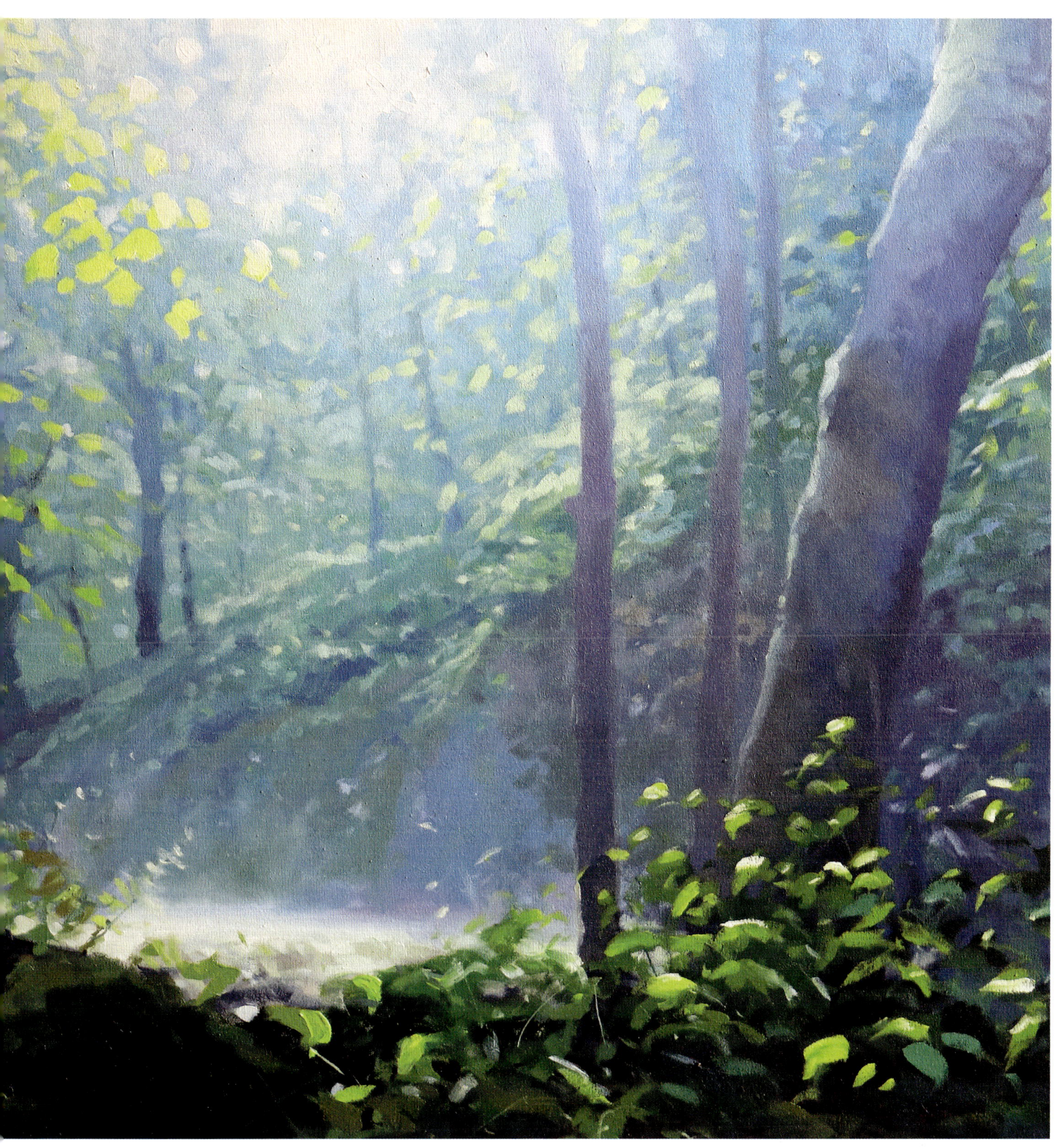

COMPOSITION

I tell people about the 'three Cs': composition, colour and contrast – and the first is the most important. For any painting to be successful it needs a good, strong composition: it is simply the bones of the whole painterly animal!

Guiding the eye

Even if every other element is top-notch, if your structure isn't guiding the eye in an effective way, all your fine work risks being lost.

Analyse what you like about the image, then edit out anything that detracts from the energy of the composition. It is easy to miss the obvious and get distracted by the painting as a whole – forgetting the fact that you are composing a visual story.

Good composition provides a compelling journey, or 'eye path', around both the surface of the canvas and through the illusory depth of the image.

Think of a focal point as the lighthouse in the ocean of your painting, drawing the eye and keeping it from drifting out of the painting. Not every painting has an obvious subject, however – so when deciding on your focal point, ask yourself these questions:

- Why am I painting this image?

- What stood out to me originally?

- How can I make that stand out best in paint?

Even if what you are painting doesn't sport an obvious focal point or particularly strong subject, you can still use good design to make the most of what you have. Remember, capturing the essence of your photograph or scene does not mean copying it mark for mark.

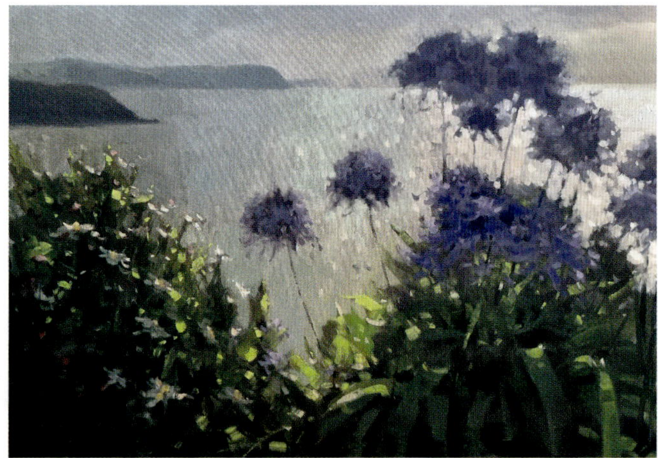

AROUND AND AROUND

In this painting, *Agapanthus*, the eye is drawn to the lightest area in this painting (behind the flowers on the right) but there is plenty to keep the eye pulled away and drawn back around the image.

Leaves, daisies, stalks, headlands and cloud shapes all work to make that path for the eye. The brushwork helps too. The sea could have been still, flat – instead I filled it with downward brushstrokes to help the flow.

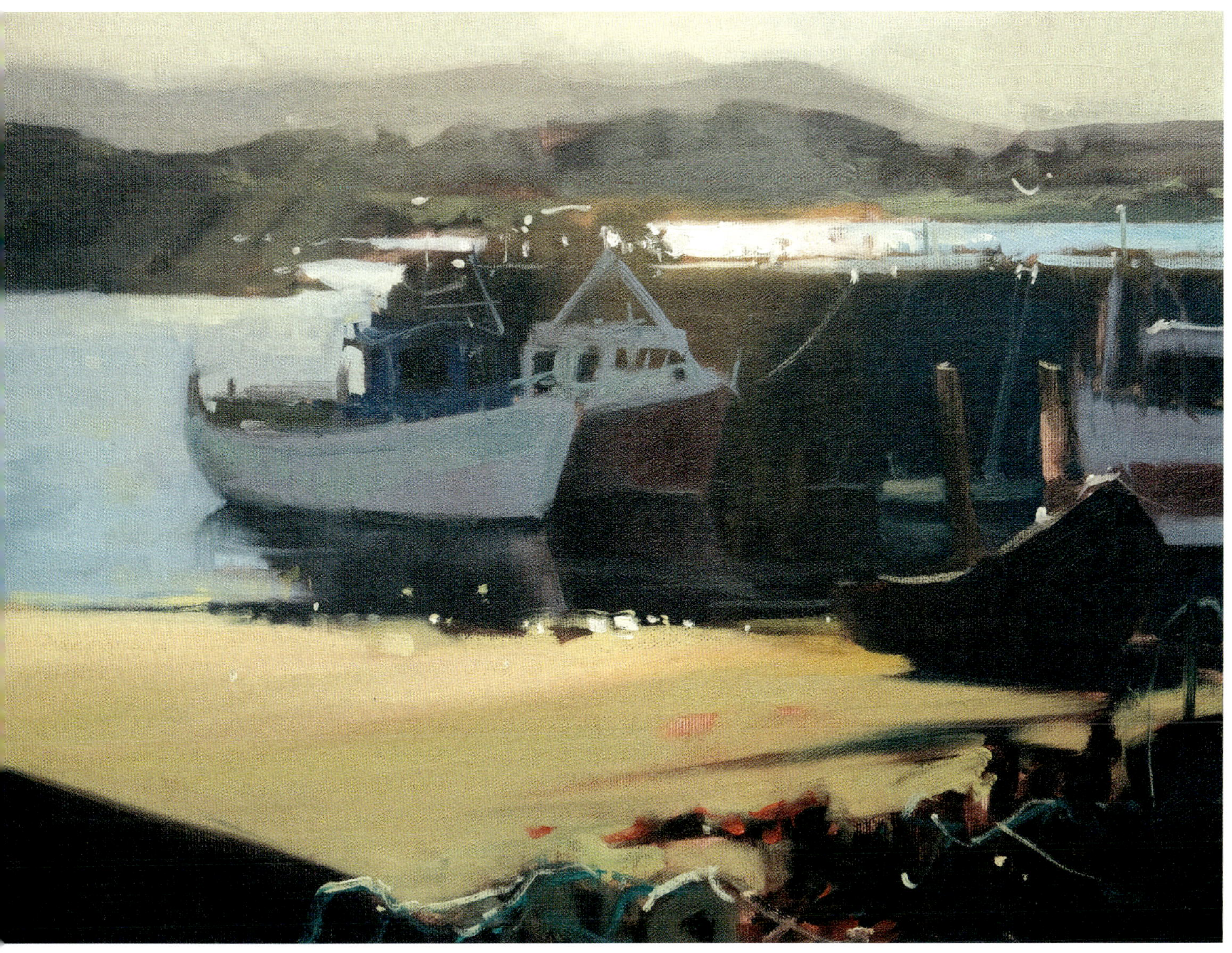

A JOURNEY FOR THE EYE

Have a long look at this painting. The composition is designed to zig-zag your eye both two-dimensionally around the canvas, and three-dimensionally through the scene. Subjects and brushwork angle towards each other and there is a sense of constant movement. Your eye does not stop wandering around the picture! It is drawn most strongly to the lightest area on the water, but little elements pull you away again: the verticals behind the foreground boat, the seagull and sparkles, the ropes.

West Coast Harbour
40 × 30cm (15¾ × 11¾in)

Compositional tips

Avoid a central focal point It seems to be natural for us to want to place our subject centrally, be it the setting sun or a vase of flowers. It is neat and symmetrical and our focus is given pride of place. Central subjects call the eye straight to them, like a bull's-eye on a dartboard, and this works well in advertising design, when you have a message you need delivered very quickly.

A speedy glance, however, is precisely the opposite of what we want! Our object is to entice the eye to linger, with all elements leading it around the focal point. We want a visual story, not a marketing message.

Make things unbalanced A horizon or vertical line too close to the centre of the canvas will split the image into two, reducing the overall impact. Your painting can be beautiful within each of those two halves, but the draw of the eye path around it is lessened by the symmetrical pull of each side.

As appealing as those two halves might be in their own right, you should aim to highlight the area that counts the most – it will be more impactful as a result. If every element is treated with the same level of importance, you overwhelm the eye and consequently create a flat painting.

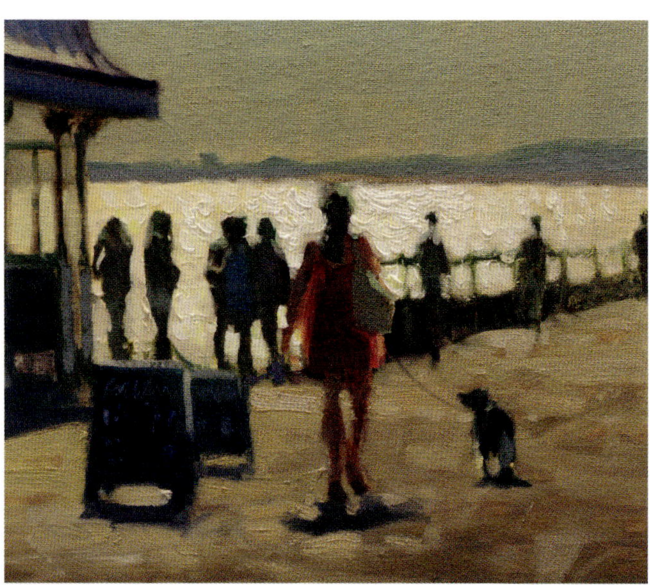

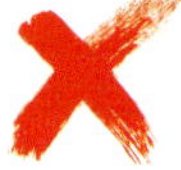

The figure in the red dress is the focal point in this painting. Here she is central, with the dog and the sign both angling in towards her. This placement reduces the compositional energy of the painting. The eye isn't drawn to anywhere else except the focal point – so while it might sell the dress, it doesn't help the painting!

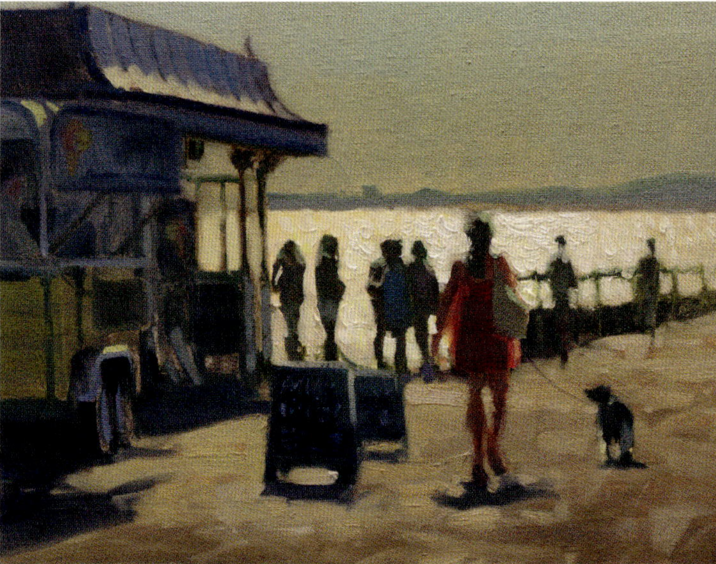

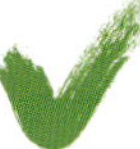

The original painting, Sun, Sea and Ice-cream, in full. The red dress is still the main focal point, but now the elements are weighted differently. She is off-centre, as is the brightest light in the distance. The eye is encouraged to follow the shapes and angles around and through the scene. The difference is subtle but the consequences for the painting are vital to its success.

Make connections Once everything is safely off-centre, all that remains is to connect the areas of the image. This compositional connection can be accentuated subtly through colour, texture, brushwork, light and the subject itself. The objective is always that strong path for the eye: a flow and a point of interest. If you can get good design in from the start, your work will be all the stronger.

The rule of thirds The rule of thirds simply means to avoid central horizons or verticals, keeping the focal point off-centre. Pop a three by three grid over your image to see how the composition is working. It is just a guide, however – as evidenced in the original painting on the right, higher horizons work for when the subject demands more attention, like a big roiling sea (or lower, for dramatic skies).

The idea is to strongly weight the image one way or another, so you avoid the image folding in on itself at the horizon point.

Keep the main focal point off-centre,
and remember the rule of thirds – it
is as simple as that.

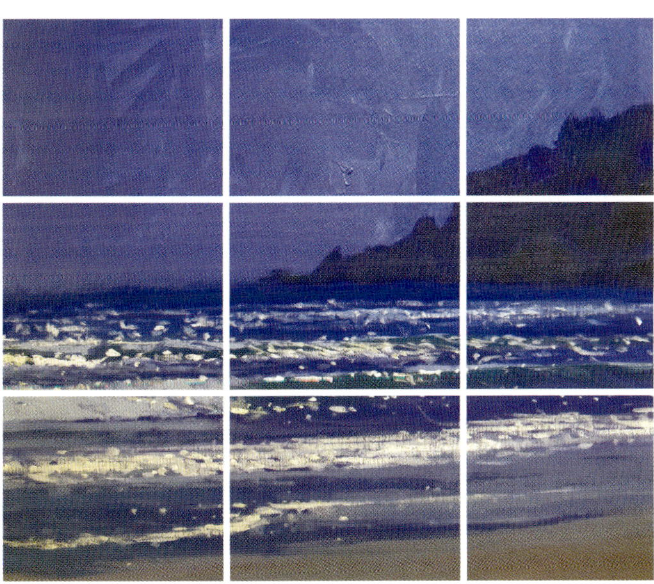

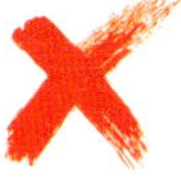

You need to use the elements of the painting to tell the viewer where you want them to look. Here, the central horizon cuts the painting in half. The sky and sea have equal weight, and there is a battle for the viewer's attention.

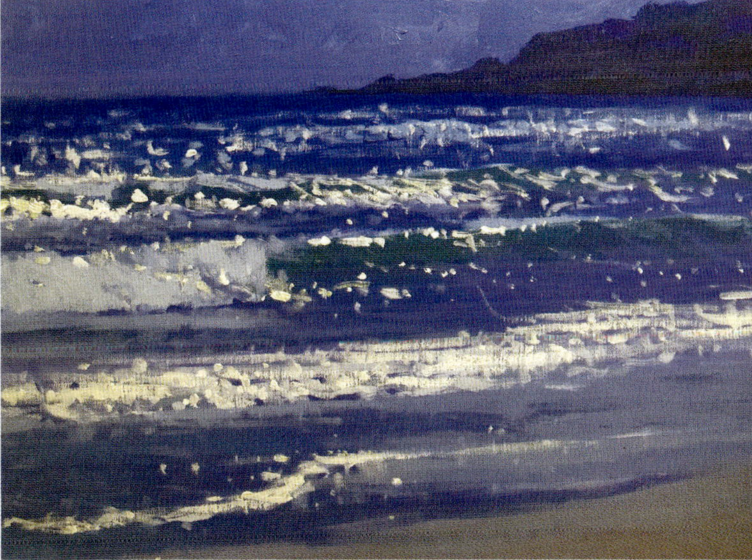

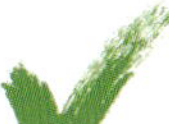

In the full painting, the horizon line ensures far more weight and attention is given to the sea.

CONNECT ALL AREAS OF THE PAINTING

Scenes with obvious focal points – structures, people, trees – lend themselves well to the creation of a decent path for the eye. This is because the individual elements can be placed around the painting with one dominating the rest. It isn't always so straightforward, however. Sometimes you have to manipulate the subject to enable the strongest painterly design.

When I paint outside, connections between elements are the most important aspects I look for. In the painting below, I increased the prominence of the pine tree and enhanced the reflection in the water, creating a strong vertical to connect the foreground, mid-ground and background. Increasing the size of the background hill and sharpening the gradient of the land made them stronger shapes in the composition, which means they support the tree better.

We are not tied by what we see or what a photograph tells us. Exercising our knowledge for strong design will result in art, not just representation.

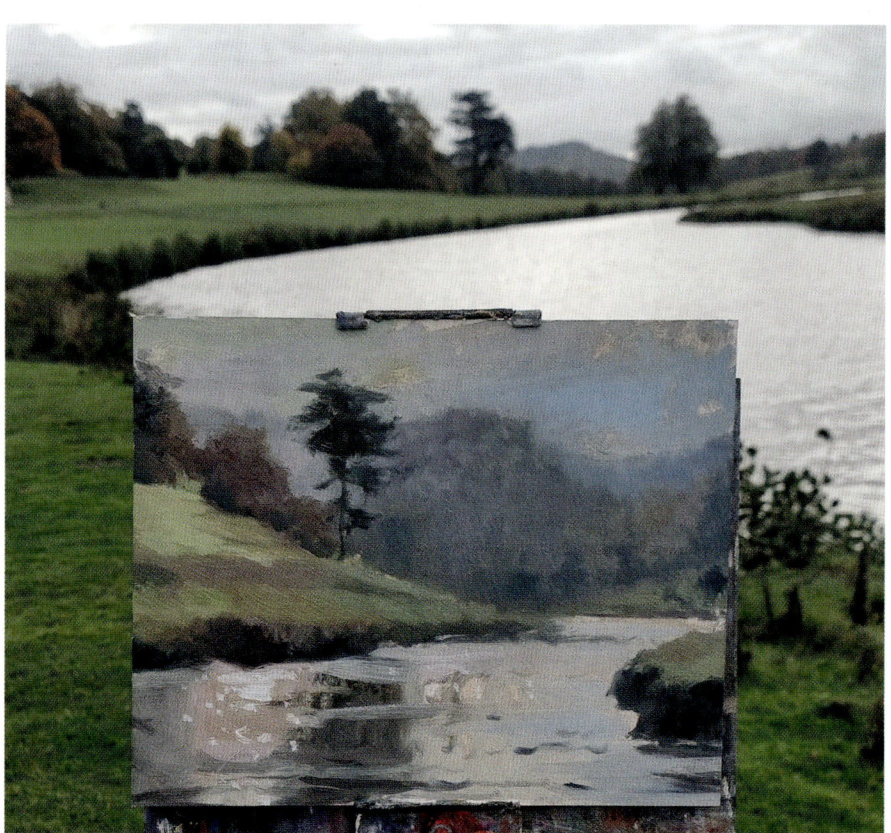

My Favourite Tree   *30 × 24cm (11¾ × 9½in)*

This plein air *painting – which began* contre-jour, *though ended in a rather grey day – shows the river Derwent at Chatsworth* .

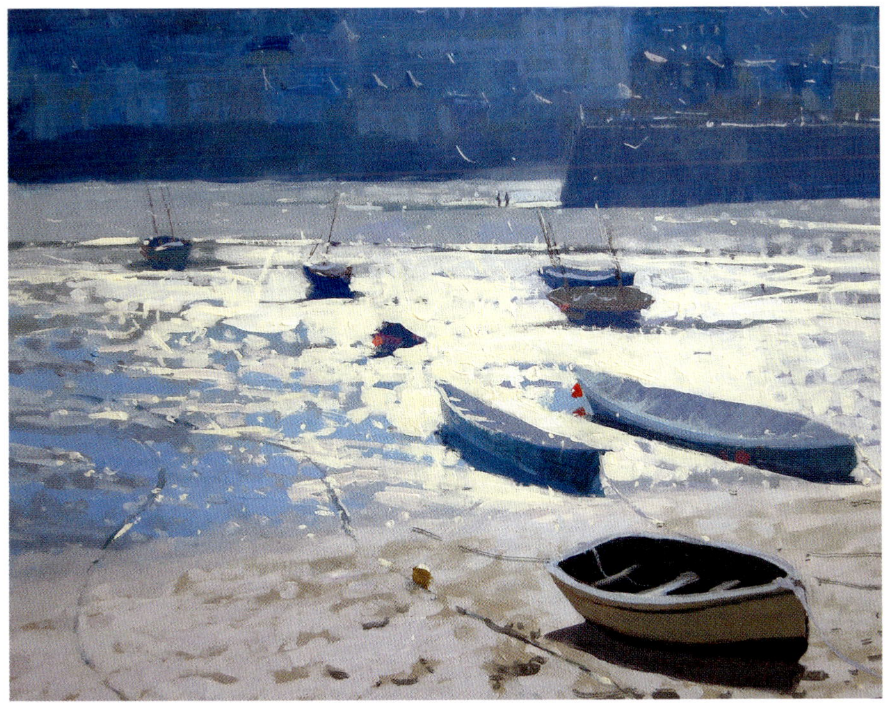

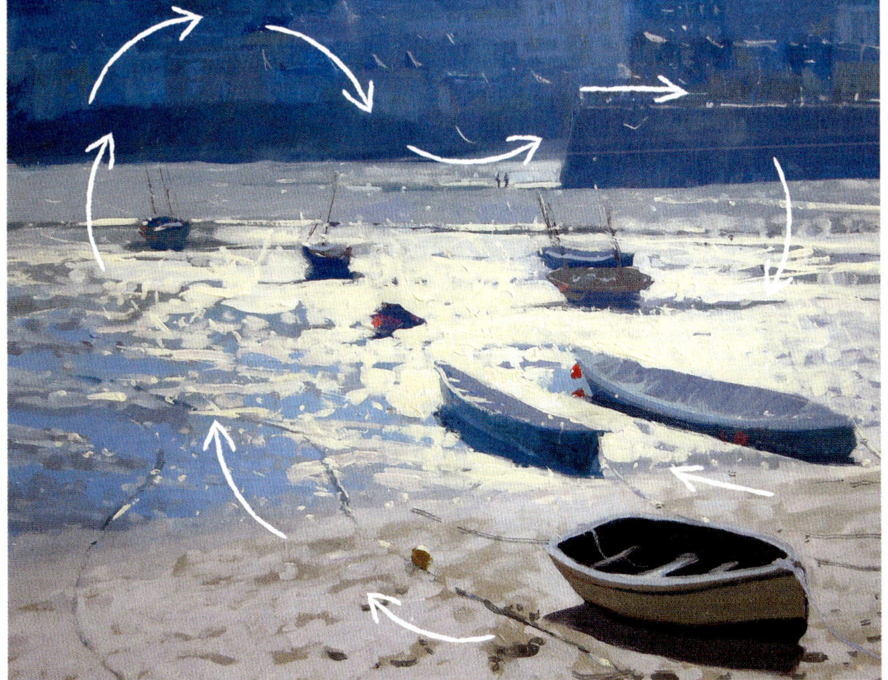

GET CONNECTED

This painting has a strong visual current guiding the eye. It doesn't have a single focal point as such – instead the composition flows between each connected element.

Everything is working to guide the eye around and through. The foreground boats and ropes lead the eye in, their angles all pointing to the top left. The shapes of the blue water and warm sand stabilize the lean by pushing the eye to the right. The eye hits the background town of St Ives and moves right and down, via the highlights on the roofs and the haze of the sun above. It then reaches the people walking right, and takes our gaze and imagination beyond the harbour wall.

COLOUR

Colour is the second of the three Cs. Seeing and identifying colours, whether from photographs or life, takes practice. It requires a mix of observation, recognition and knowledge of what to look for.

Colour is only revealed to the human eye through light. The quality and temperature of that light will affect the object of study. Surrounding colours and anything in our peripheral vision, including our own vibrant clothing, will affect both what we see and how we judge. Does this matter? Yes! Colour is not an absolute, and being aware of this is important when you are depicting light on a two-dimensional surface.

Be aware of your own preconceptions when judging colour. We all jump to conclusions. It is easiest to make this mistake when an object is known for its colour – a yellow banana, white snow, blue seas, green grass or brown tree trunks. Yes, these objects can appear to be these colours… but this is certainly not set or unchangeable. Never assume you know the colour of a thing before you have studied it in its context. The power of what we think we know can prevent us from even trying to activate our observational skills.

This knowledge is what stops me from giving out fixed 'colour recipes' for certain subjects when I teach. Clouds depicted perfectly by ultramarine blue, burnt umber and white one moment, will be a completely different mix the next. And on another, important note – you and I will make different sense of those colours. Just as our thoughts, concepts and styles are distinct from one another, we all see and interpret colour differently. When we paint our perception of the view before us, we are sharing our unique way of seeing.

PALETTE

This shot of my palette shows the messy, intuitive nature of my mixing. I have provided suggestions for colour mixes in the projects, but I strongly encourage you to work out mixes yourself from observation and matching – it's much more interesting and fun!

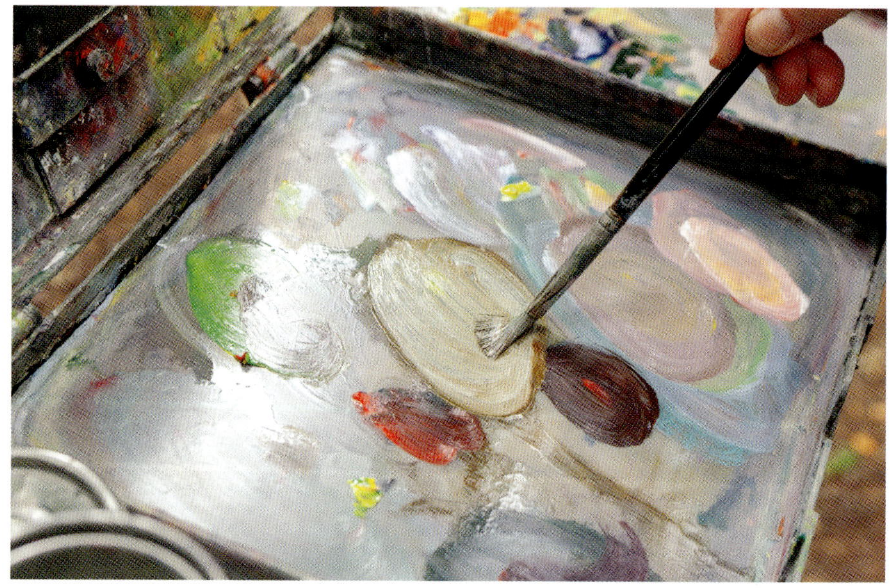

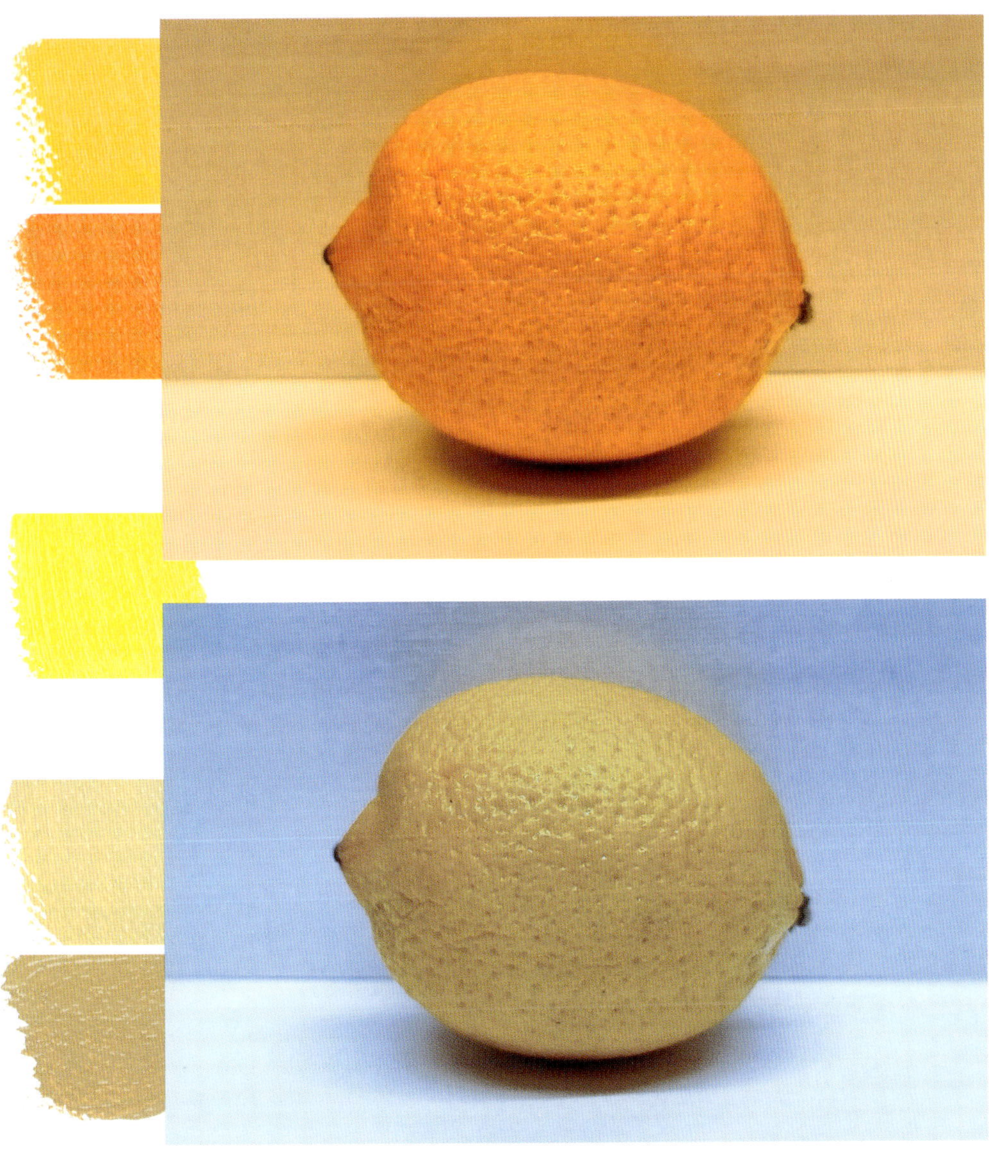

Oranges and lemons?

How often would you see a lemon in a fruit bowl and reach for 'lemon yellow' paint without thoroughly analysing its actual colour?

Pictured above is that same lemon, photographed in warm (top) and cold (bottom) lighting. There is a swatch alongside each, showing the highlight and shadow colour. The middle swatch is a pure lemon yellow from the tube, for comparison.

While we would still describe the lemon as 'yellow' in each of the photographs, the actual colours are much more varied than you might have expected.

How to see colour clearly

'There are two things in the painter, the eye and the mind; each of them should aid the other.'
Paul Cézanne

Trying to ignore the 'but grass is always green!' voice can be tricky, but there are ways we can activate our observational skills. My most useful studio painting aid is to 'abstractify' the image by turning the photograph upside down. Making things abstract, or at least unfamiliar, can make the shapes of a scene clearer. It also allows us to see darks, lights and colours more truthfully.

I first used this method for portraits, at the beginning of my career as a painter. When working from photographs I found that I would always see the cheek and nose area as longer than it was. This error became obvious when I compared the photograph and painting upside down, so I decided to work like this from the start. It was so effective for seeing subtle colour transitions in skin tones, that I began to use it with my landscapes too. Try it with your own photographs.

- First, study an image the right way up.

- Name the colours, as best you can – dark grey-blue, mossy green, and so forth.

- Number the colours – from darkest to lightest. See the *Tonal Seascape* exercise on page 28 for help with this.

- Turn the photograph upside down, and repeat the steps above.

Your interpretation of the scene will now be secondary to your observational eye. Often you will find that some of the 'blacks' are lighter than you think, the colours less defined and more grey. The colours in the image are more tonally complex, when compared to your first impression.

OTHER APPROACHES

There are other ways to really see when we look:

- Use a small viewfinder to isolate colours and persuade the brain to see a colour distinct from the subject.

- When painting outside and trying to discern subtle colours, you can't turn the landscape upside down – but you can tip your head on one side.

- Try viewing the painting and photograph in the mirror.

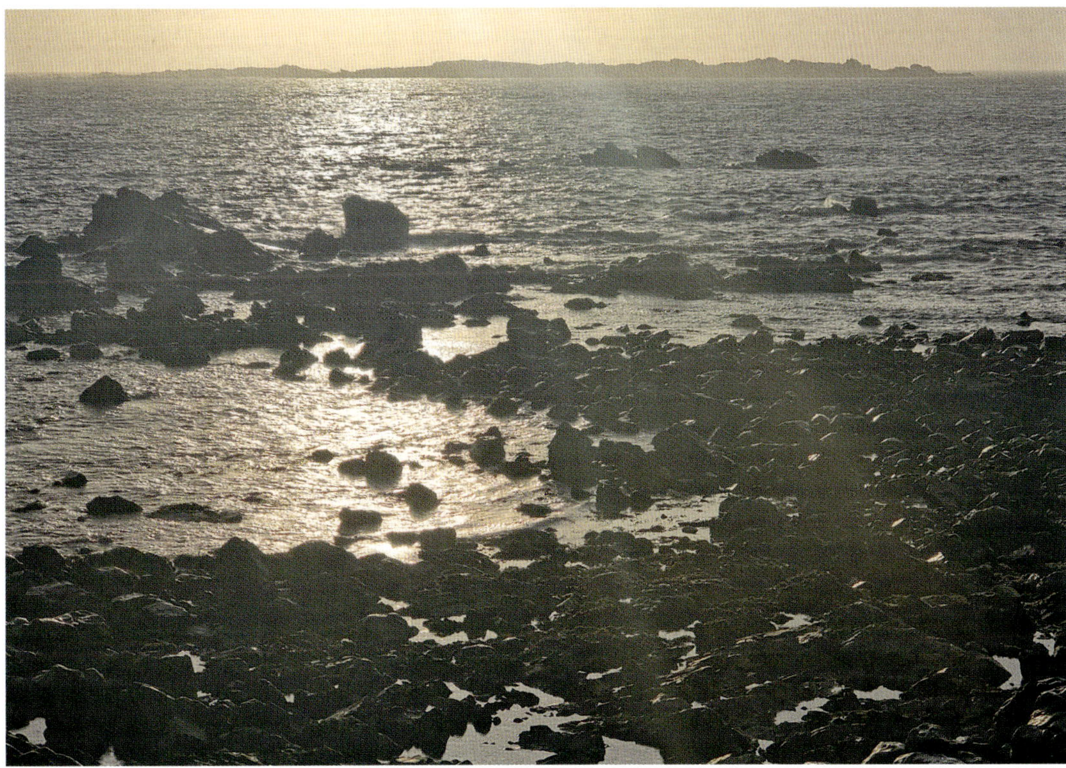

As an example, let's look at the image above and study the colours. At first glance, we might assume that the rocks are all black, the sea bluish with a white reflection and an orange sky.

Now turn the book upside down and try again. It becomes more obvious that the black rocks, while dark, are not all one temperature or the same colour. The close-up detail below, and the swatches of colour I mixed reveal that there is so much subtlety of grey out there in that glorious landscape!

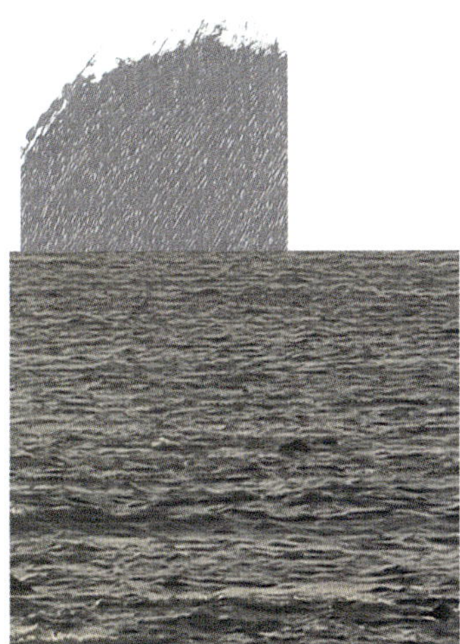

The seemingly 'blue' sea is a muted midtone grey.

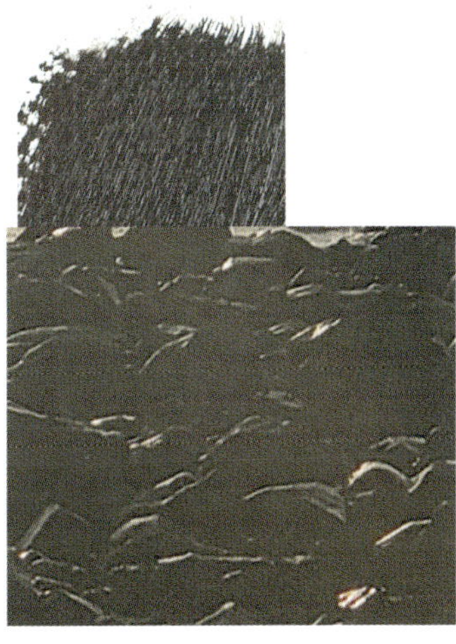

The 'black' rocks aren't nearly as dark as you might expect.

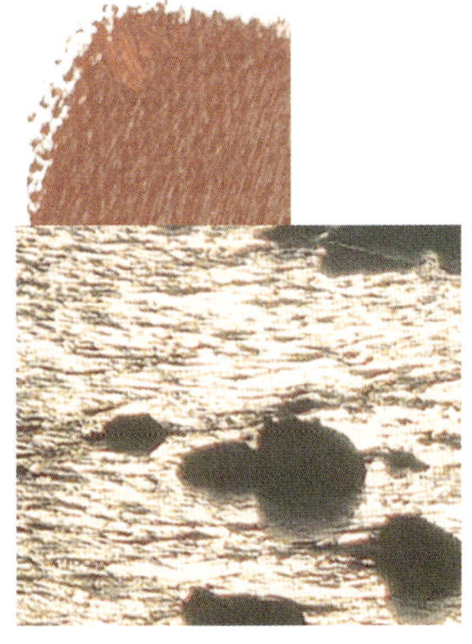

The shadows in the water reflections are a surprising grey-orange.

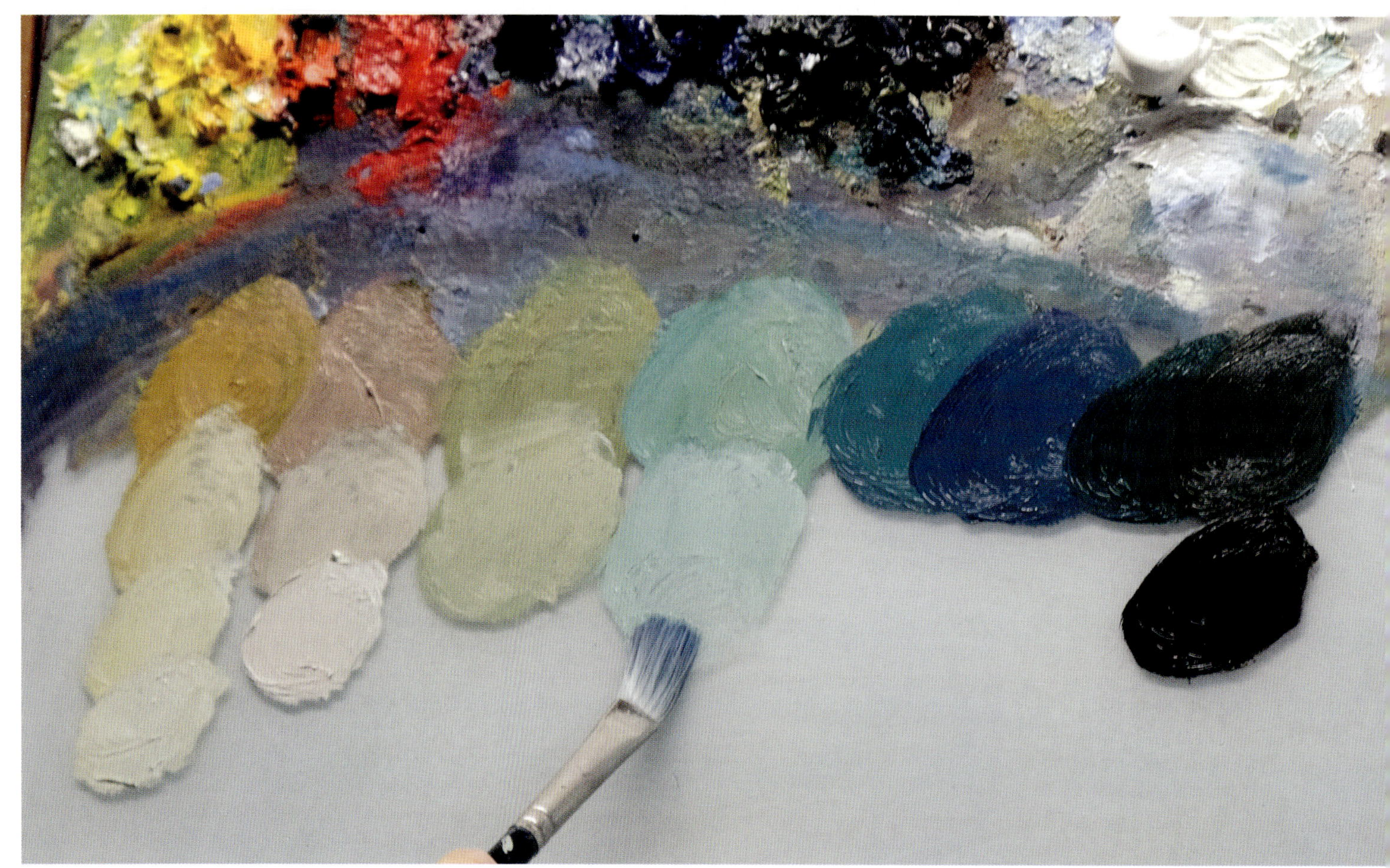

Mixing colour: a rainbow of greys

Grey is desaturated colour, and essential for *contre-jour*. Understanding its power is the key to understanding painterly light. I am often asked how to mix grey, or brown (also a grey, just a warm one), and the answer is simple. Grey is always a mix of a primary with a secondary – or in other words, a combination of all three primaries.

With the right amounts (and bearing in mind the tinting ability of each colour), through mixing yellow, red and blue you will find a very serviceable black. Add white, and you have a grey. If your grey is 'too red', add its complementary: green. If it is too warm, add blue. Whatever your mix is 'too much of', add the opposite colour to grey it back.

Desaturated greys are easy to manipulate by adding more colour, while bright lights and saturated colour lose effectiveness if they are muddied. Save adding white till last, as it is hard to get back to a real dark once you have added white to the mix. If your colour is too light, you may need to start a new mix with a clean brush and fresh colours.

BASIC MIXING CHART

I often play with new colours, but my preference is for mixing colour opposites from my basic palette (see page 25) to make versions of my favourite colour: grey.

Experiment with your own colours – it is an excellent way to get to know them!

This mixing chart is the key to my process. I make a lot more mess than this on my palette, but effectively this is it!

Mixing a primary with its complementary will give you a grey. You can lighten these greys further and tint them any way you choose. The results (see right) are subtle, beautiful, and easily achieved.

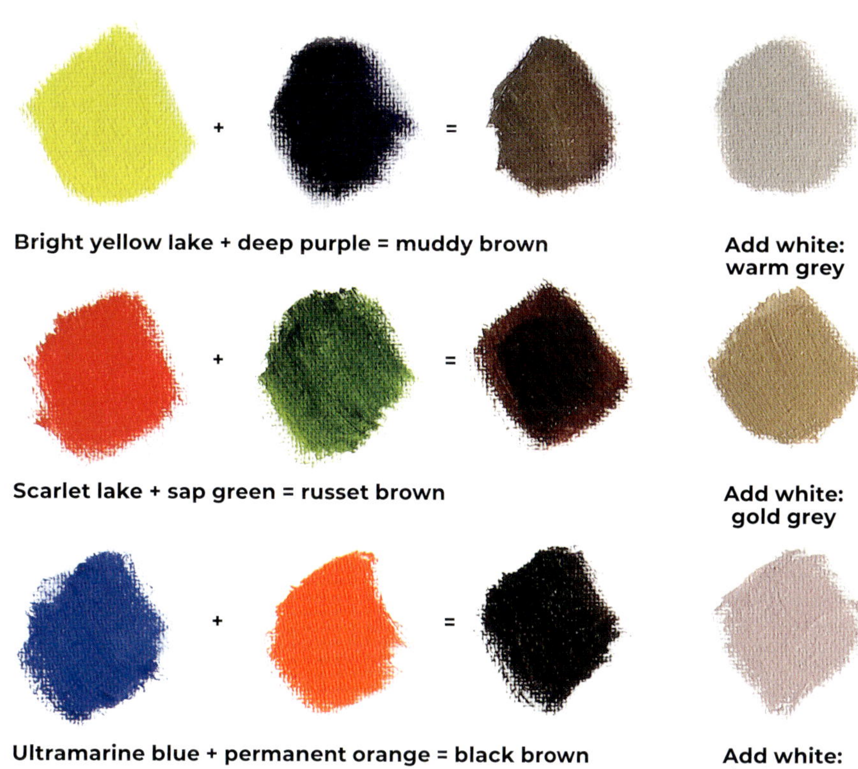

COLOUR WHEEL MIXING CHART

This takes the process to the next step, mixing the other six colours on my colour wheel (see page 27).

Note that the names of the resulting grey mixes are my own.

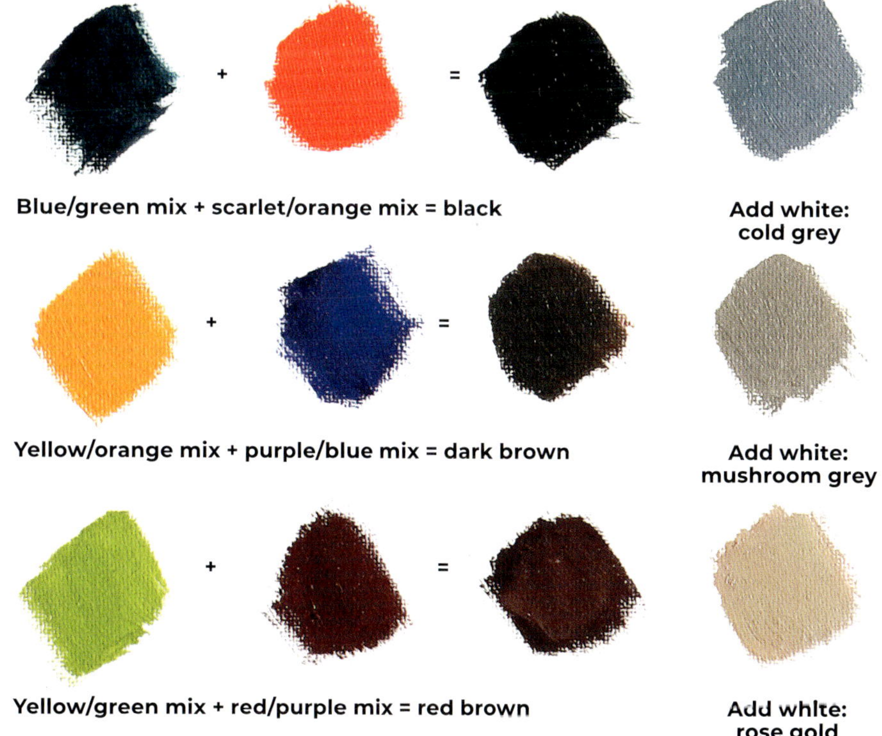

CONTRAST

The last of the three Cs; the word contrast makes most of us think simply of light and dark, especially where *contre-jour* is concerned.

I think of a successful painting in terms of a collection of contrasts, each adding to its interest and character. The key is to look for as many ways as possible to make that focal point sing. I aim for the following contrasts in all my work.

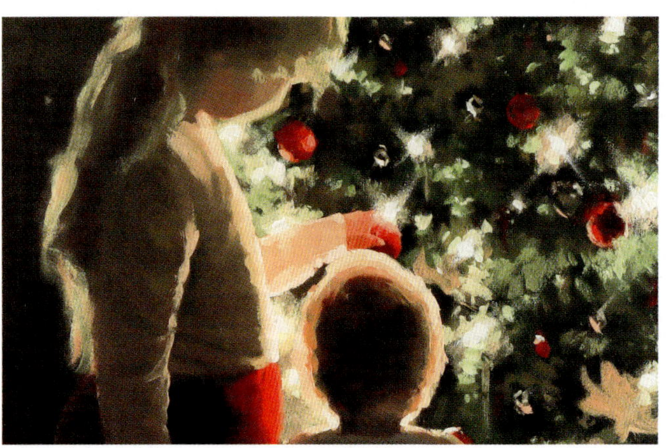

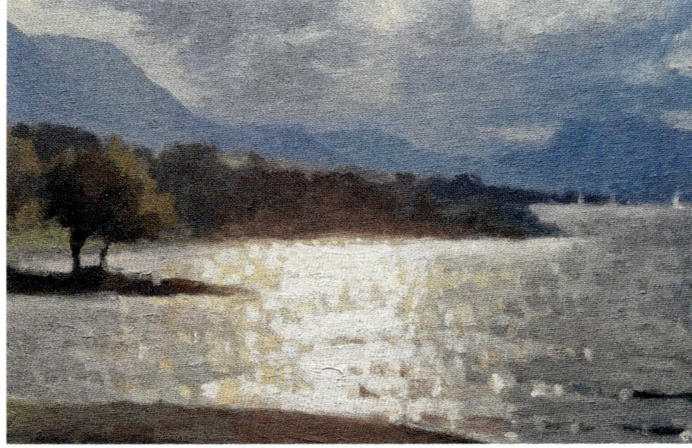

LIGHT AND DARK

I love *chiaroscuro*: strong lighting contrast used to dramatic effect. Think of the works of Rembrandt, or Caravaggio – rich blacks surrounding figures in a pool of glowing light.

Lights simply look brighter when contrasted against dark tones – a key element in *contre-jour* – so having the lightest and darkest values next to each other in a painting makes the lighting pop.

WARM AND COLD

Cold colours are there to make the warm colours look warm, not just 'orangey'. Warm colours draw the eye and so can push cooler tones into the background – perfect for creating the illusion of depth in the landscape.

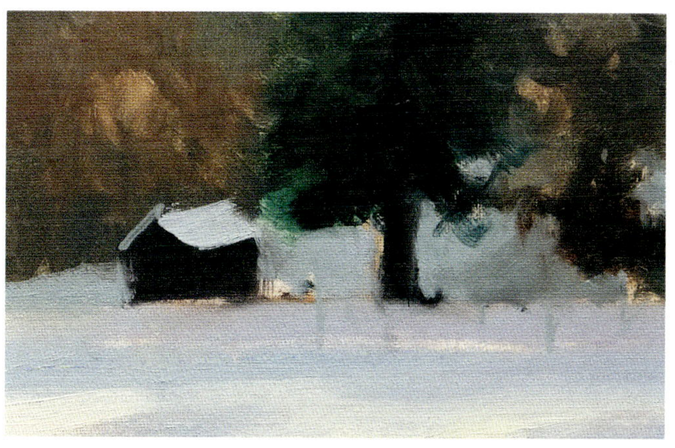

OPAQUE AND TRANSPARENT

Glimpses of a visible, transparent underpainting can provide a fresh dimension to a painting, through its contrast with opaque overpainted areas. The detail here shows flashes of the pink-tinged underpainting around and between the building, tree and snow.

As you paint, watch for these unpredictable moments of surprising beauty – pause often so you don't accidentally paint over them.

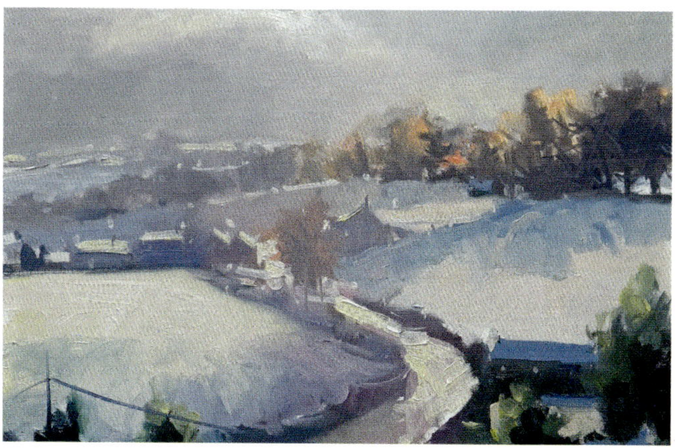

SATURATED AND GREY

In terms of lighting, paintings awash with pure saturated colour can be flatter and give less impact. Greys provide the stage for the star that is colour, and help that colour to pack a punch and stand out.

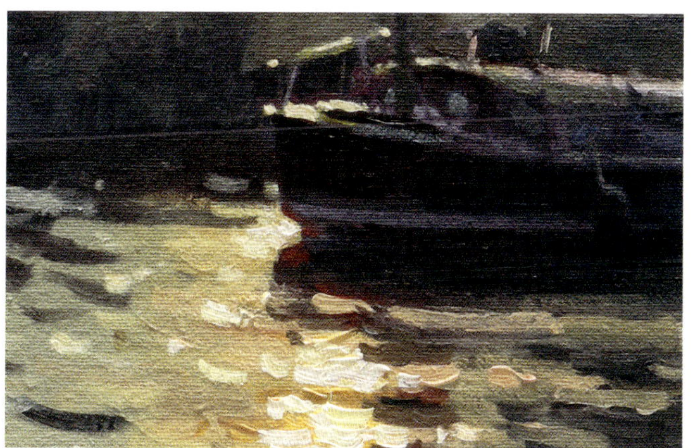

THICK AND THIN PAINT

For depth and compositional focus, using thicker paint provides another useful way to define your focal point simply because it stands proud of the thin. In my *contre-jour* work, I find the lighting illusion is more effective with thick, flat lights; unbrushed and unsullied. The louder I can make those highlights shout, the better.

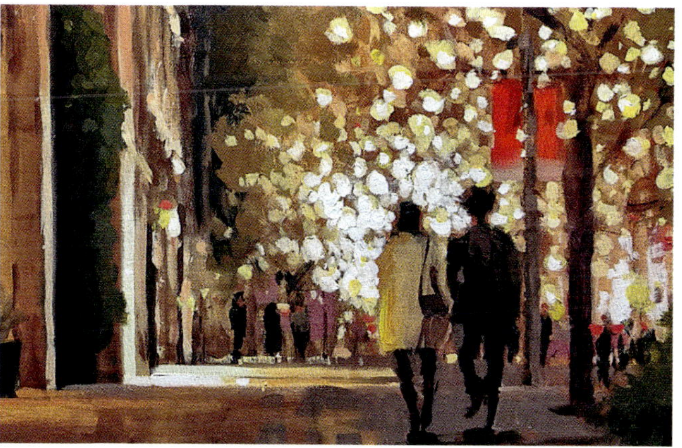

DETAIL AND SOFTNESS

If there is too much detail, the impact of a painting can be lost. Keep in mind both depth and the focal point when you are making any hard edges – ask yourself if that area really needs to be sharp. If it's in the background, or outside the hot zone, chances are it should be softer so the compositional focus is not lost.

USING THE THREE CS

It is worth repeating that all the rules of composition, contrast and colour are fluid – this is art, after all. Understanding the guidelines will make your ideas visually stronger – but it will also enable you to break any rules well.

Assessing your reference

It is worth analysing our photographs to see what we can achieve with them. It requires a bit of imagination to work out what each offers in terms of light, colour and brushwork before you launch into painting.

Our photographs can sport the most wonderful subjects and composition, but can often be lacking when it comes to colour. Photographs often benefit from a digital push in order to make them good as reference for a painting. This is especially true when working from *contre-jour* photographs – they can be bleached white and extremely uninteresting.

We'll look further at photography later on – but when you take photographs with an eye for a painting, always think analytically. Use what you know about composition, colour and contrast. Is there enough of a story to play with? Does the scene have a wide tonal range of dark to light? Is there enough temperature contrast to make the warm light sing? There is so much you can do once you let your painterly knowledge into the game.

Enhancing your reference

I recommend adjusting a *contre-jour* photograph so that the colours are warmer, more saturated, and the darks less black, as I've done in the example below. I have darkened the whole image so that highlights are more prominent. There are plenty of intuitive, free phone apps available to enable this.

This method doesn't create a more attractive photograph, but that is not the object of the exercise. Once you've got the image, don't forget that you can digitally play around to make something more useful than the original photograph. Always exercise your artistic licence, and celebrate the freedom of paint!

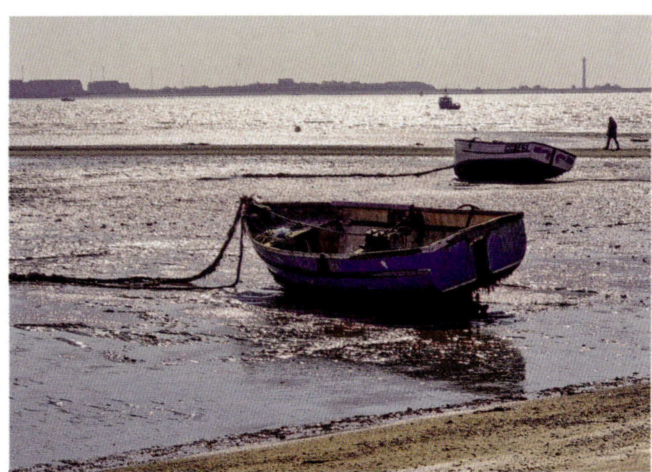

The original photograph.

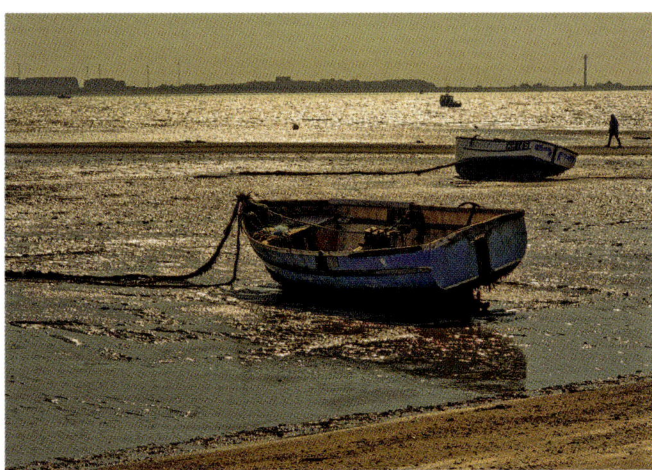

The darkened photograph.

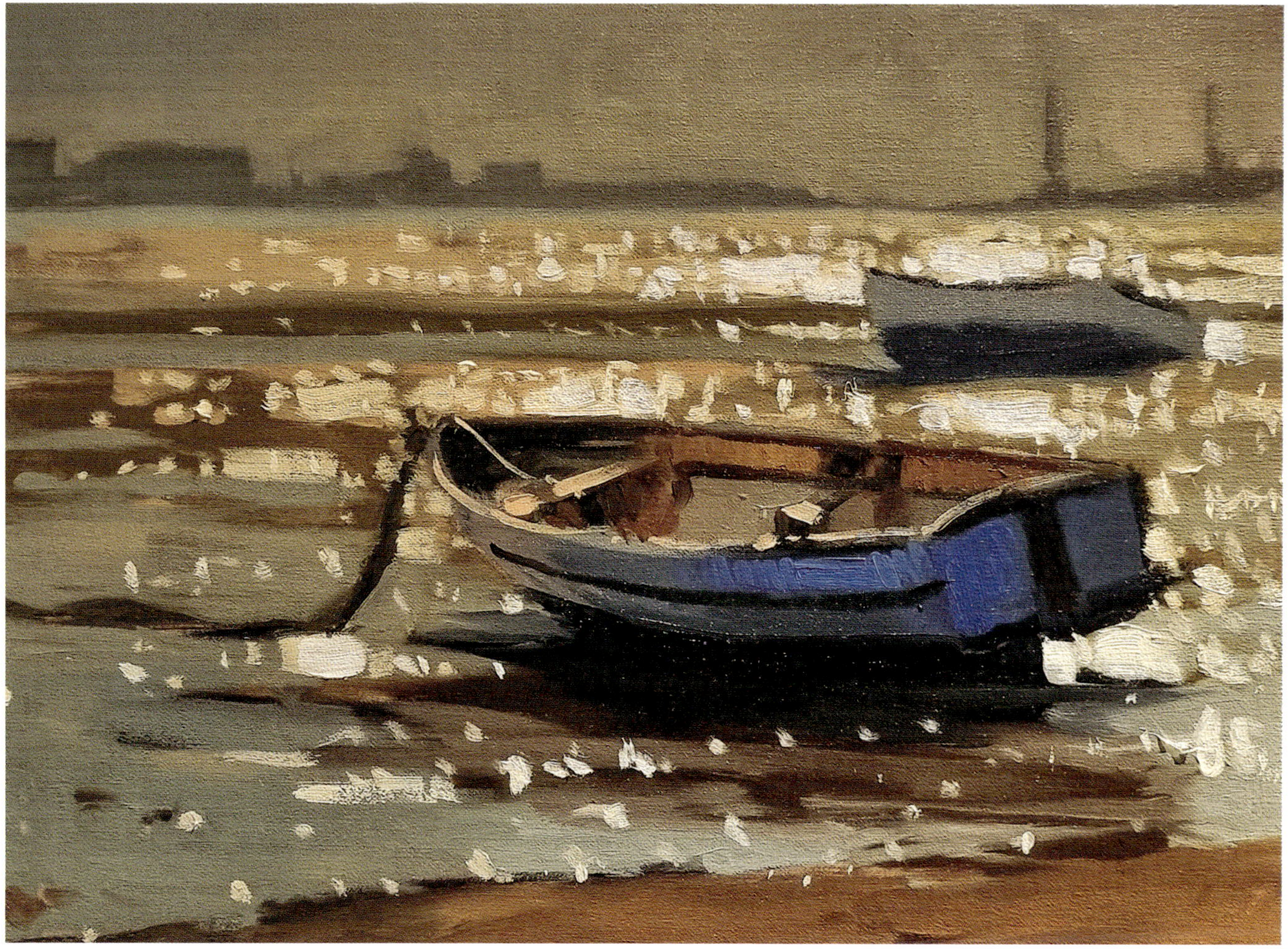

Using your reference

The success of the lighting in this painting relied upon two things: the contrast between light and dark, and the relationship between the two colour opposites: the burnt orange and the blue of the boat.

The surrounding complementaries of cool greys and warm browns make a balanced, supportive setting for these key elements. I made the boat colours even brighter and more saturated than in the digitally altered photograph, in order to make the play of colour stronger and more exciting.

The tonal range is wide, with the darkest shadows underneath the boat contrasting well with the brightest lights on the water. The brightest lights are in thick, luscious paint, standing proud against the flatter greys of the distance.

Low Tide, Harwich
40 × 30cm (15¾ × 11¾in)

THE APPEAL OF THE OCEAN

We now have everything we need under our belts to start – and we'll begin with a subject that's close to my heart. My love of *contre-jour* was sparked by my love of the sea. I have stared at it since I can remember, and am entranced by its every mood. I could talk about it for several chapters, but suffice to say, nothing stops me in my tracks like the light on the waves. I find it unendingly comforting. The sparkling sea, with that direct reflection of the sun, draws us into that warm, all-encompassing light. All those little lights are telling us so much about the currents, wave patterns, wind and noise. The colour of the sea tells us about the temperature, the quality of the light and time of day. The shadows show the strength of the light, the height of a wave, the depth of the water.

With every new attempt at capturing this subject, I look for a better illusion of light, warmth and movement on the canvas. I want to feel that I am there, squinting, with the salt and the breeze on my face!

It seems to me that there is always something new to learn about special effects of colour and light. Shown here are some close-ups from recent seascapes where a little bit of magic has happened.

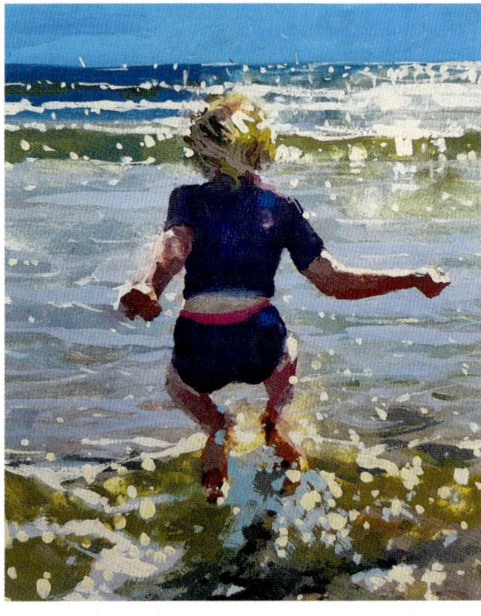

Jumping waves on a sparkly summer's day – surely one of the best activities.

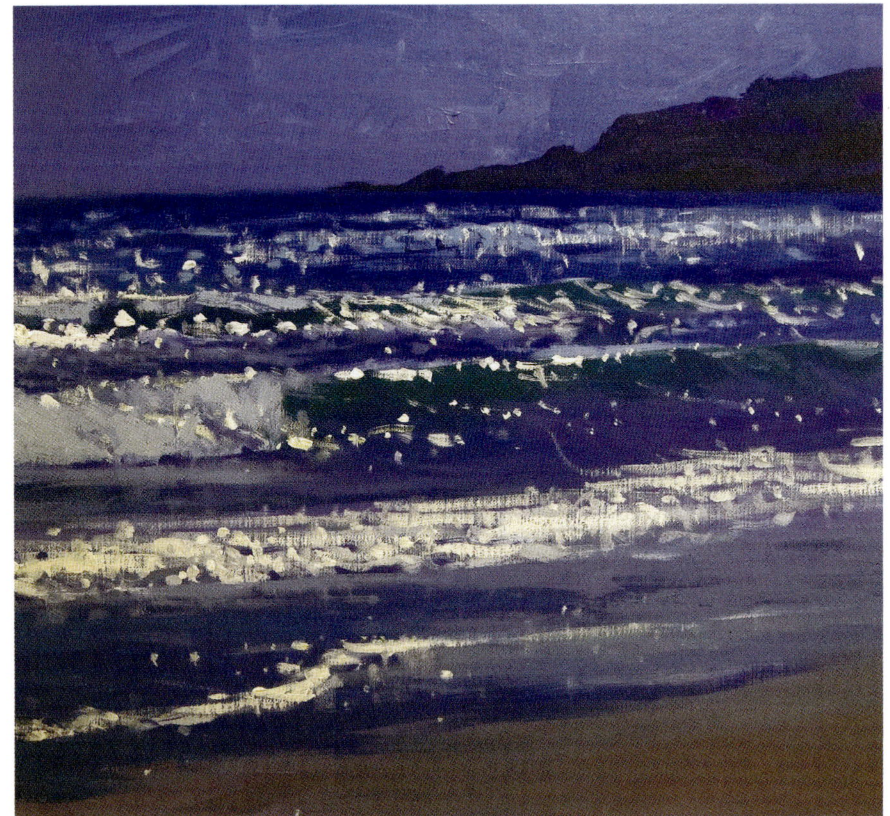

I love the grey foam in this painting, and how it affects the highlights.

This was a studio painting from a photograph, which at first glance seemed entirely blue and white. I knew I had to give prominence to the reflective light, and pick out the waves. The addition of cold green brought form to the wave faces, showing where the water became more transparent. Greying the crashing foam and accentuating its own reflection in the water then allowed the yellowed white highlights to glow.

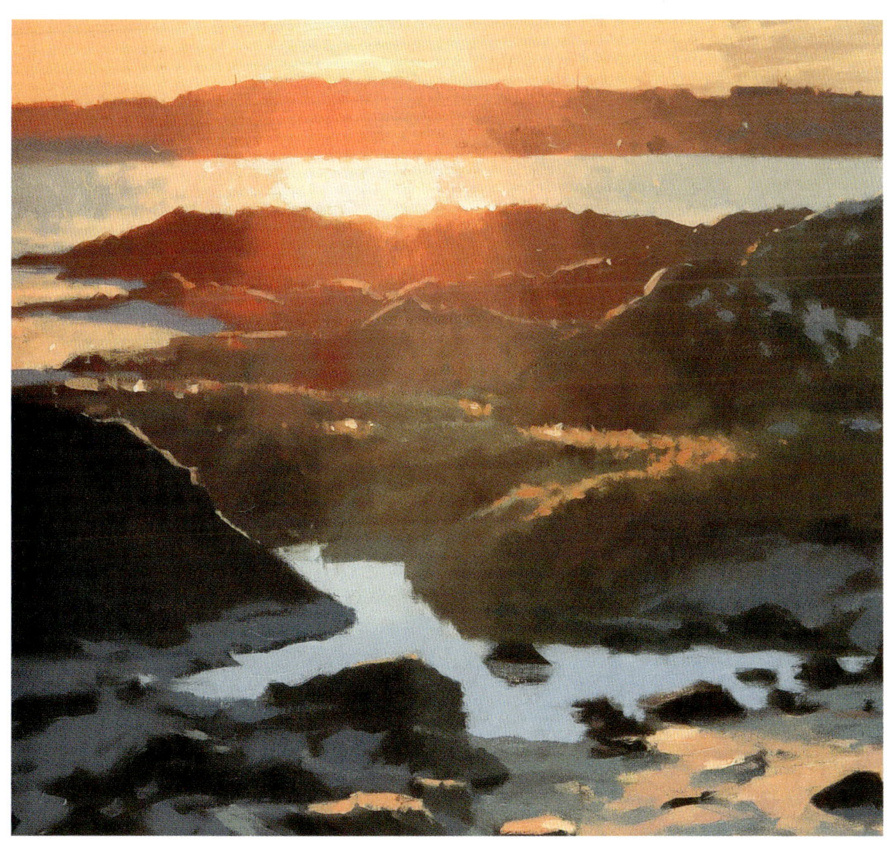

This painting is a perfect example of complementaries doing their job!

Sunsets can be overridingly orange. It is important to find the cooler temperatures, both for contrast and to grey the orange outside of the brighter zones. This ensures you don't lose the painterly impact. The cold blues in the foreground and green tones in the haze here allow the orange, pinks and russets to sing.

The sparkle itself is white mixed with a touch of yellow, sat on a bed of very light yellow/pink. This is cooled with the tiniest touch of blue. The blinding brightness is due to there being only one loud area of light, with the odd spark dotted about.

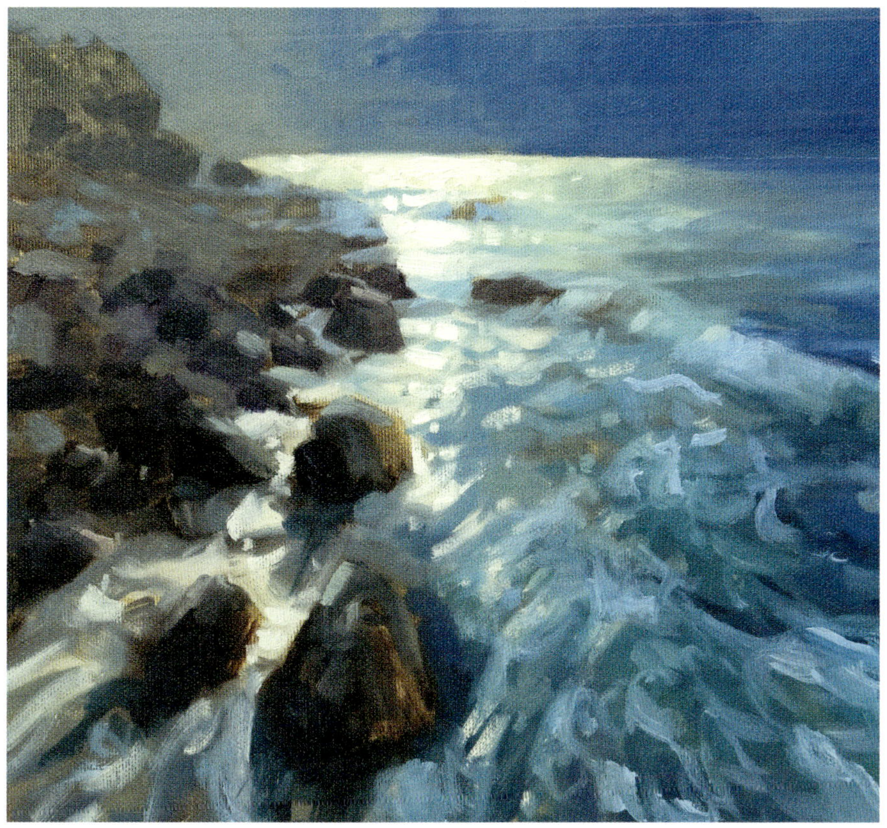

I make most of my discoveries in painting outside, in that intense rush to capture changing light. A photograph will never capture what our eyes can see.

On this occasion, the stormlight was intensely green-yellow, the sky a dramatically green-blue. Everything, including the light, was cold! I found that the transparent umber warmth of my initial sketch was the perfect complement to the opaque, icy tones, so I kept much of it in and then reproduced this in a larger studio painting. It's all about balance.

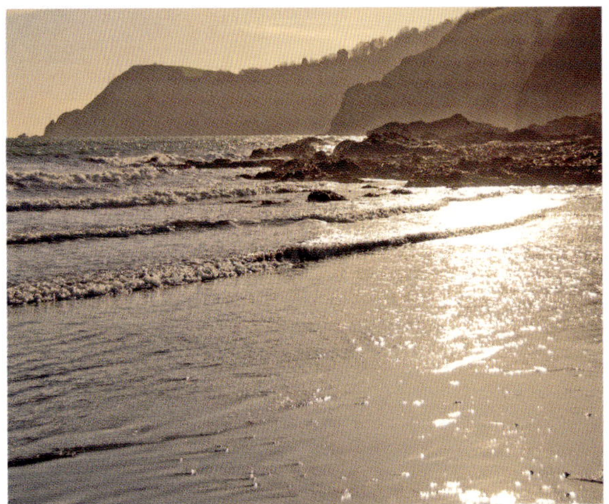

THE SPARKLING OCEAN

The ultimate in sparkly light! Painting Polkerris, a coastal village in Cornwall, UK, will show you how to develop zones of colour gradually in order to depict hazy sunlight and distance. Building on the *Tonal Seascape* exercise (see pages 28–31), this project will gently introduce you to bringing colour into your work, and it will also give you excellent practice in mixing all those greys.

The project is broken down into broad stages, with explanations of what needs to be done at each stage for this painting so you can follow along. Alongside these instructions are my notes and thoughts on more general aspects of painting similar subjects, so you can explore further on your own.

You will need

30 × 24cm (11¾ × 9½in) canvas board

Brushes: 12mm (½in) flat brush, 12mm (½in) bristle flat brush, 6mm (¼in) filbert, small rigger, small fan brush (optional)

Paints: titanium white, bright yellow lake, scarlet lake, deep purple, ultramarine blue, sap green

Low-odour solvent

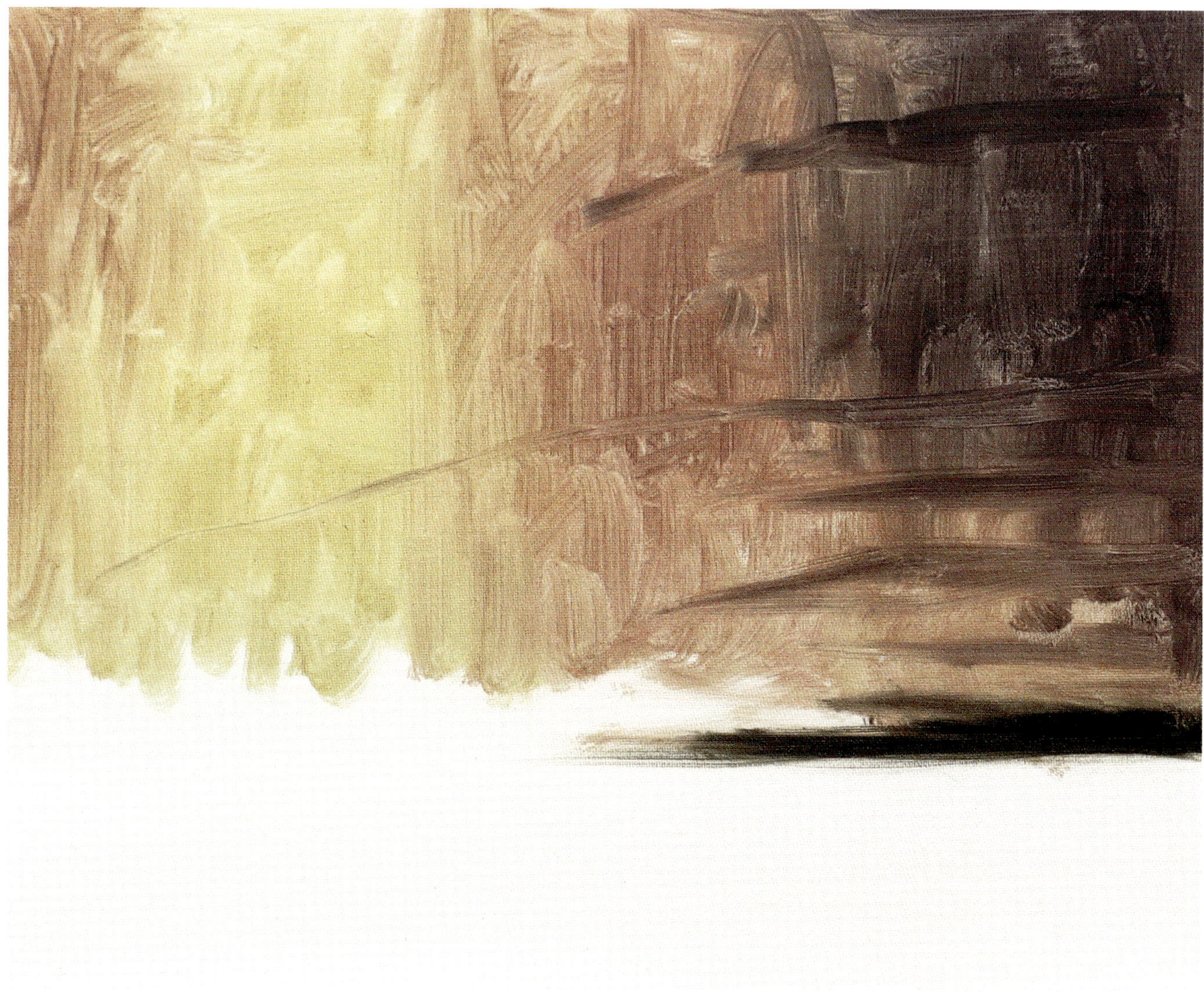

FIRST STAGE

In the initial stages of covering the canvas, we will create one thin mix at the beginning, and develop it with addition of other colours until the white is covered. This will result in colour harmony across the painting.

· Turn the reference image (see opposite) upside down. Working upside down will help you to establish colours and loose shapes quickly and without interpretation, giving you a solid base for more intuitive development.

· Use a little solvent to create a thin mix of bright yellow lake, scarlet lake and titanium white. Starting from the left-hand side, brush this on using loose downstrokes of the 12mm (½in) flat brush.

· Add a little more scarlet lake and a touch of deep purple for the next colour zone, then a little more purple and yellow for the darkest colour on the right.

· Add a touch of ultramarine blue to the mix for the darkest colour on the horizon, and paint some horizontal waves to cut across the vertical brushwork.

Brushwork and the sea

I used a mix of synthetic soft and bristle brushes for this project. Soft synthetics allow for smooth colour placement of background and sky, while bristles allow for a more impasto texture and brush marks of opaque, bright light or crashing waves.

For this sort of scene, I would typically use a 12mm (½in) soft flat for the initial stages, followed by a filbert for more defined marks. I'd keep a small rigger/liner in my brush bag for those final marks and splashes, too. I also find a soft fan brush useful for reflections beneath waves.

Soft flat

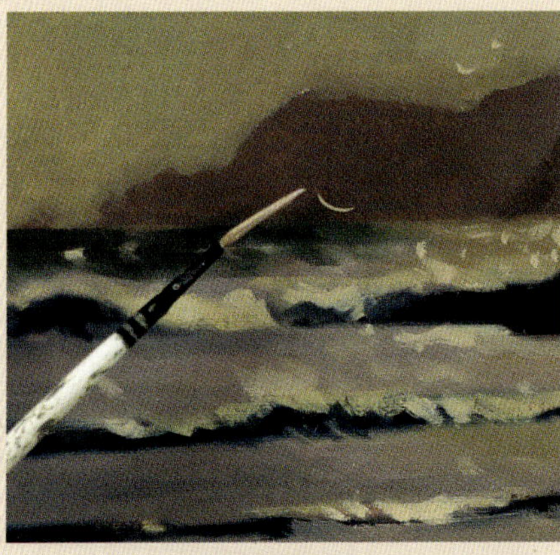

Small rigger

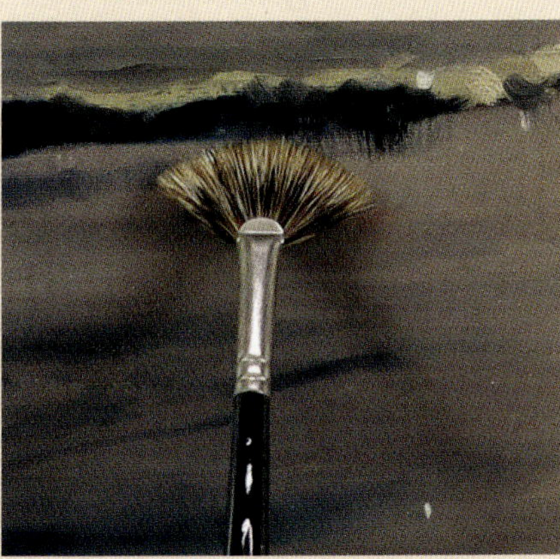

Fan

A brush can be so much more than a drawing tool. Brushwork is a language in its own right – one we will explore throughout this book, as each painting brings unique opportunity for individual painterly expression. Where the sparkly sea is concerned, here are some ideas for marks and strokes you can employ to strong visual effect.

Flat brush: brushed on downstrokes perfect for the base of a flat, reflective sea. Horizontal strokes cutting across it speak of waves and currents.

Flat brush: blocky 'paint placement' Using the face of this brush with opaque paint is perfect for the brightest reflective sparkle.

Filbert brush: angled strokes Using the side of this brush at an angle makes for great foam on the face of a wave.

Rigger brush: dabs and dashes Irreverent dabs and dashes made with flowing paint will add the atmospheric noise so well – smaller sparkle, distant birds, tiny splashes, loose highlights.

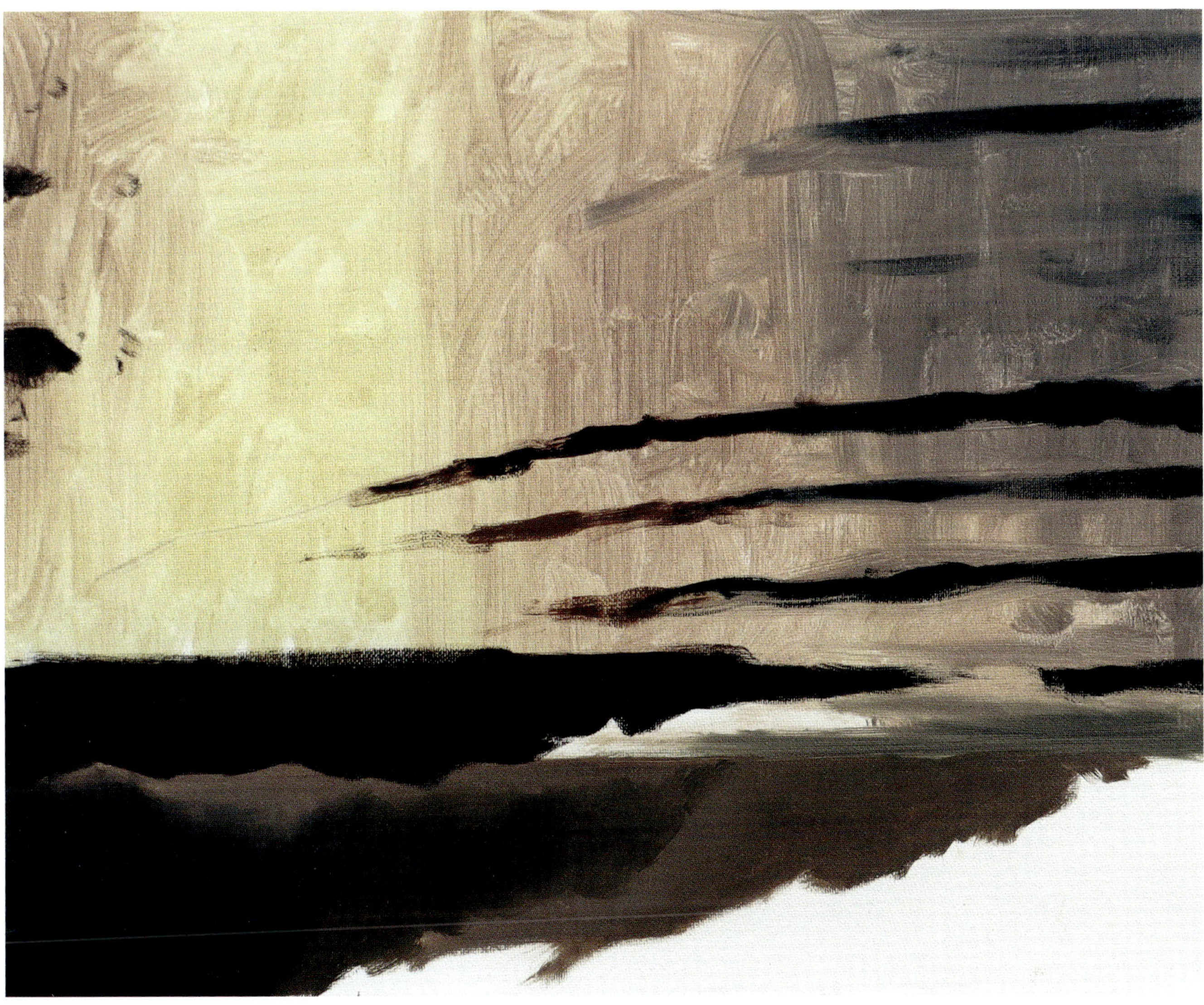

SECOND STAGE

You don't have to thin these background colours as much as in the first stage, as they won't have to support another layer of paint. Each time you add a colour to the mix, do so carefully, as you want the blend to evolve slowly to represent distance and hazy light. Too much, and the harmony will be disjointed.

- Still working with the image upside down, mix scarlet lake, bright yellow lake, deep purple and titanium white to make a dark grey for the most distant headland. Reserve some of this colour to one side, too.
- Add more deep purple and bright yellow lake for the middle cliff, and more ultramarine blue for the nearest.
- Next, mix scarlet lake, bright yellow lake, deep purple and ultramarine blue for the darkest rocks – note there's no white in this mix – and also pop this in for the waves.
- Using the reserved distant cliff colour, paint into the waves nearer the light, and the area above the darkest rocks.
- Now the canvas is almost covered, turn it the right way up.

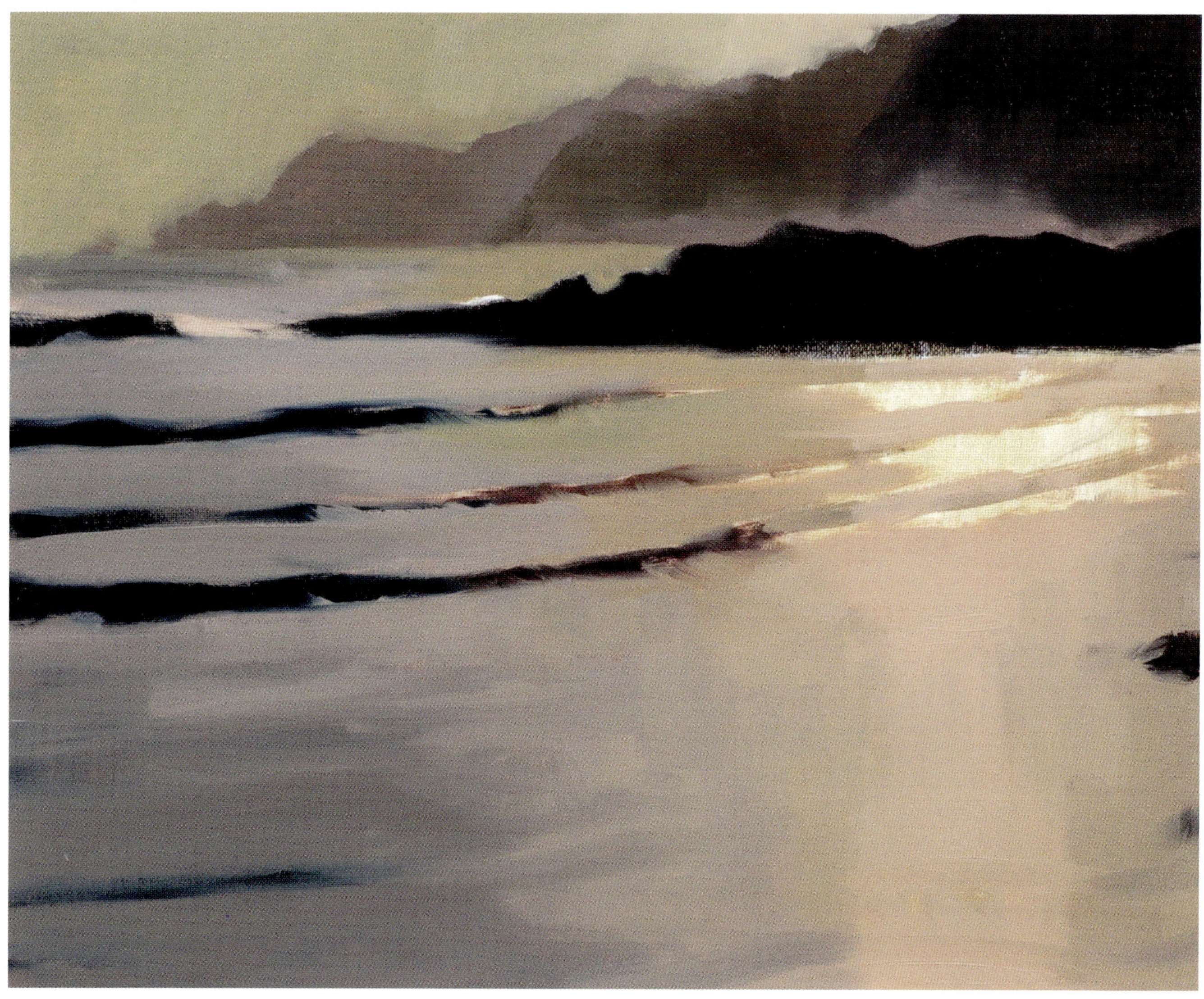

THIRD STAGE

I like to paint the sky in after the land because distant edges are softened by the haze of dust and moisture in the atmosphere. This is especially true in contre-jour *where the light catches all. Since atmospheric light affects our view of distance so greatly, it makes sense to me to make the sky subtly dominate by using it to shape the land.*

At this stage in a painting, I don't know how much of the underpainting will survive; it is down to the individual feel of each painting.

- Using very little solvent, mix titanium white, scarlet lake and bright yellow lake for the central zone of light. Place this horizontally into the wave faces, but more vertically/blockily into the wet sand lower down the painting, so you don't lose the sense of a reflective surface.
- Add a touch of sap green into this mix, for the area to the left.
- This also makes a great colour for the sky, so block it on at the top of the painting, adding a little more titanium white and scarlet lake on the right-hand side, and a little more sap green on the left. Brush it into the land, for a soft, blended edge.
- Finally, add a little more scarlet lake and ultramarine blue for the coolest areas of the sea and beach.

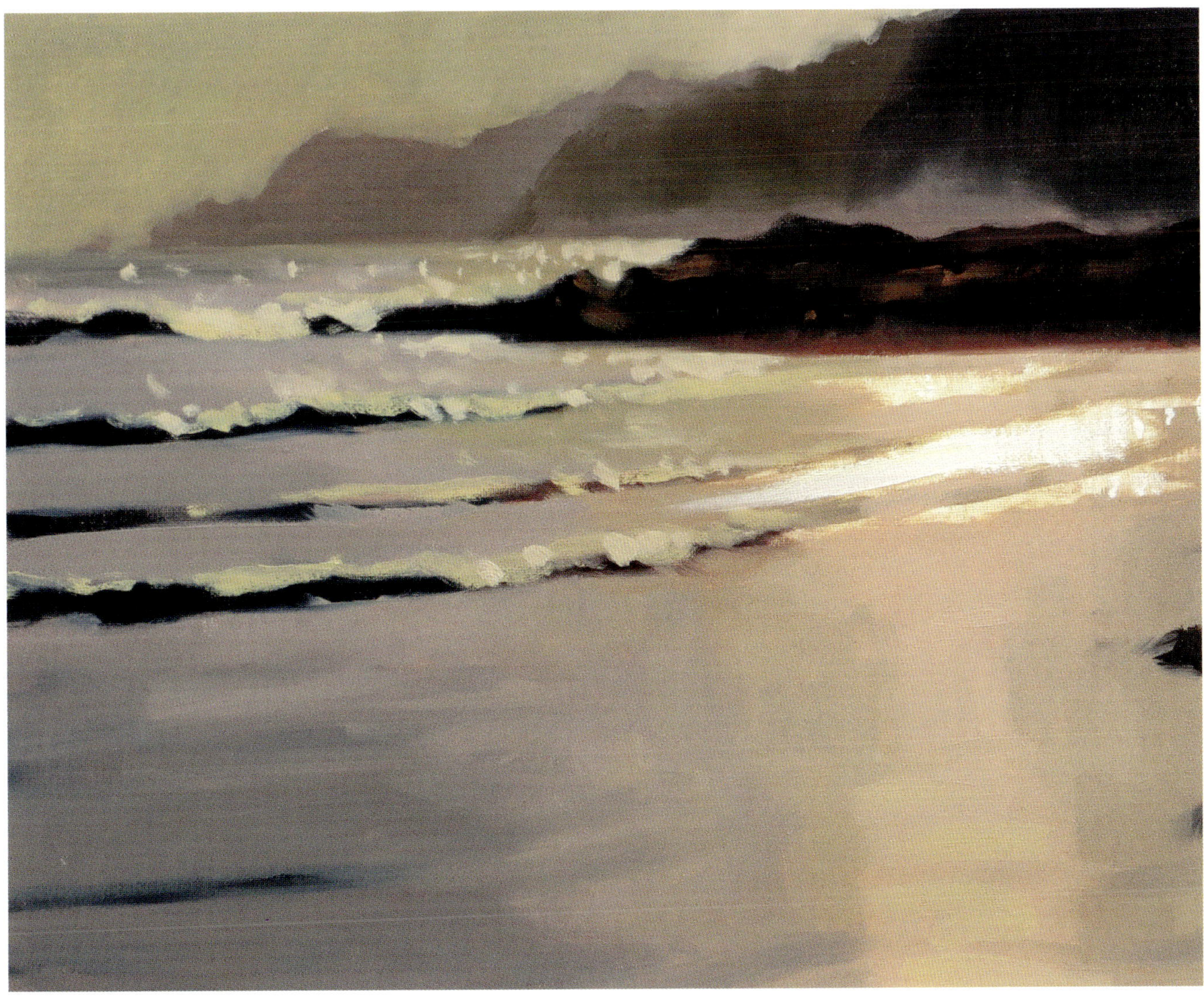

FOURTH STAGE

I changed my brush for this stage, switching to a small filbert. This is the point at which I add the first highlights in the painting – not the brightest whites, but the lighter, warmer colours that make highlights look like light and not just white paint.

- With only enough solvent for flow, create a mix of bright yellow lake and titanium white, then add a touch of scarlet lake for warmth. Place this lightly along the tops of the waves using the face (not the end) of the filbert.
- With more paint than before, place diagonals of colour to represent the breaking wave, using the side of the filbert. Brush a little of this yellow tone into the foreground sand, too.
- Mix in more white and add a few little blobs for light and noise on the water.
- With a clean filbert, mix scarlet lake, bright yellow lake and a touch of deep purple. Brush this into the base of the darkest rocks and add a few notes to their tops. This vibrant colour makes a dark surface look as if it is being lit by bright light, adding to the illusion.

The many colours of white

It is worth covering some extra ground on the wonderful non-colour of white. One of the easiest paints to reach for; white is often overused when simplifying and summarizing what we think we see. White snow, white surf, white sheep, white clouds, white sunlight, white clothing – anything that is an indeterminate, light colour is often portrayed with white paint straight from the tube. Perhaps this is in part due to the watercolour method of using bare white paper for the lightest areas – a beautiful technique, but perfectly suited to that medium, not oils. If you want the illusion of *contre-jour* light in oils, you must be fully in control of the lighting through control of your palette.

As we've already seen with the lovely lemons (see page 43), every colour is affected by surrounding colours and background light, and the battle with our perceptions is just as strong. White is no different. As with any colour decision, think before you paint. How clean, cold and empty would the light and surrounding area have to be in order for your subject to warrant being painted in pure titanium white?

Next time you get to a public gallery, wander through and look really closely. You might be surprised at how little pure white is used in the paintings. I think of it as the icing on the cake – the final touch at the end of a careful process.

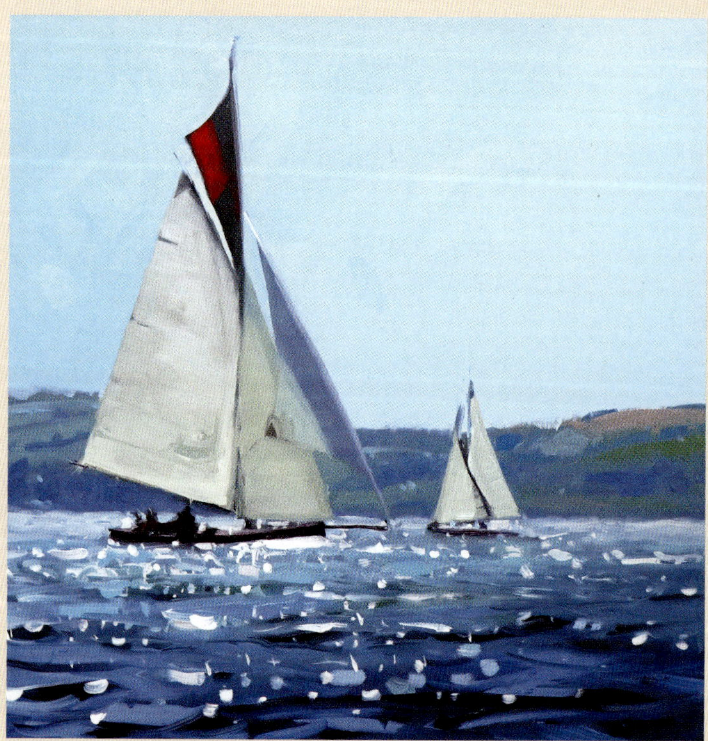

Full Sail, Carrick Roads

50 × 40cm (19¾ × 15¾in)

White sails, white sparkles… but not one of these areas is actually pure, clean white!

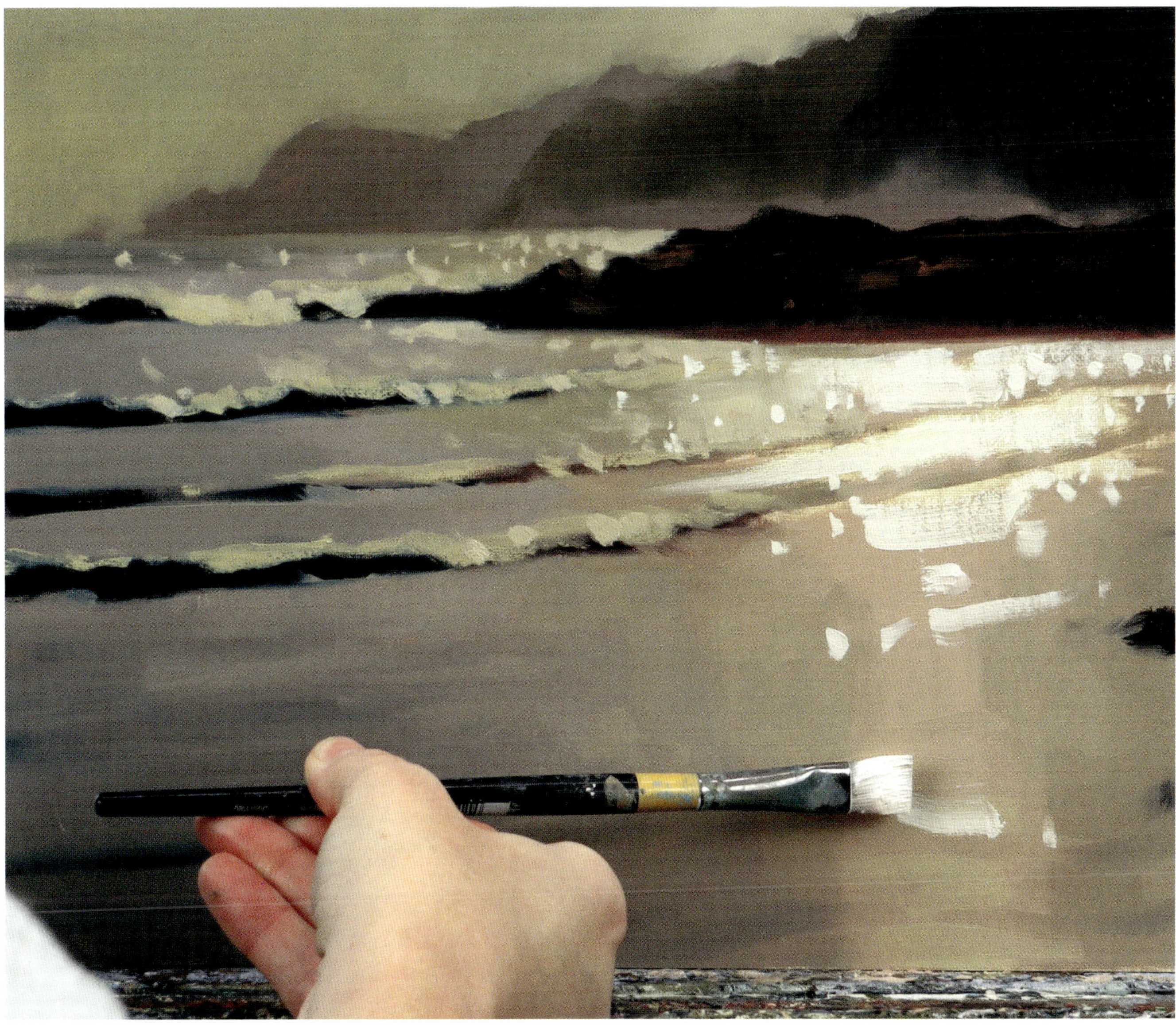

FIFTH STAGE

It is coming together! This is the really exciting stage where you discover if the work you have done has been enough to make that tinted white look like light.

· Mix plenty of titanium white with tiny touches of bright yellow lake and scarlet lake. Use just enough solvent so that the brush will let go of the paint.

· Use the face of the brush, handle adjacent to the canvas, and place on blobs, blocks and oblongs of this mix. Don't revisit what you have painted in order to neaten or brush about – this will mix the highlight with the colour underneath, and turn to mud. Little defects usually don't need neatening, especially when you're painting a wet beach on the glare of the sun!

· Angle the brush a little, to use the corner as a way of applying smaller blobs. I like these shapes to be amorphous, undefined; they feel more realistic. The shape of the sparkles describes the nature of the reflective surface – which is anything but regimented and neat.

SIXTH STAGE – REFINING

This stage is where I really slow down on a painting. It is about standing back – a lot! – to help you decide whether the original idea of your painting is there, and making the finishing touches. Your painting will be finished when you're happy.

Here I wanted a little more light contrast and a little more atmospheric noise. Your example might need some other slight tweaks, so think carefully about how you proceed with your painting.

· Using the mixes on your palette, bolster any darks on the left which need strengthening to make the light pop. Use this to add a few more filbert marks to the foreground to help draw the eye into the composition.

· Use a 12mm (½in) synthetic bristle flat to lay down thick titanium white, tinted with the tiniest bit of bright yellow lake, into the central part of the lit area where the reflection of the light is strongest.

· Finally, with some flowing titanium white tinted with scarlet lake and bright yellow lake, add some flecks, dots and dashes to represent gulls and spray.

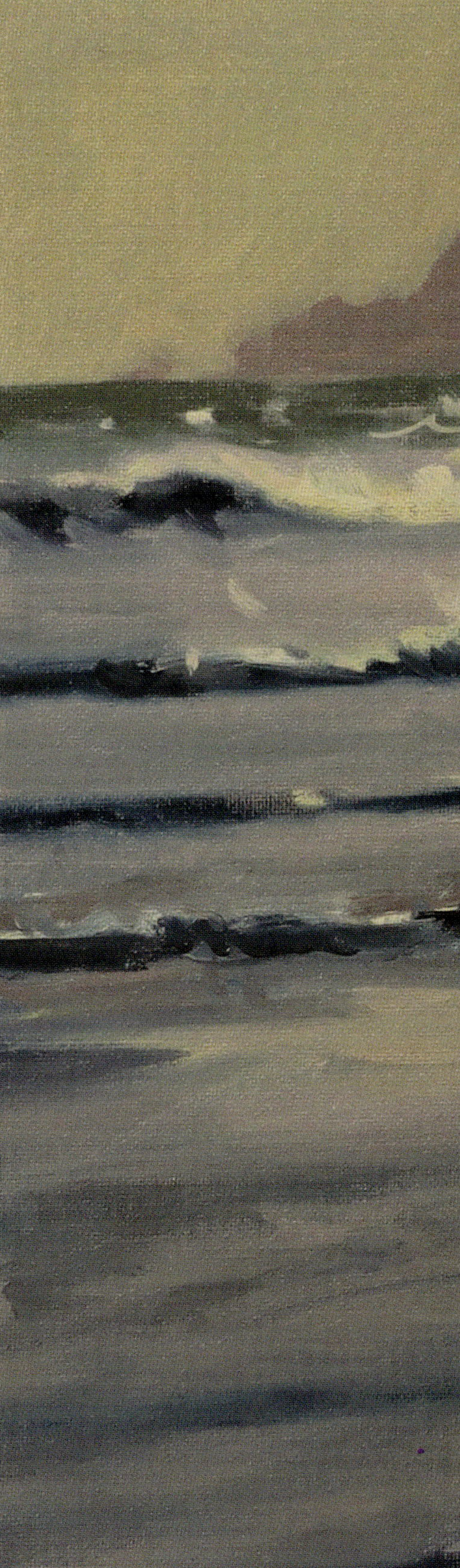

Notes on finishing

After completing a painting, I take a break from it and come back later to see if the buzz of happiness is still present. If it is, then that painting is signed there and then.

Sometimes, however, there will be elements that niggle. The trick is to decide whether they genuinely detract from the painting as a whole. It is easy to end up so overly focused on one element that you lose the original energy and beauty.

Instead of fiddling with the painting, I find it best to take mental notes to apply to your next piece. Here are mine, for this painting:

A little of the underpainting remains visible, providing a hint of a glow in the waves in the sunlight. I like it, but I wonder if I could have left more! I don't mind telling you that this is an area I want to push in my own work: creating a more interesting surface through contrast.

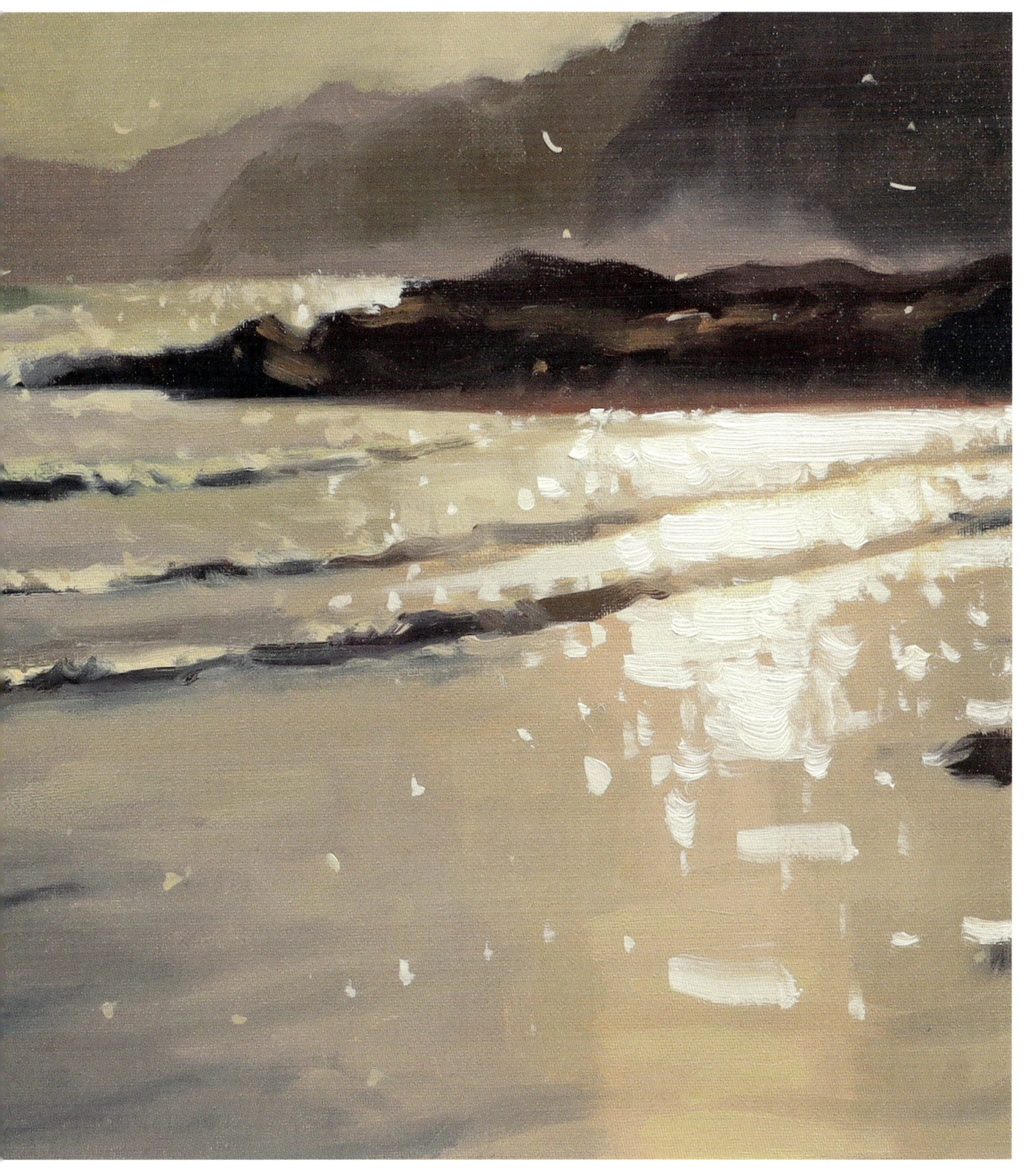

The finished painting

EXPLORING THE SEA FURTHER

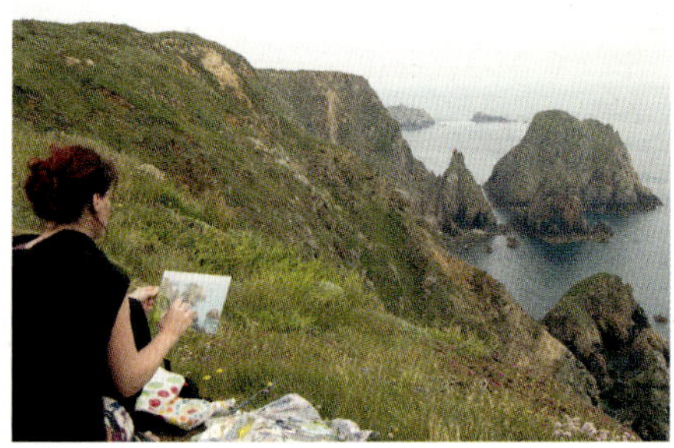

In my earlier years as an artist, the open sea was almost all I painted. This obsession undoubtedly helped me in my study of light. A great big sea without landmark or subject can seem daunting, but that empty, reflective ocean full of 'white' is actually the perfect subject for studying all those *contre-jour* lighting effects.

Look for patterns For a cohesive finished painting, making sense of the patterns helps. Try to discern the rhythmic space between waves. Note where the rocks and shore are interfering with the flow, and spot the way the colour of the water responds to the light depending on the colour and depth of the sea bed.

Establish a focal point I always want one dominant feature to slightly anchor the eye. In this example, I placed the main breaking wave along the edge of the top third, within the off-centre light, as my focal point.

White Without the colours of the land or foreground beach, a *contre-jour* sea can appear quite devoid of colour and full of the aforementioned bleached white. In this painting, I zoomed in on the lit area, so that a large area of the painting is within the complex, hazy zone along the edge of the sunlight. This meant that I could focus on all the subtle colour and temperature relationships in the spread of tones representing 'white' across the painting.

Brushwork Brushwork is vital to describe form when there are no real hard edges in a painting – as it the case with the open sea. The angles tell us of distance, and how the water is moving, the texture shows us the state of aeration, the blocky, 'placed' strokes illustrate light.

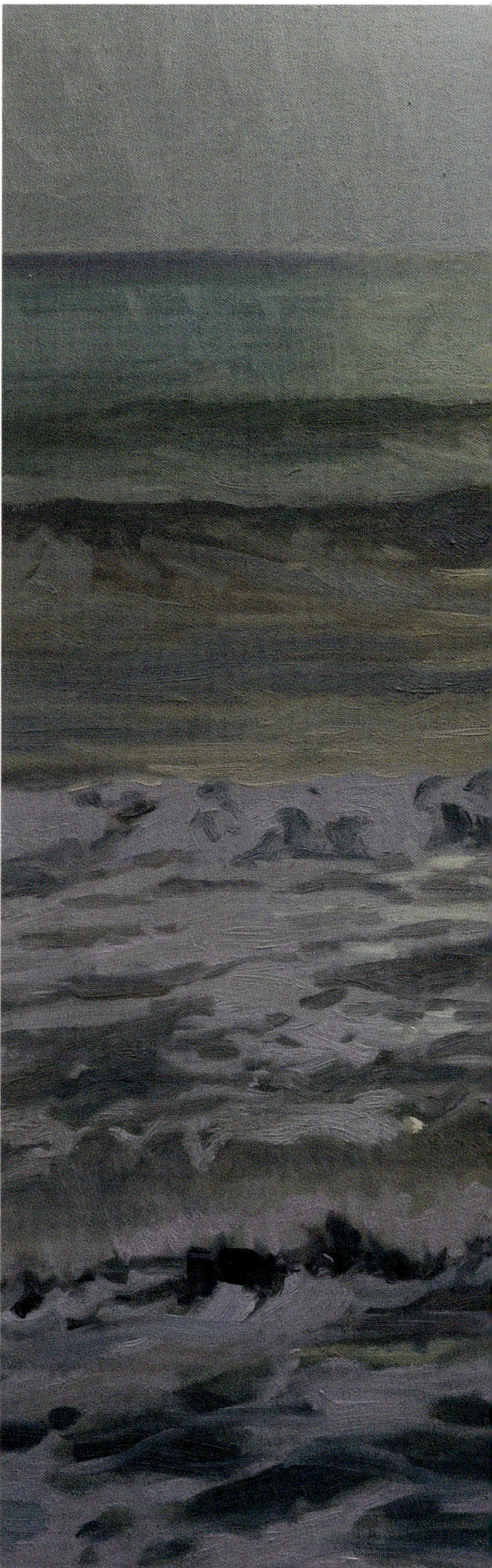

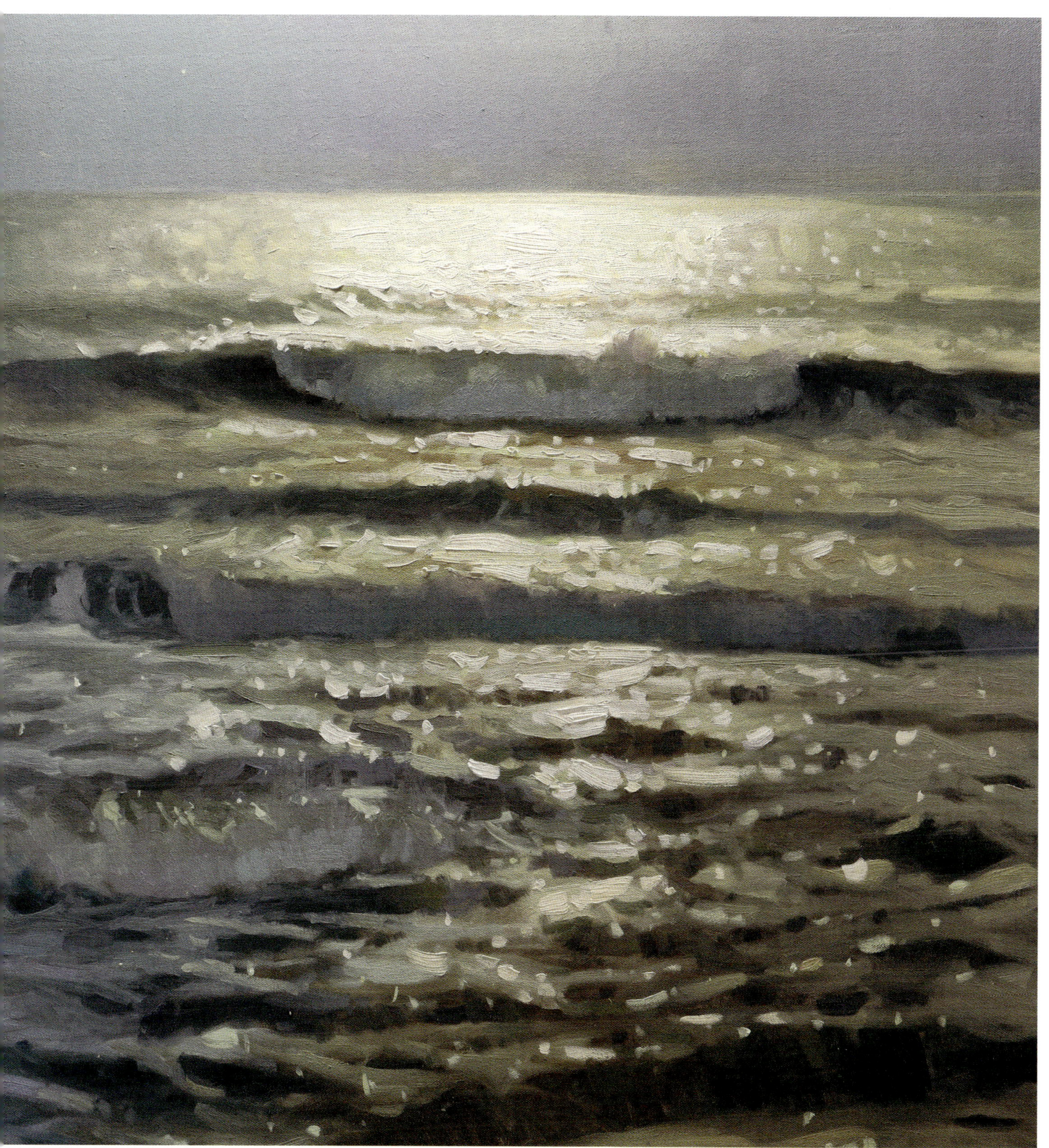

Evening on the Wild Atlantic Way 100 × 80cm (39½ × 31½in)

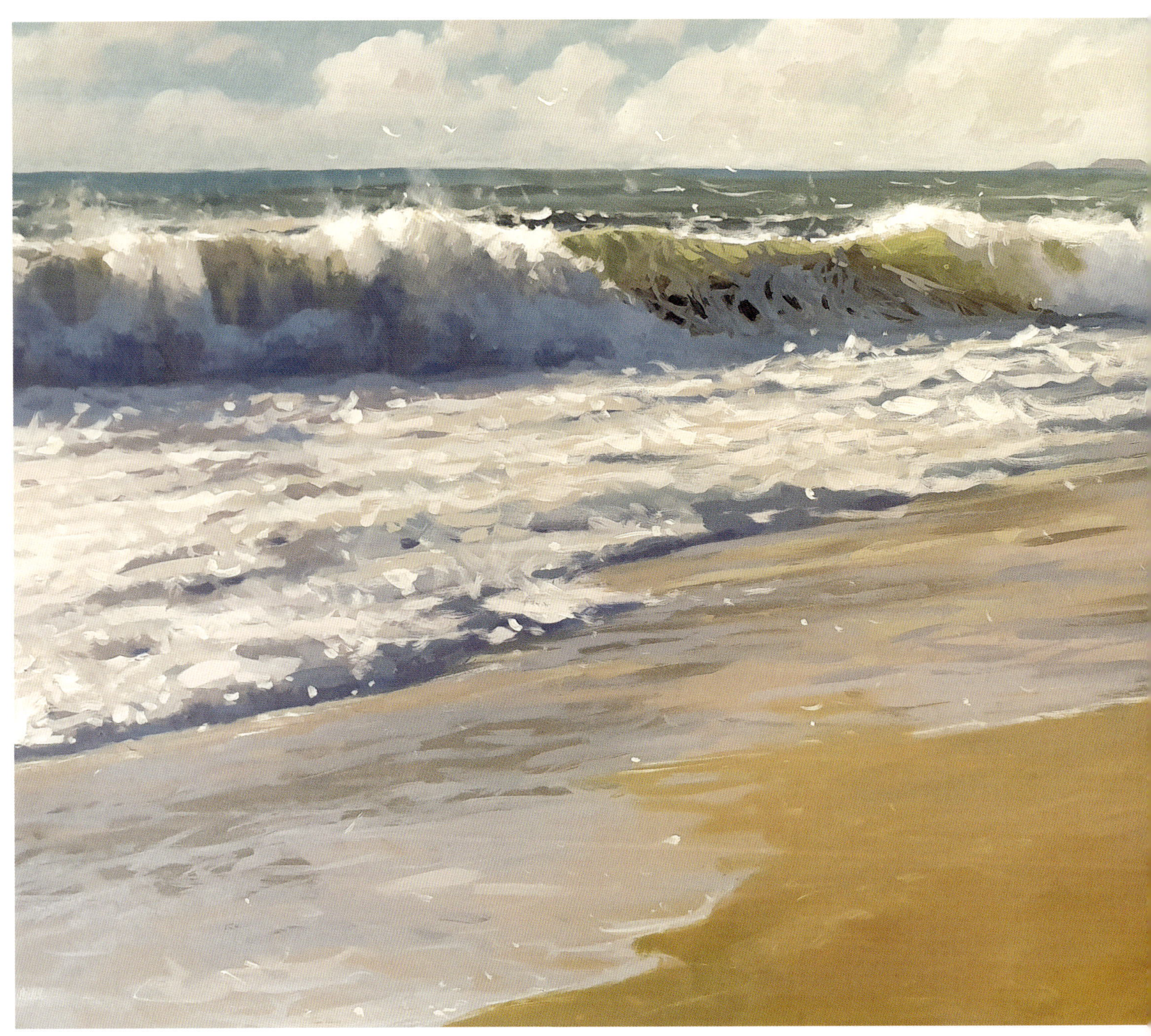

Llanddwyn   *120 × 80cm (47¼ × 31½in)*

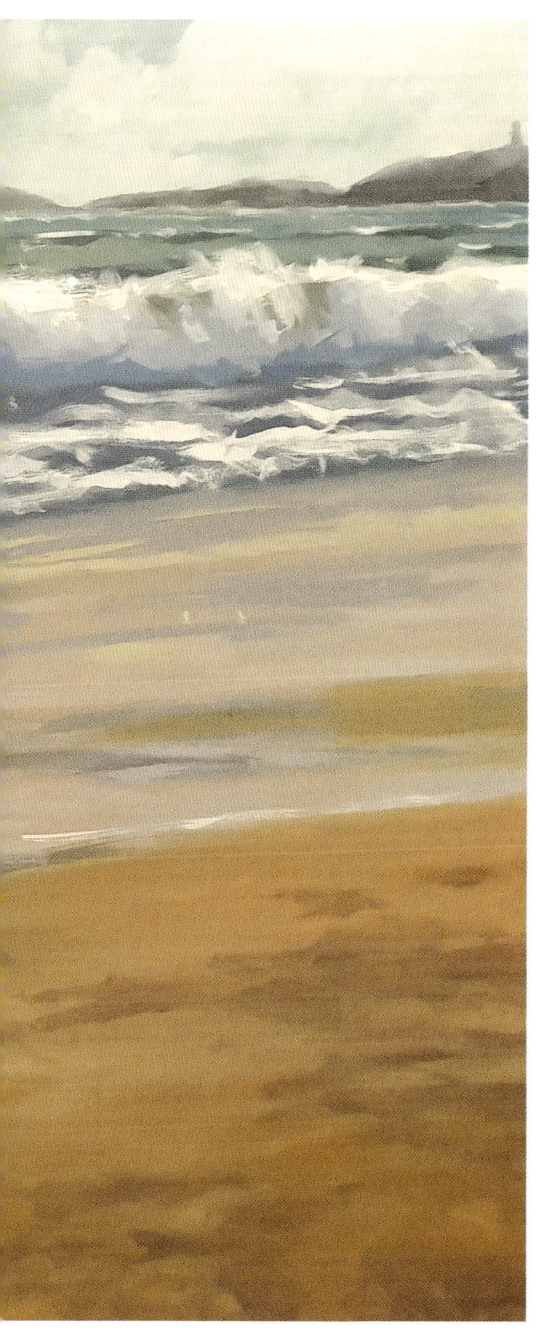

The rhythm of the sea

All-enduring muse of so many artists, the sea is one big capricious character – and never more exciting to me than when it is turbulent.

I wouldn't say understanding the sea is necessary to convey your response to it – but when dealing with realism and the illusion of light, it is worth developing your knowledge of its behaviour.

Professional photographs often show an idealized version – perfect waves, clean white foam, blues, golds and turquoise. Even stormy scenes are somehow sanitized, as clean lines and strong design appeal to photographers, too! The sea, like everything, is much messier in real life. I like trying to capture that; although it isn't always easy to find the composition, or make sense of the movement. Every time I paint the ocean *en plein air*, I learn something completely new.

If you can, spend time staring at the ocean, focusing upon colours, shapes, patterns and form. Watch the waves gather and peak as they break; the foam rush into a shoreline swash; the strength of the backwash and undercurrents. Notice the lumps and bumps and bubbles, muddy foam and weedy shallows. Find the colour of the landscape echoed in the deep; call all the frothing 'whites' by new names.

This doesn't apply solely to the sea. Whether outside or in the studio, have a mind to the whole, living nature of your subject, whatever you are painting. It will influence your brushwork and consequently inject movement and life into your work.

Anatomy of a wave

Peak (1) The wave peak is pushed up by the circular force within, whipped by the breeze. It breaks apart with gravity as it grows in height in the shallows. It provides an opportunity for highlights and cool shadows. For this effect, scrub the edge of a filbert or flat brush lightly along the edge.

Face (2) The face of the wave is created by water being drawn up. The pitch gets steeper as the wave nears the shallows, and its colour will be influenced by the lighting, sky colour, water colour and the sea bed. To paint the face, use filbert/flat brushwork. It sweeps up noticeably towards the top, becoming flat and indiscernible for any transparent water. A rigger or the corner of a flat can be good for that snaking foam, but keep it soft if it is in the background.

Trough (3) The trough refers to the calmer space in between waves, where any foam stretches out and snakes up the face of the wave behind. The water here is usually flat and, if not filled with foam, will reflect the colour of the sky. Use long, sweeping brushstrokes for this.

Break (4) The rising sea floor or rocks will slow the base of the wave, and the wave height therefore increases until it breaks, causing foam, the colour of which will be influenced by lighting, water and sand. Foam is aerated seawater – a mass of bubbles and droplets caused when a wave breaks apart. In this case, the wave is breaking against a large rock – so the foam is exploding out at various angles. My take on painting it is to treat it as one bundled mass – and not try to paint (or even spray) a million, separate tiny dots. It can make a crashing wave appear weightless and fluffy. If you have stood in the face of a crashing wave, you know it's heavy!

The break is an opportunity for some lovely *contre-jour* greys. I use a flat brush and the side edge of a filbert for some scrubbing and placement of opaque marks. For the highlights and spray, I use the corner of a flat brush and a small rigger, making sure marks are not regimented – the water is flying about, and in no way neat or tidy.

Swash (5) The foamy rush that snakes through rocks, bubbles over pebbles and eventually washes back into the face of the next wave is known as swash. Make the brushwork reflect this movement – varying flat 'S' shapes are great for the approaching edge of the foamy water. Use big loose strokes of a filbert to retain the sense of movement. The colour is highly influenced by light, shore and sky colour.

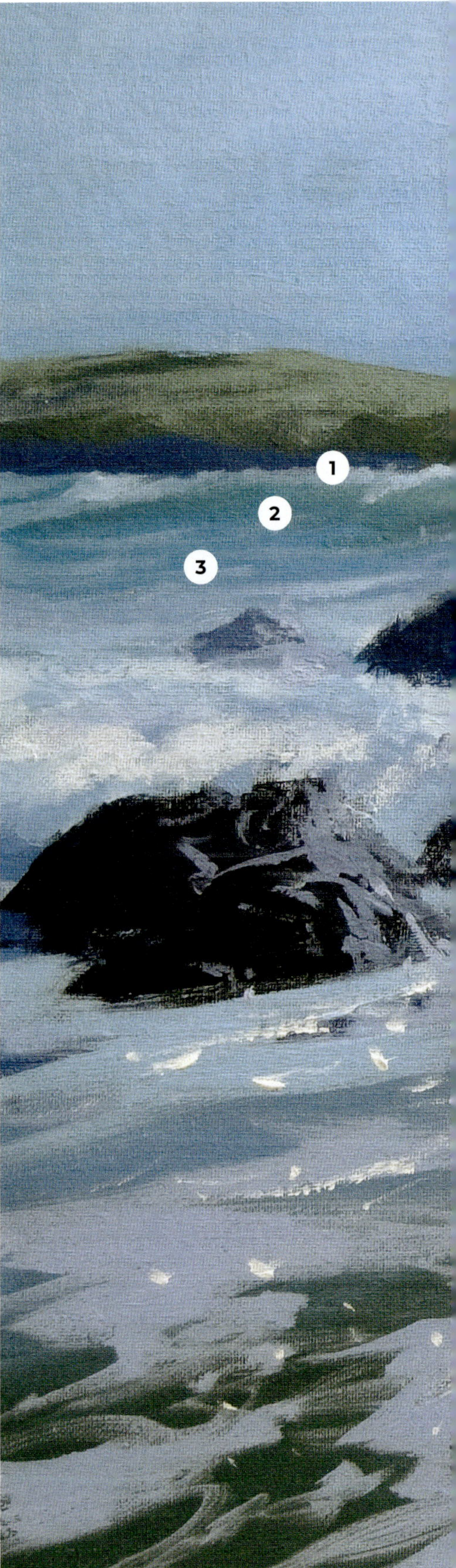

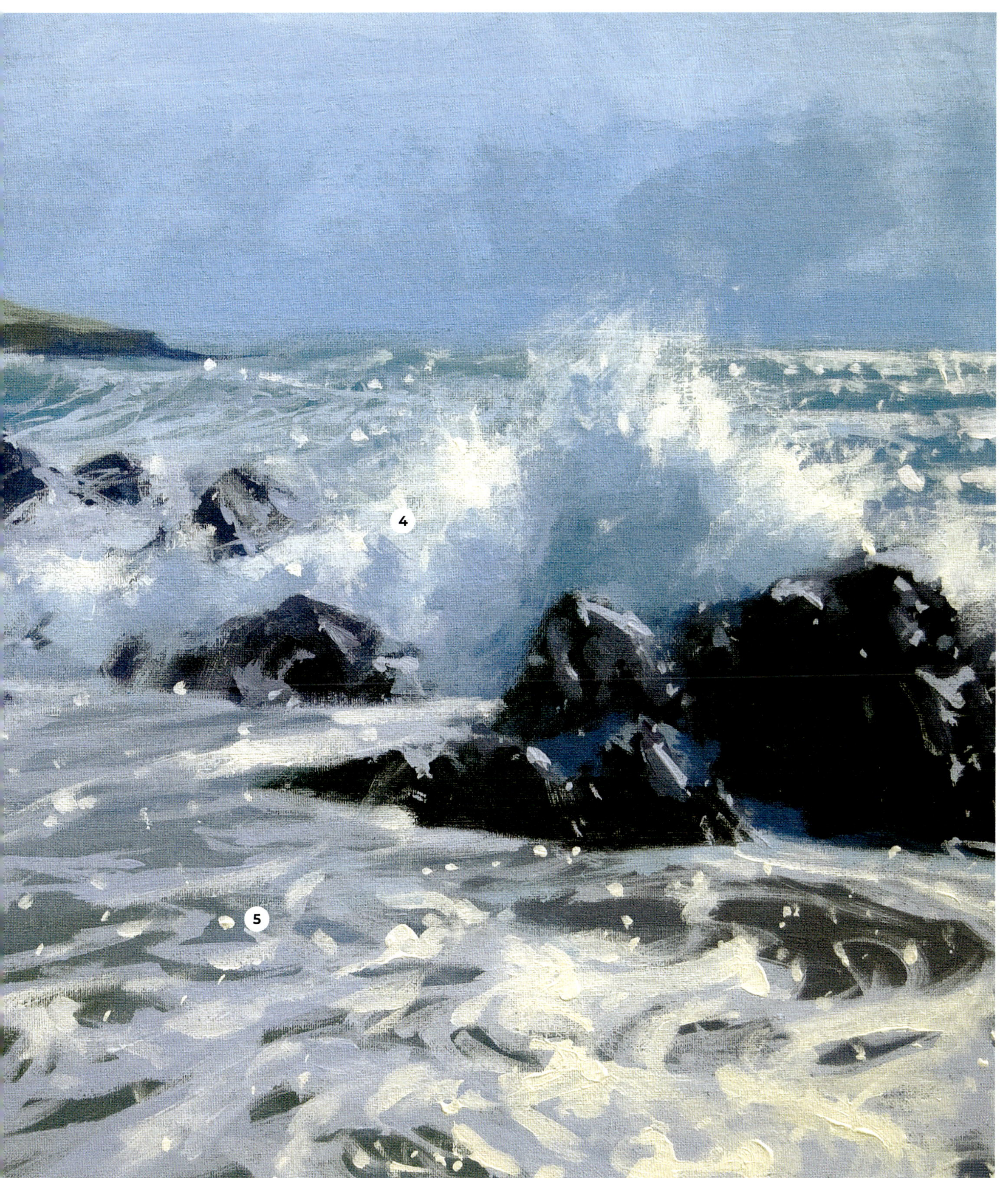

Tywyn   50 × 40cm (19¾ × 15¾in)

Seascapes and perspective

For large scale *contre-jour* sea paintings like *The Saddles and Long Island Rock*, it is helpful to take into account linear perspective – the illusion that straight lines converge in the distance. It will be there in all representative paintings with an authentic sense of depth and scale. It can be a challenge in seascapes, as you tend to have fewer reference points than in, say, a street or woodland.

Good perspective draws a viewer into the scene. I approach it with intuitive understanding, rather than mathematically accurate theory. Instead of heading into architectural drawing or three-point perspective, here are my basics:

Shapes Shapes look smaller when further away. This is obvious, but easily forgotten when it comes to painting the sea. In this example, look at the angled highlights on the foreground waves, showing their shape as they reflect the light. It will look exactly the same at the other end of the bay – but we can't possibly see that from our distant perspective. Therefore it gradually becomes a flat area of light, giving a sense of distance on the water and the illusion of a foreground below us.

Detail Detail diminishes with distance, especially when you're looking into the sun! Again, we know this in theory, but when faced with painting a truthful representation of an image, it can be so tempting to put in every last descriptive stroke. This can skew both the sense of depth and perspective. Keep it indistinct and minimal – our imagination will engage and make up the rest, just as it does when we view objects from a distance in real life. As with the dots and dashes of farms in the painting opposite, this then feels more authentic to the eye and adds to the illusion of depth.

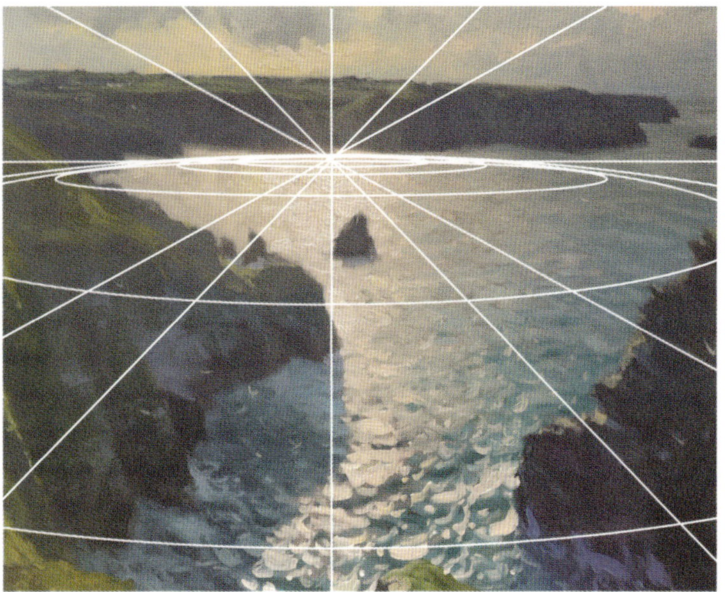

Vanishing point The visual to the left is what I see with my mind's eye when I look at the light on the ocean. I pick a point on the horizon where the light is brightest, then imagine lines radiating out from that point, like sun rays. I organize the scene into circular zones of distance with their centre at this point, and employ those angles, subtly, in the brushwork.

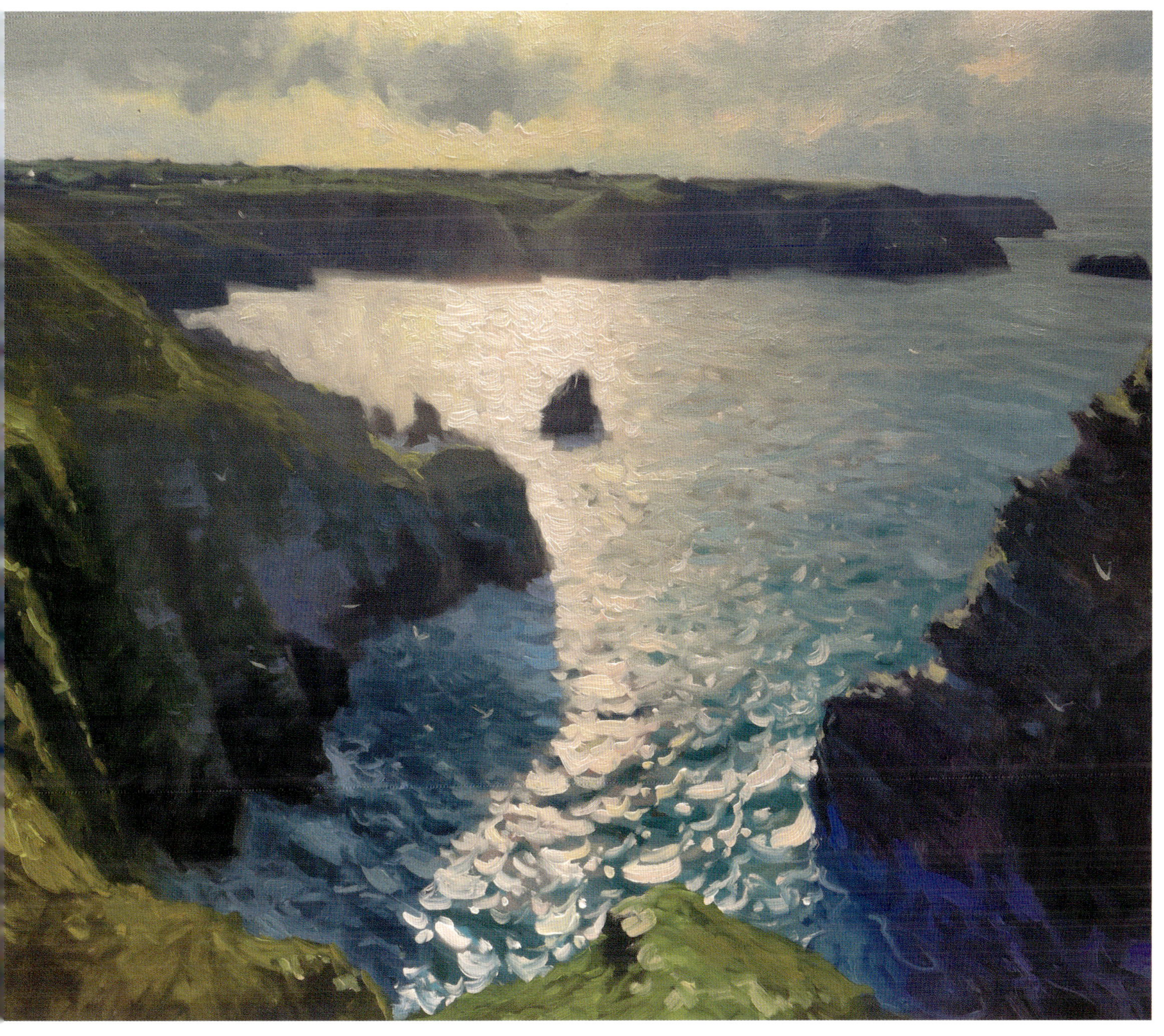

The Saddles and Long Island Rock   100 × 80cm (39½ × 31½in)

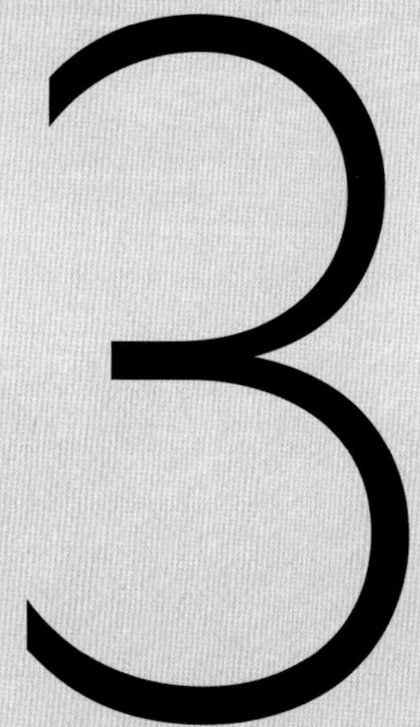

SIMPLIFICATION

'Simplicity is the greatest adornment of art.'
Albrecht Dürer

Most artists I meet are seeking to enhance their painterly language by simplifying their brushwork. *Contre-jour* lends itself well to reduced detail, as it gives you opportunity to say everything through colour, design and shape, rather than drawing. It certainly doesn't mean carefree brushwork, however – quite the opposite. Good form is essential to guide the mind's eye. I see it as a game – how little can I say to express the most possible? How accurate can each brushstroke be?

When well designed, a painting with an intentional lack of detail can create a strong sense of a single glimpsed moment. There is a timelessness in this kind of 'memory capture' that has universal appeal – when the detail is less defined, a wider audience can more easily relate to it. Each one of us can project our own experiences onto the painting, filling in the missing detail with our own experiences and memories. To my mind, when detail is lessened, the emotional appeal grows.

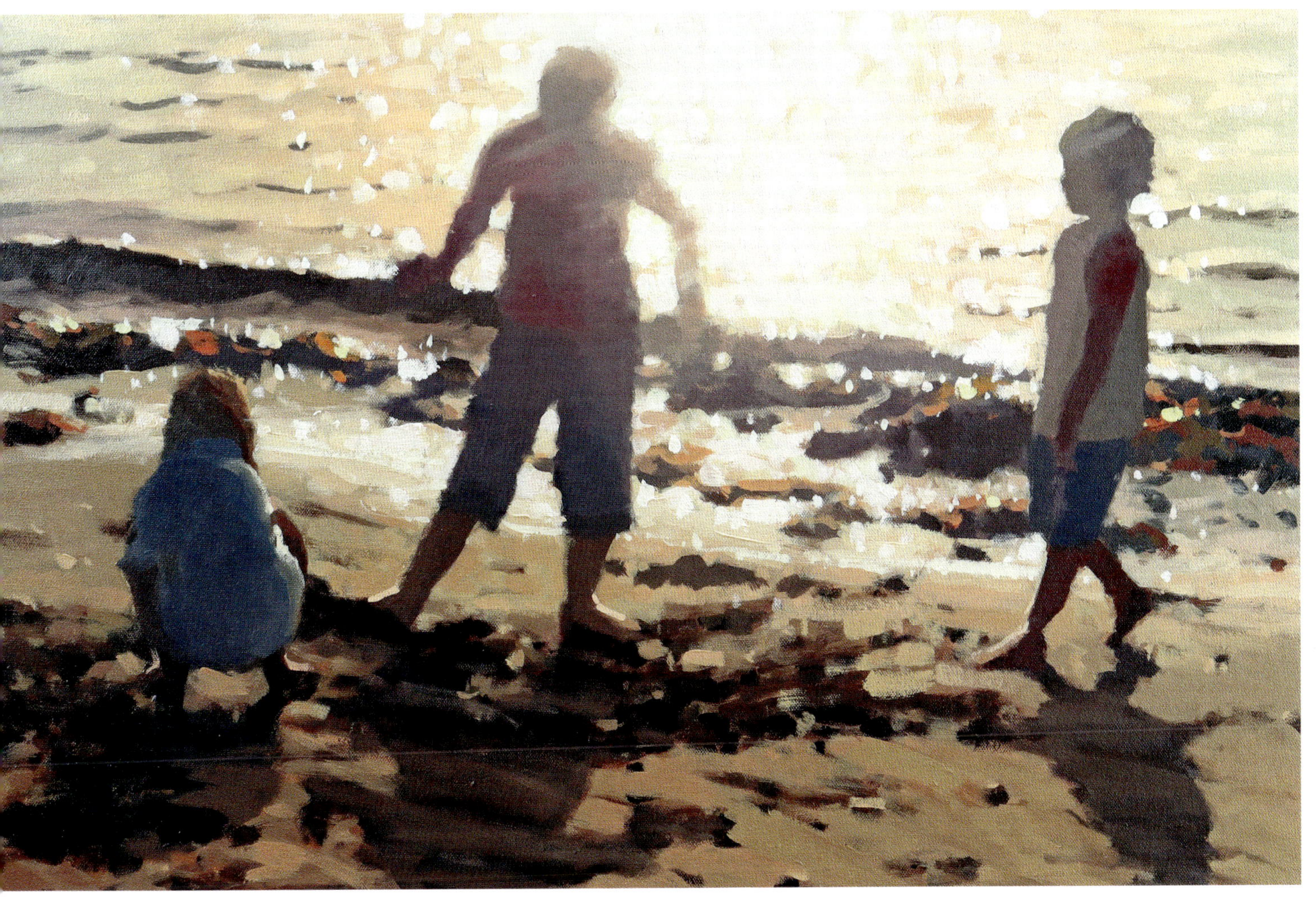

Playful Evening, Gurteen

76 × 50cm (30 × 19¾in)

The middle figure has no features at all, and yet we can tell so much about him through lighting and shape – and of course, our own imagination.

The warmth across the top of his head and the lack of neck shows us that the head is looking down. The right arm shrinks at the shoulder, showing us that the arm is bent with the elbow pointing back towards the sun. Angles and positioning show that the weight is on his slightly bent left leg, the right dragging through the sand. If there were much more detail than this, the sunlight wouldn't look as strong – instead, there is enough truth in form to carry the impression.

Colour, texture, brush direction and tone define each aspect, rather than descriptive line. The level of detail is constant across the painting, creating a credible 'moment' and freeing the imagination to interpret.

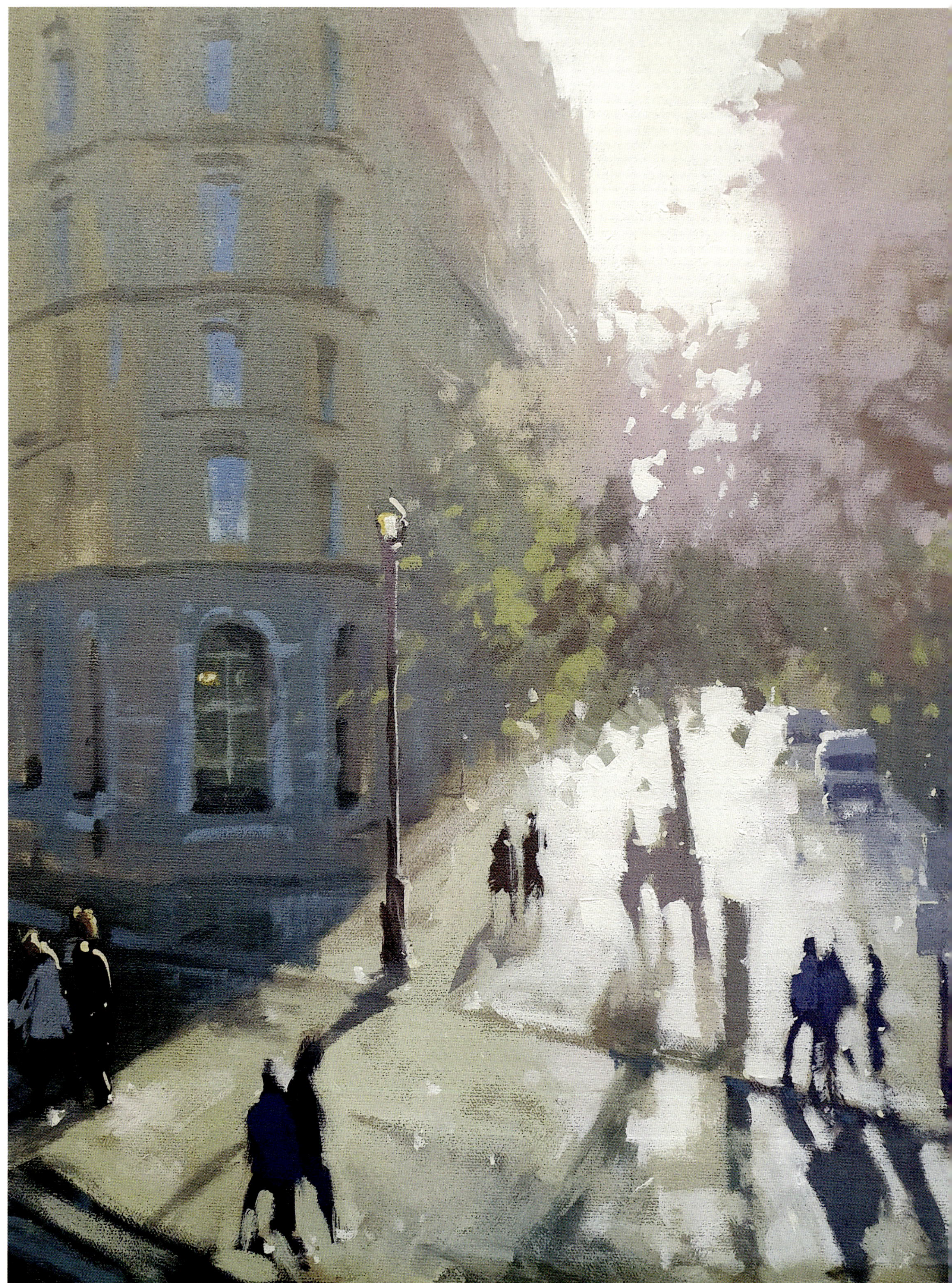

Autumn Sun, London

40 × 50cm (15¾ × 19¾in)

Scenes such as this are full to the brim with detail. I wanted to include just enough to give the impression of a fleeting glimpse into the sunlight while walking by. Working with the reference photograph upside down helped me place the main shapes, but once I had turned it around, the temptation took hold and I filled in all sorts of areas with descriptive brushwork.

Towards the end, I found that the building was too weighty and over-detailed, standing proud from the rest of the painting. With a cloth and solvent, I wiped away much of the face, then went back in with a large brush and a focused mind. The end result is balanced and atmospheric, with nothing pulling too hard on the gaze other than the light.

SIMPLICITY AND SACRIFICE

I love to paint, and happily paint pretty much anything – but the real drive for me is to create work that draws others in, to relate and to connect with my way of seeing.

Getting something said in a single brushstroke is our aim, but the ability to make that perfect stroke is the culmination of a journey. It is a learned skill. You might get one or two happy accidents, but you'll never complete a successful painting relying on those! Happily, making things look simple – that is, refining and adjusting until the painting appears as you wish – can work just as well. The rewards are for getting it right, not getting it right first time.

Oils are the perfect medium for painterly deconstruction. I often find, when I reach the end stages of a painting, that I have lost control of the narrative a little. It happens so easily, as we become absorbed in our craft and fascinated by painterly reproduction of each element. As good as all those descriptive marks may be, areas can quickly become too busy, the painting too flat, and the impact reduced as a result. This doesn't mean the painting is ruined. Balance can be regained with the removal or softening of certain areas.

Don't be afraid to sacrifice strong areas of work for the sake of the painting as a whole. Think of it like cooking a meal and adding all the amazing herbs and spices to it at the same time – any appealing flavour will be lost. Keep stepping back and remembering the original point of your painting, and use that cloth/knife/ big unwieldy brush to get some focus back into your work.

LIGHT AND FACES

Contre-jour portraiture doesn't just allow us to omit detail, it demands it. The *contre-jour* illusion requires light to seem powerful; after all, looking into the light is a blinding experience! If we deny that power by overly detailing hazy areas, the authenticity of lighting will be lost. Get those simplified marks on as accurately as possible, and they will say enough.

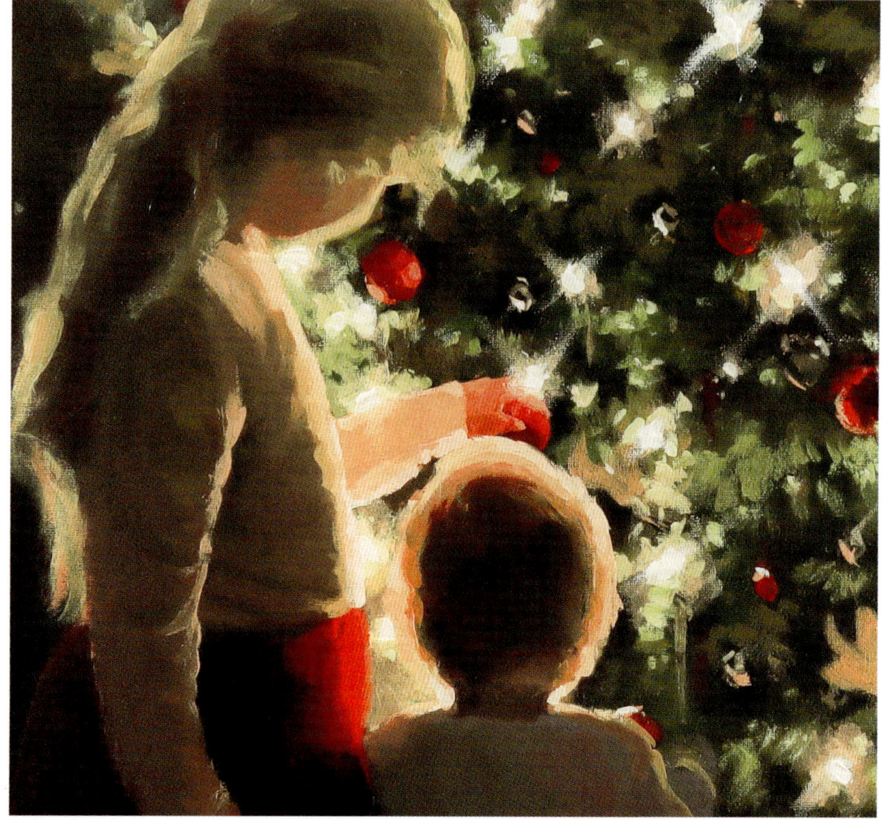

Sometimes features would actually detract from a painterly atmosphere, as they always draw the eye. I increased the lighting from the tree to soften any detail otherwise needed in the girl's face and hand. This resulted in a more timeless, relatable image. The portrait is now more about light and movement, rather than photographic recording – although retaining enough accuracy in shape to ensure likeness.

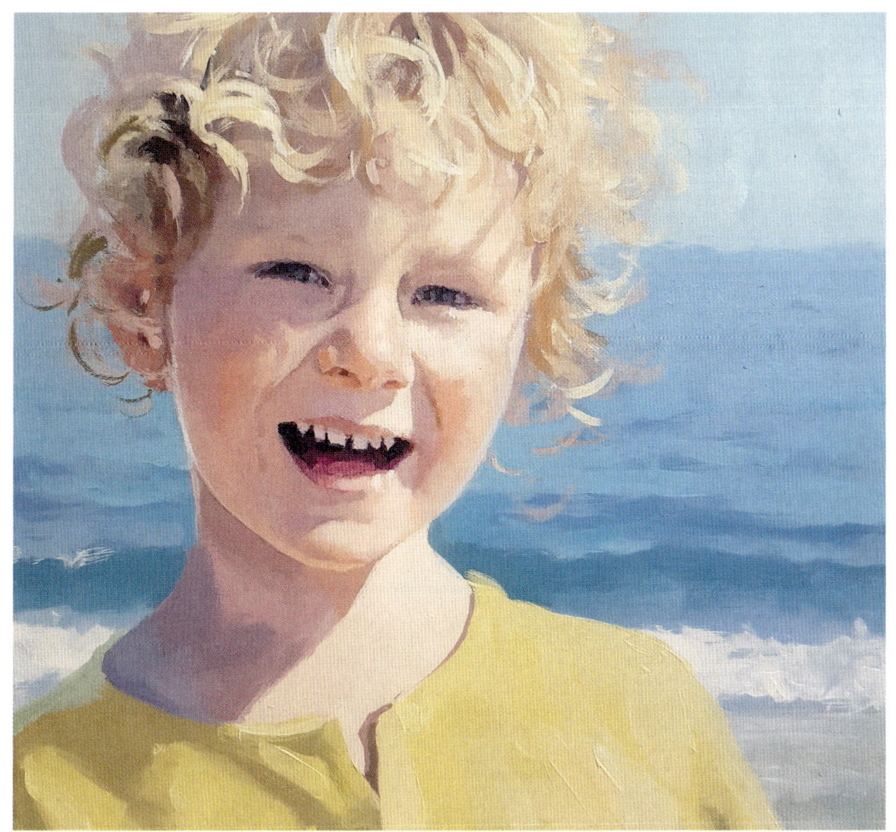

A commissioned portrait with a slightly softer contre-jour, the light placed a little further to the top right. I've included this image as most of his face is still in shadow, with colour and strong light defining the features. The accuracy in likeness is there, but the detail is soft and implied. I find this the easiest way to paint portraits! Shape and form must be right – but there's still room for atmosphere and movement.

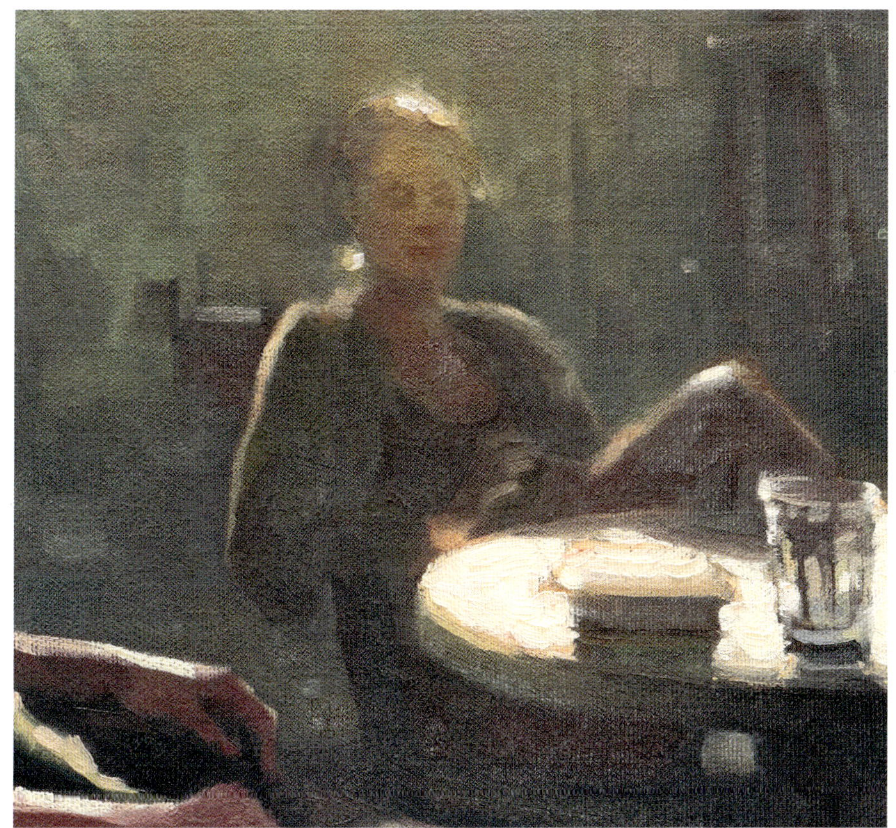

A portrait of my youngest daughter with very minimal brushwork! A few salient shadows in the face, all low contrast and soft edges, tells us as much about the quality of light as the features themselves. This is the vital balance I try to strike – a conversation between light and detail that results in faithful representation of a real moment in time and space.

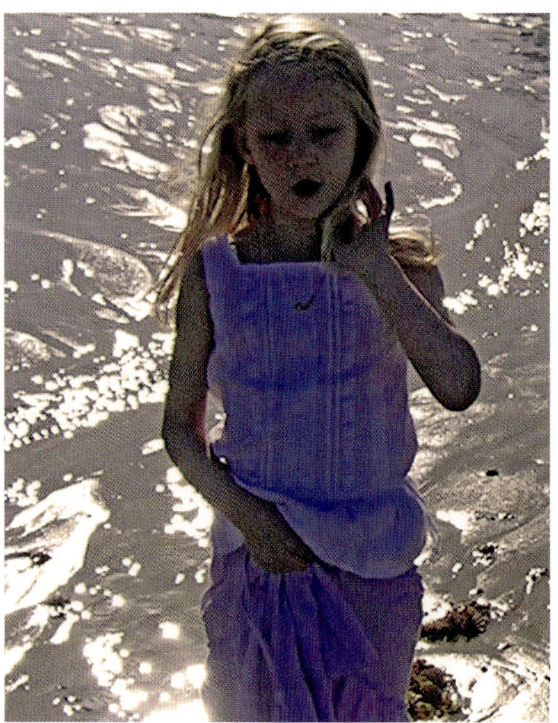

PORTRAIT

'Simplify, omit all but the most essential elements.' **John Singer Sargent**

I have so many photographs like this, of people set against the backdrop of sunlight! The subtlety in colours and temperature is endlessly fascinating, and make it a great challenge for our next project.

I'm keen to encourage mixing from your own observation, so there are fewer 'colour recipes' than in the other projects. Don't worry – every colour in a *contre-jour* face is some kind of grey; and so a good starting point is to mix red, green and white together to get an initial tone and then compare that to the colour on the reference photograph. Using this mix as a basis, you can tint, lighten or darken it as you go.

You will need

30 × 24cm (11¾ × 9½in) canvas board

Brushes: two 12mm (½in) flat brushes, 6mm (¼in) filbert, 3mm (⅛in) round

Paints: titanium white, bright yellow lake, scarlet lake, deep purple, ultramarine blue, sap green, phthalo green, burnt umber

Low-odour solvent

Watersoluble coloured pencil

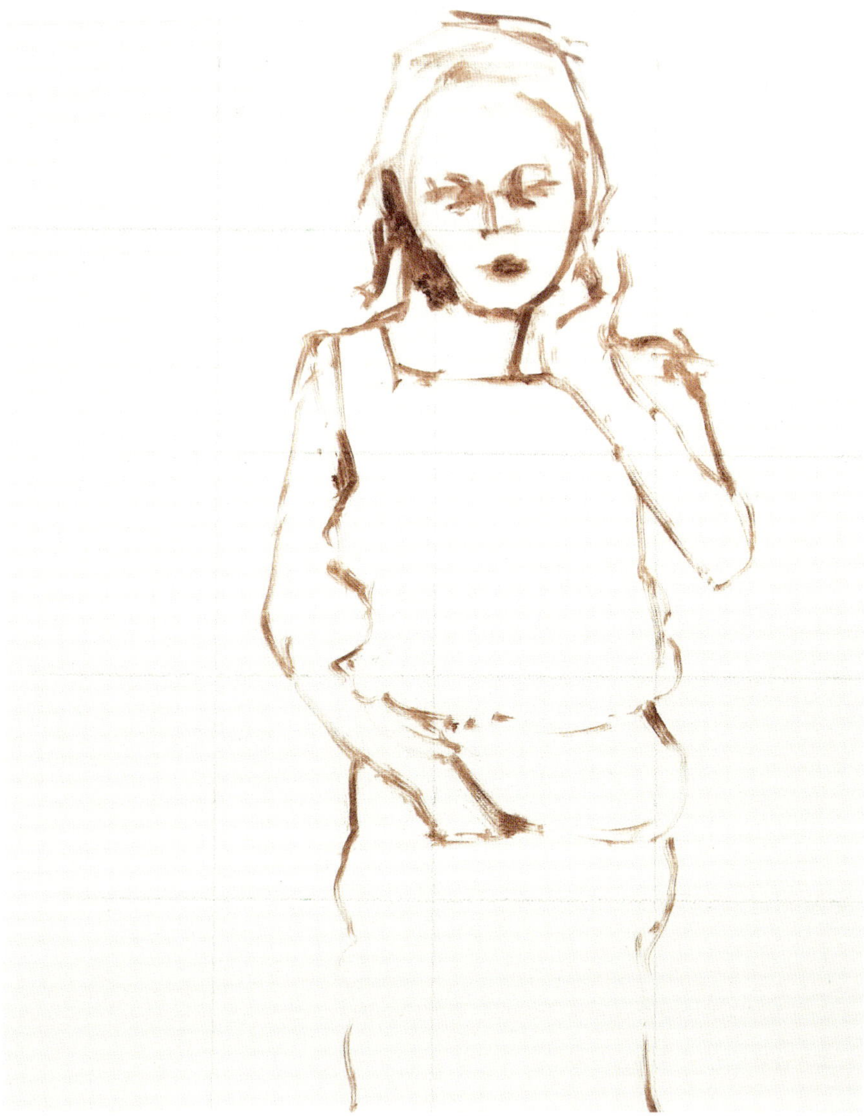

FIRST STAGE

My aim with portraits, whether contre-jour or fully lit, is to prioritize lighting, movement and moment above detail. Try to adhere to this painterly direction all the way through the process. Knowing what you want from any painting before you start makes decision-making much easier as you paint.

I always use a grid where close-up faces are involved, no matter how loose the likeness required. If things aren't quite in the right place, people can start to look quite odd!

- Lay down a five by four grid using faint pencil lines.

- Prepare thin burnt umber and use a 6mm (¼in) filbert brush to establish a simple framework. Simplify shapes as you go – the overriding aim of this painting is atmospheric light, so don't be tempted to overcomplicate it.

- Once this framework is in, I move on to the colour – there is no need to fiddle around too much at this stage.

Brushwork and the portrait

It is so easy to convince yourself that every line and shadow must be reproduced in paint! Choosing a brush that discourages fiddling by making it physically harder to do really helps. The best way to avoid multiple small, hard marks is to stick to as large a brush as you can feasibly manipulate for the task. For most portraits, I find my trusty 12mm (½in) flat brush does the job perfectly. While unwieldy for sensitive details, it forces me to question whether those marks are necessary to the painting as a whole.

Deciding where defined edges will be in the portrait is another point of restraint to consider. Don't have them everywhere – as discussed earlier, edges have more impact within the composition if they are contrasted with soft, 'lost' edges. Most edges can be blurred and lost, as long as there is some definition showing essential form. A bit of scrubbing across edges with a small filbert can bring magic to an otherwise static portrait.

Here are some ideas for which brush to use for which stage, to ensure a clean, fresh finish.

Small filbert This sort of brush is great for sketching out the initial shape of a figure, and filling any complex areas.

Flat Useful for laying down the largest shapes you can see with a flat brush – reducing any detail to areas of colour.

3mm (⅛in) round Excellent for adding a touch of definition – but use it sparingly, only when necessary to correct angles or hone shapes. Carefully place your salient paint marks, rather than brushing paint around in an effort to find what works. Once your figure is laid in, a 3mm (⅛in) round brush is great for a touch of definition, but don't be tempted to over-correct. It is better to remove paint with a cloth and place fresh marks, than keep fiddling with a small brush: the paint will become muddy, and the area will stand out uncomfortably.

Small rigger I like to use a small rigger for the final few flourishes and details. No matter how thick the paint is, a rigger loaded with thin, opaque paint will apply it beautifully with a light touch.

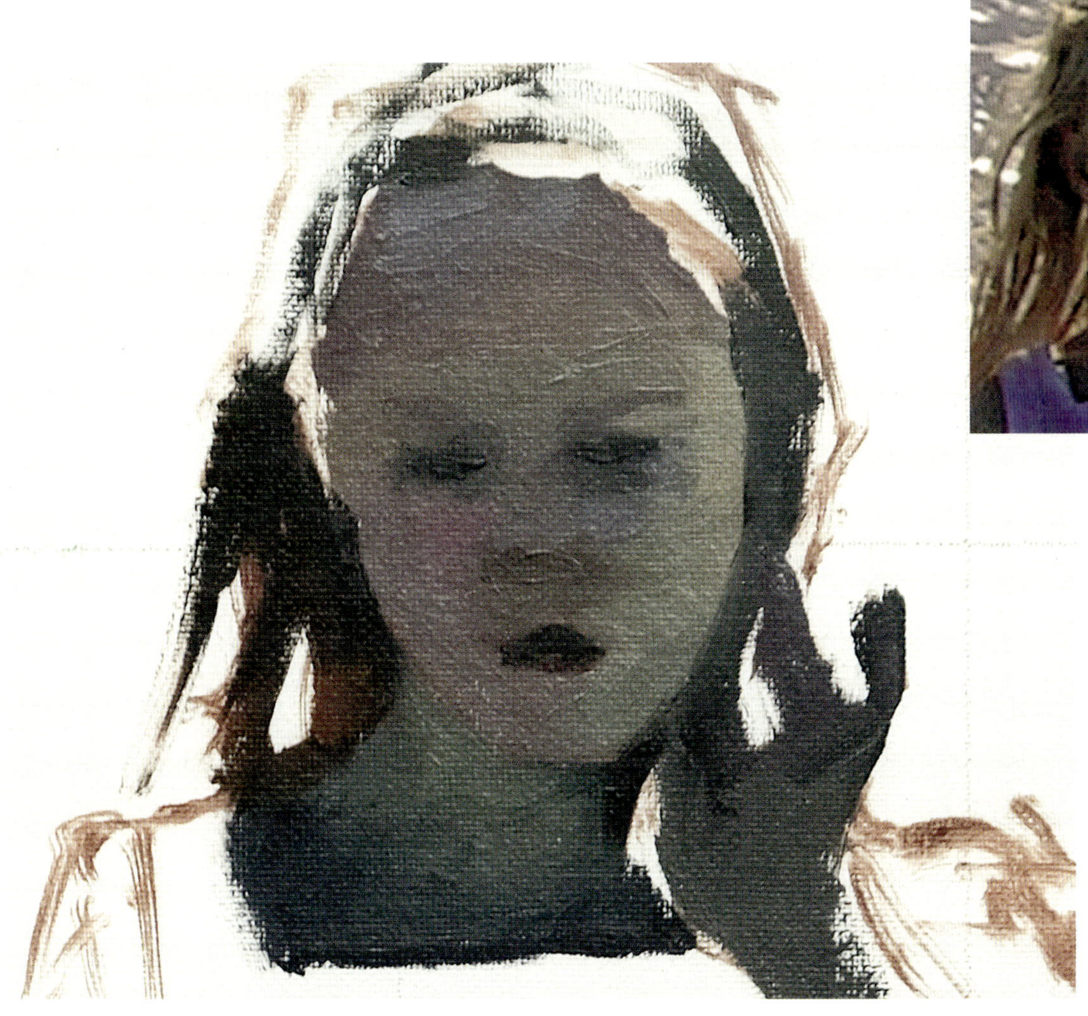

SECOND STAGE

In this stage, we concentrate on the colours of the face – overall, these are muted and grey, as you can see in the detail of the photograph.

As you are mixing your paints, remember to look for temperature differences in the colours. Think about the nature of the face and how lighting will affect it. Any lighting variation on the face will be because of the sunlight bouncing off the sand around the figure, and this must be taken into account.

It is tricky, but try to see just the colours and marks!

- Continue to work upside down, preparing your mixes by matching them to your photograph. Using a thin (just a touch of solvent) combination of scarlet lake, phthalo green, bright yellow lake and titanium white, and the 6mm (¼in) filbert, mark in the features and shadows of hair and hand.
- Lighten this mix with a little titanium white, as a starting point for the flesh tones.
- Using close observation and colour matching, start to fill in the face and neck with the filbert and a touch of solvent.
- There isn't a lot to go on, so any subtle difference you see, use! The left of the face has more scarlet to it, the right more yellow. The top of the head has a little purple and white in the mix; the neck has a green tinge to it.

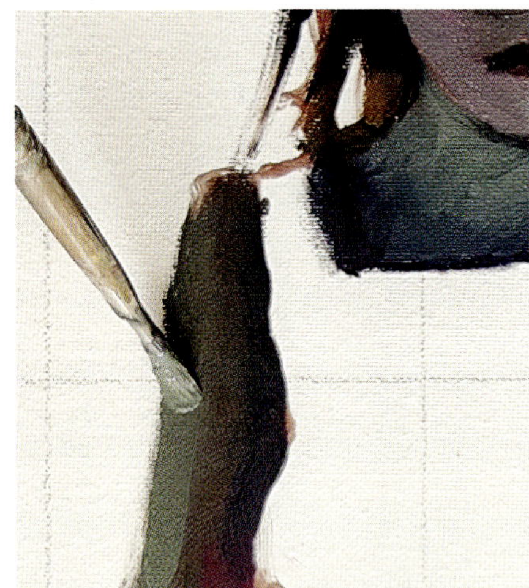

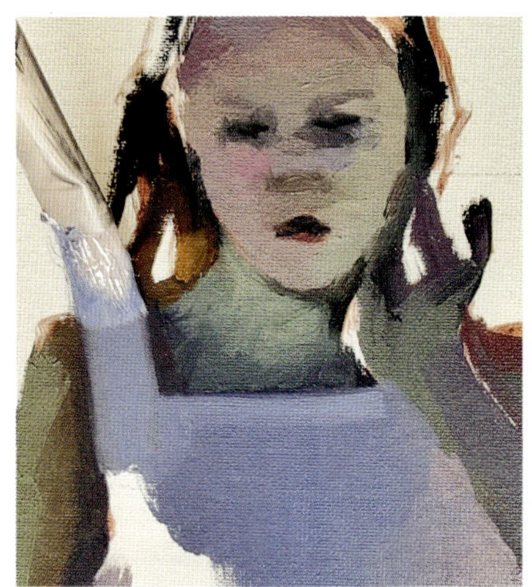

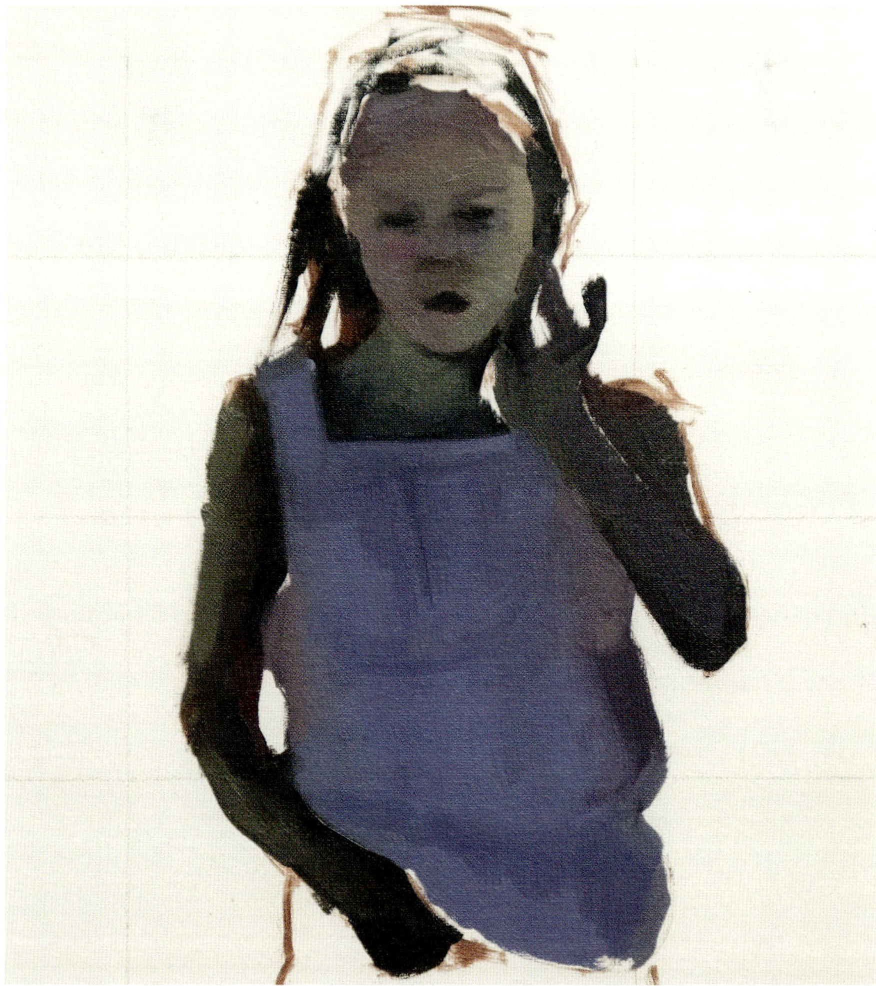

THIRD STAGE

With the crucial element of the face established, it's time to turn to the rest of the portrait.

Aside from a few salient areas, we don't want the same level of detail in the clothing or anywhere else, or we risk distracting from the focal point of the face.

- The colour on the arms is similar to the initial dark tones on the face, so use the mix on your palette as your starting point. Alter it according to what you observe.
- There is a hint of green in the arm on the left of the picture and in the palm on the right. The arm on the right of the picture has warmer tones, so add a little more scarlet to the mix.
- Try to keep brushwork a little looser on the arms as opposed to the face, by placing the paint instead of scrubbing it on (see upper left detail).
- Once all flesh tones are finished, switch to the 12mm (½in) flat brush for larger marks, such as the blouse (see lower left detail). Mix ultramarine blue, deep purple and titanium white for the blouse, adding burnt umber to the mix for the shadows.
- For the areas where the sun pokes through under the arms, mix deep purple, bright yellow lake, scarlet lake and titanium white.

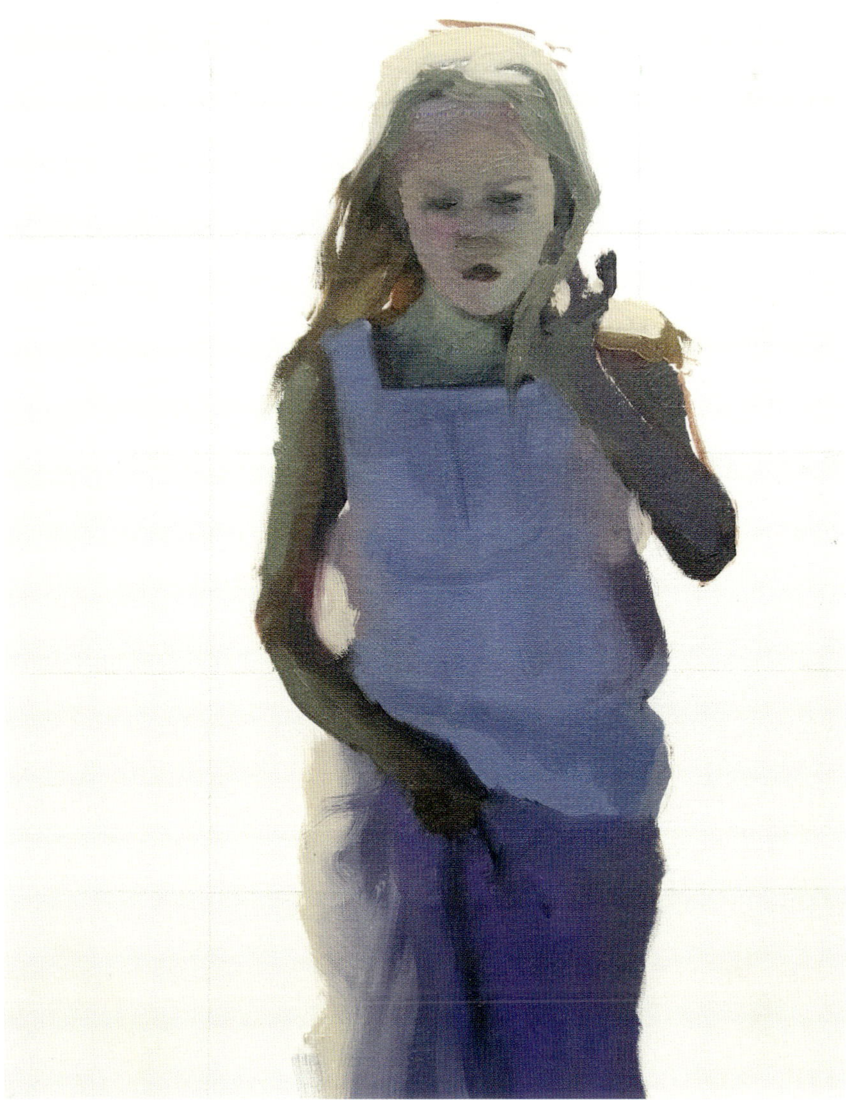

FOURTH STAGE

A friend saw the painting at the end of this stage, and asked why all the colours were so dark and dull. These comments can sometimes floor you a little! Remember: context is everything. It is harder to judge values when you are still faced with an eyeful of white canvas, even when you know what you are looking for.

We already know that the source image works well, so put your trust in the method: once the background is added in the next stage, the colours will make complete sense.

- Continuing with the flat brush, use a mix of deep purple, ultramarine blue and titanium white for the skirt. Add more deep purple and ultramarine blue with burnt umber for the shadows.
- With the round brush, mix bright yellow lake, scarlet lake and deep purple for where the back light is coming through in the shadows of the hair. Use this mix to warm the flesh tone on the inner arm on the left, and on the shoulder on the right.
- Now for the colour that blends the figure to the background: using the clean 6mm (¼in) filbert, add a mix of bright yellow lake, scarlet lake and titanium white to the top of the head, shoulder, underarms and left-hand side of the skirt.

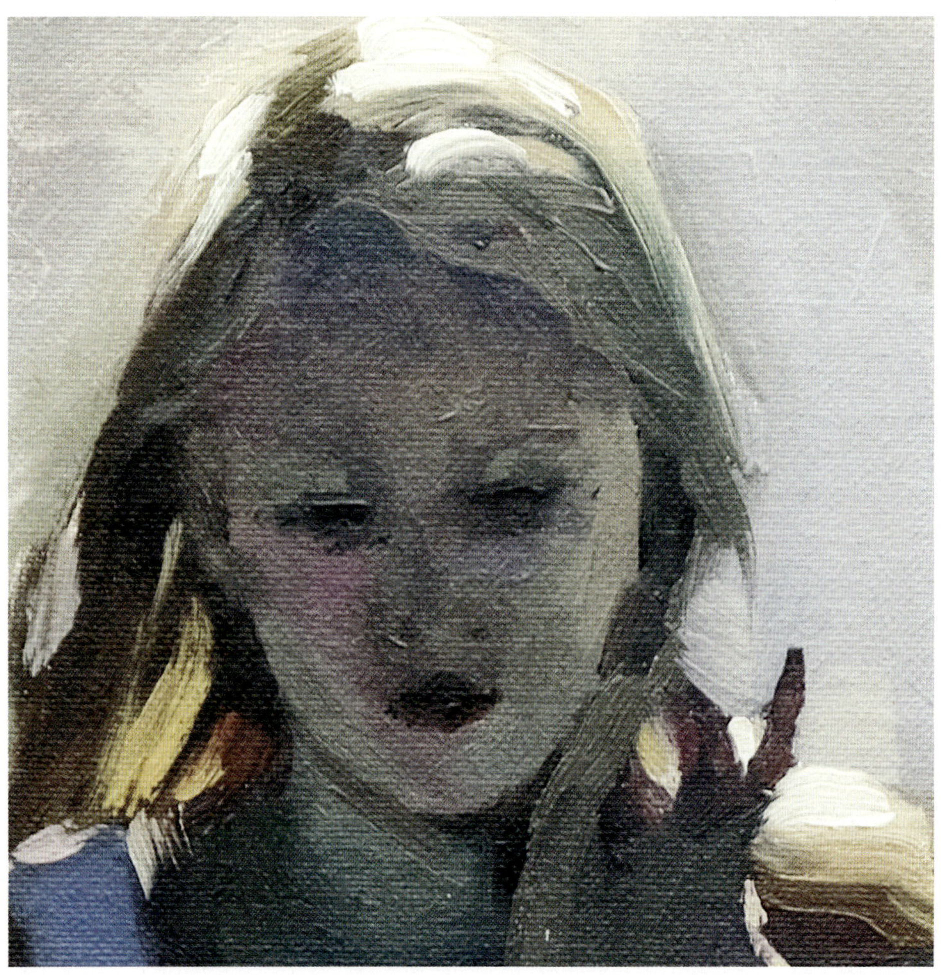

FIFTH STAGE – REFINING

And hey presto, the background greys bring it all together!

Unless a subject is too small within a painting, I will always cut the background in around it. It is important for a sense of atmospheric light, and very useful for softly honing your shapes. A bit of blur at the edges is good for that sense of movement.

When adding the background, if the paint mixes too much for your liking, just take a little off with a cloth and focus on 'laying' the paint as opposed to brushing it in.

- Prepare a light mix of deep purple, bright yellow lake and lots of titanium white.
- Use big, loose strokes of the 12mm (½in) flat brush to cut around the figure. These free strokes provide a nice contrast to the smaller brushwork in the figure. Add a bit more deep purple and bright yellow lake to the mix for the darker areas of background.
- Don't leave gaps on edges. Any merging will either add to the atmosphere or can be painted over. Barely-joined edges can stand out uncomfortably and do not create the impression of light surrounding a figure.
- Switch back to a clean 6mm (¼in) filbert to work thicker yellow into the hair, adding titanium white where it is directly reflecting the sun. Add this light mix to the right-hand shoulder, too.
- Finally, using the rigger brush and a thin, flowing mix of titanium white, scarlet lake and bright yellow lake, place highlights to the right-hand arm and left-hand shoulder.

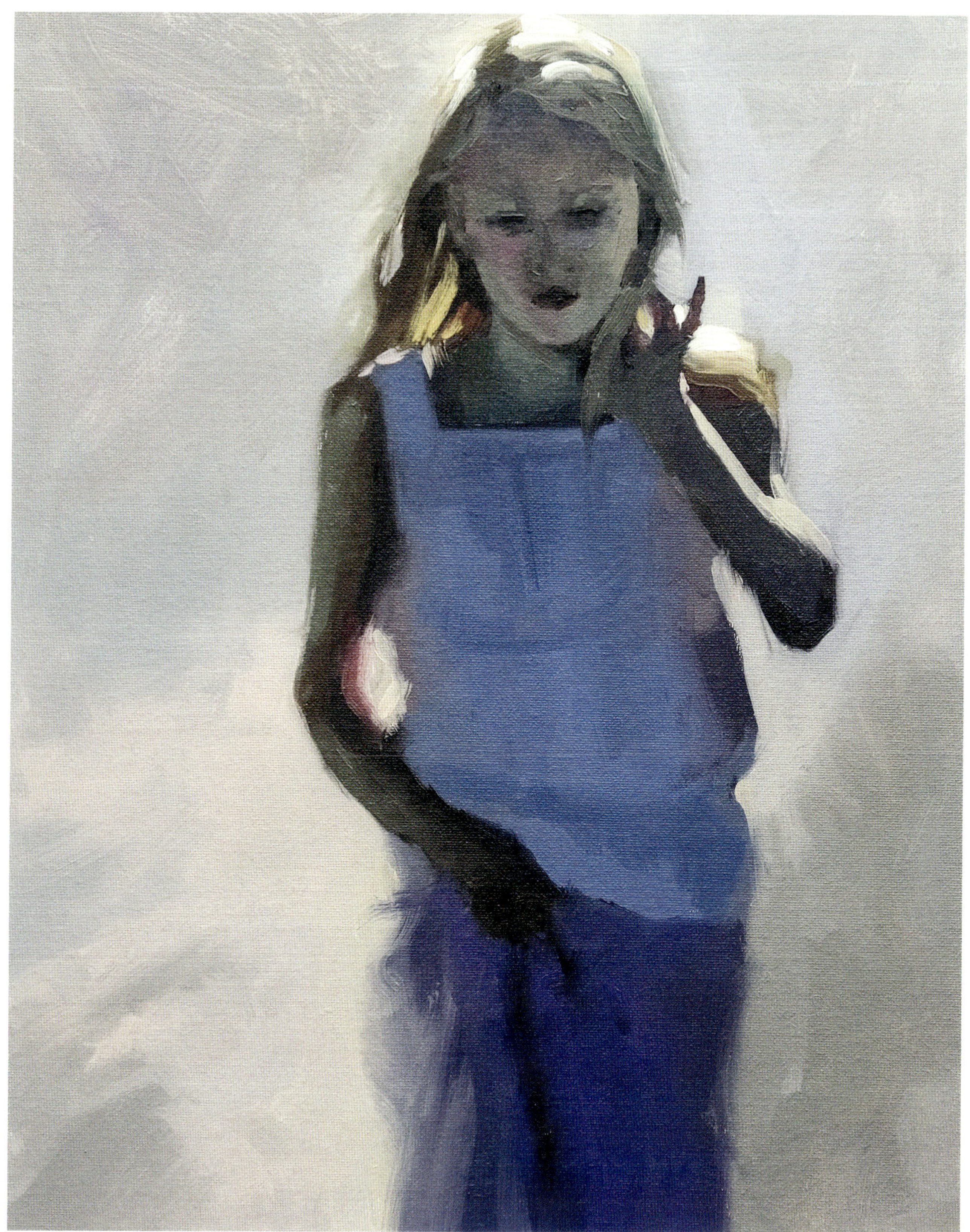

Finished painting

After evaluating this stage, I decided to keep the lighting minimal and call it finished. There is more that could be done, but is it needed? The painting is saying exactly what I wanted, simply, without any sparkly extras.

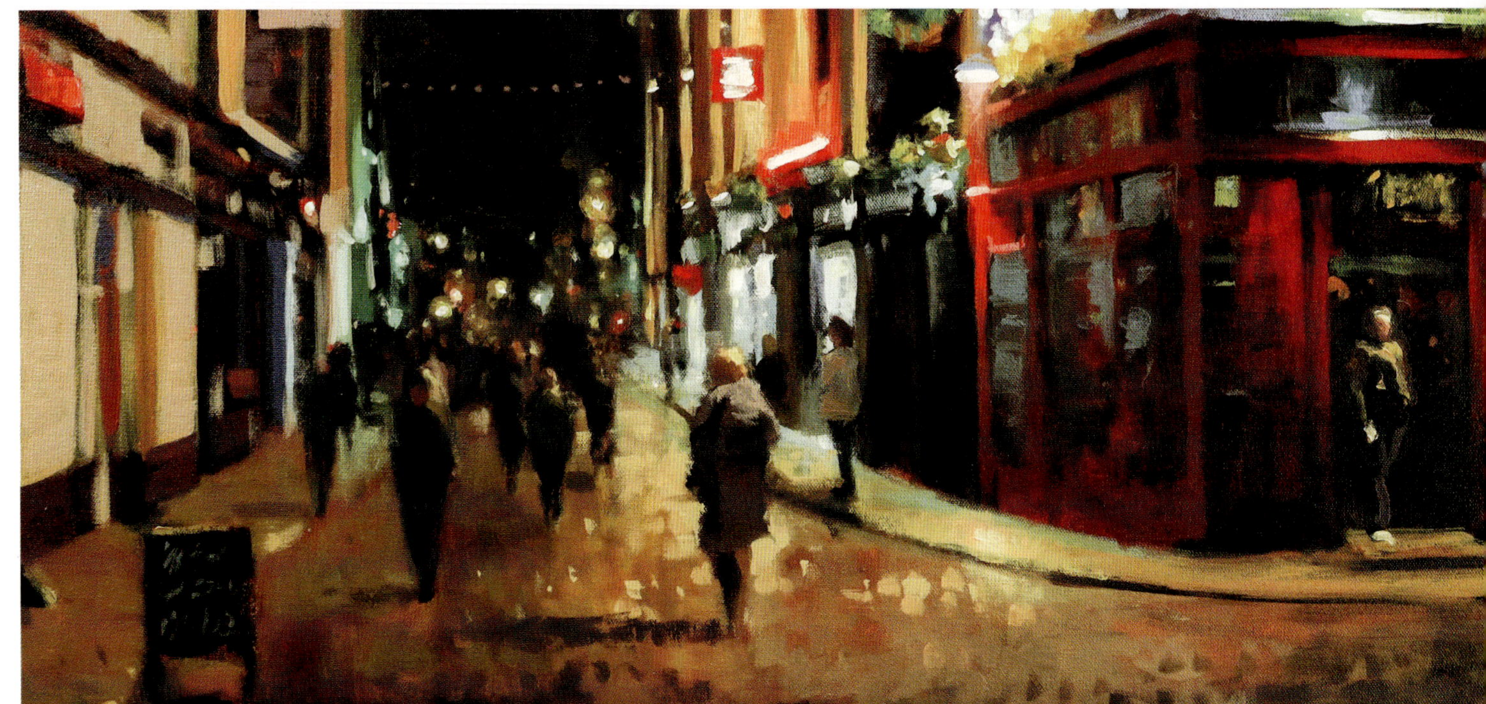

FIGURES

Figures can bring a painting to life. As incidental elements, they bring an immediate sense of sound, movement, moment and narrative. It is amazing how loose these figure shapes can be when set against light – and to my mind, the looser the better! Unlike portraits, where the person is the focus, figures in broader scenes can be treated as part of the light and overall atmosphere, rather than a separate entity to the surroundings.

Engage your imagination

Have you ever looked at a curtain pattern and found faces? Or spotted animals in the clouds? The tendency to see recognizable objects in vague, abstract shapes is called pareidolia. When we use this ability in viewing art, we become more engaged. The painting becomes more visually interesting – something to be discovered and worked out by our own mind's eye. If a subject is fully described in photographic detail we read it quickly and move on. So, if you want to create a visually engaging painting, leave some of the work for the viewer to complete.

As we know, it isn't possible to look into the light and see every last detail anyway – so we can get away with shapes and subtle lighting doing most of the work for us.

Evening Stroll, Temple Bar
Detail of the figures from the 76 × 50cm (30 × 19¾in) original.

SIMPLE FIGURE

Contre-jour figures will be greyed colours, with a bit of saturation and light on the edges, depending on the angle and proximity of the light source. My figures are typically made up of a blob, a rectangle and a stick for the head, torso and legs respectively. I then refine edges with the surrounding colour and apply any lighting. Painting them in this way makes them seem more of an integral part of the scene, rather than superimposed.

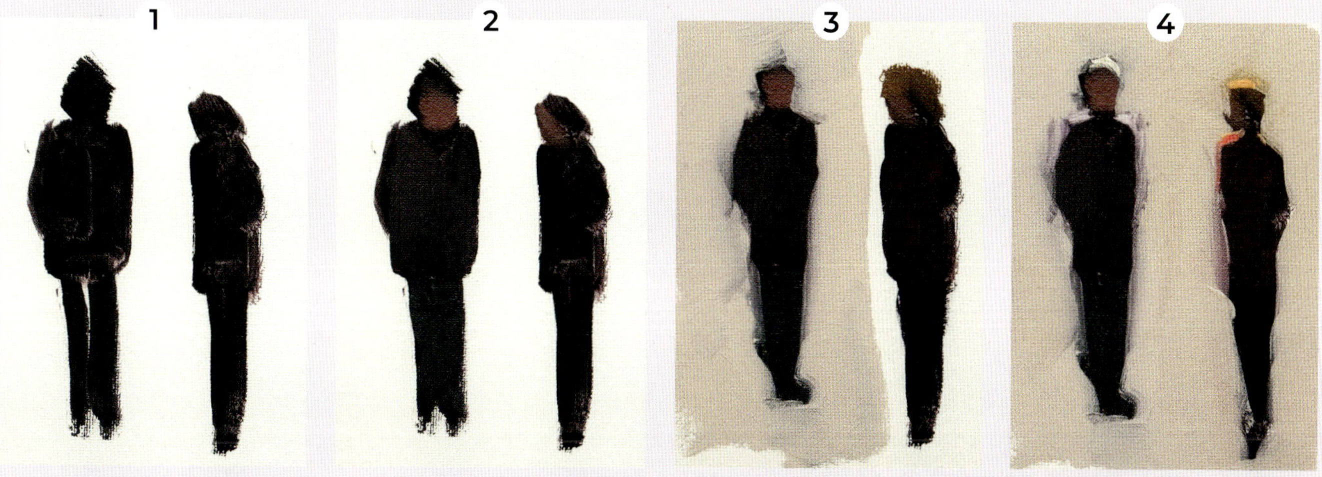

Use a 12mm (½in) flat brush for the process, to stop you drawing too precisely. It will activate your own pareidolia; and you will start to interpret and organize the brush marks so that recognizable elements appear: arms, shoulder bags, bent knees, long coats, turned heads – which you can then emphasize a little with an extra mark or two.

All of my figures in the landscape are created this way – it works! It is great fun to experiment.

1 With a 12mm (½in) flat brush, mix a dark tone of orange and purple to make a base mix. Using just four brushstrokes, paint a blob for the head, a rectangle for the torso, and two sticks for legs. Paint each figure larger than they need to be, so that you have room to cut in and shape them with the surrounding colour.

2 Touch in each face with a warm brown; then use deep purple or red tones for their coats, and greens or blues for the legs. All the colours should be a form of grey.

3 Still using the 12mm (½in) flat brush, mix a much lighter warm grey and cut in around each person. This is the moment to find out what your figures are saying! Here, it turns out that they are passers-by in the street, having a brief chat.

4 Cutting in has turned my right-hand figure into someone walking away, her back leg stepped back. Her body points away from us, her face turns to the figure on the left. Add some vibrant highlights to finish: red/white on the coat, gold on one head, white on the other. These give the impression of *contre-jour* light.

WOODLANDS

Simplification is your friend when it comes to representing the wonder of trees and the forest. Do you want to faithfully record all the massed detail of the branches, twigs and leaves – or instead to evoke their feel and presence? I would suggest that the latter is both easier and more effective if evocative atmosphere is your aim.

When painting woodlands *contre-jour*, there is an orchestra of meaningful marks to be made – it really is an opportunity to explore what your brushes and painterly tools can do. Carefully layering these areas can quickly create a convincing illusion of depth and detail.

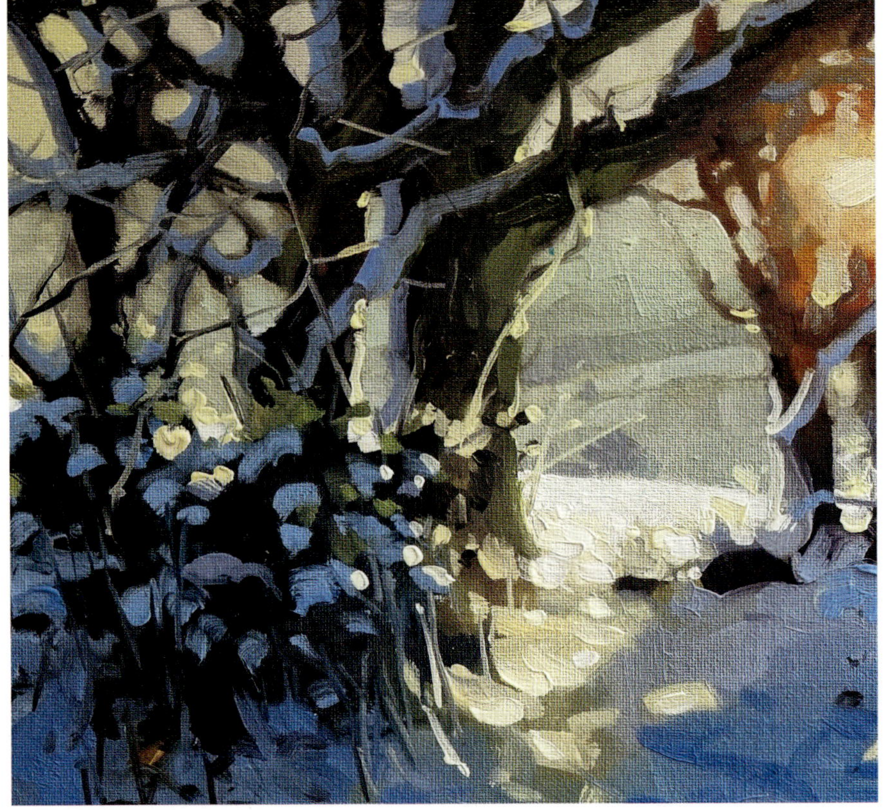

Heavy snow on grasses, sticks and twigs provides us with great opportunities to paint with big, blobby colour.

This painting was inspired by an absolute thicket of winter brambles and nettles, covered with fresh snow. I painted the bramble area and trees first in one, solid dark tone, then laid the blue blobs of snow, some greens for bark and foliage and a few stick suggestions on the edges.

The highlights were the final flourish. Layering from dark to light in this case made the process more minimal and prioritized atmosphere over detail.

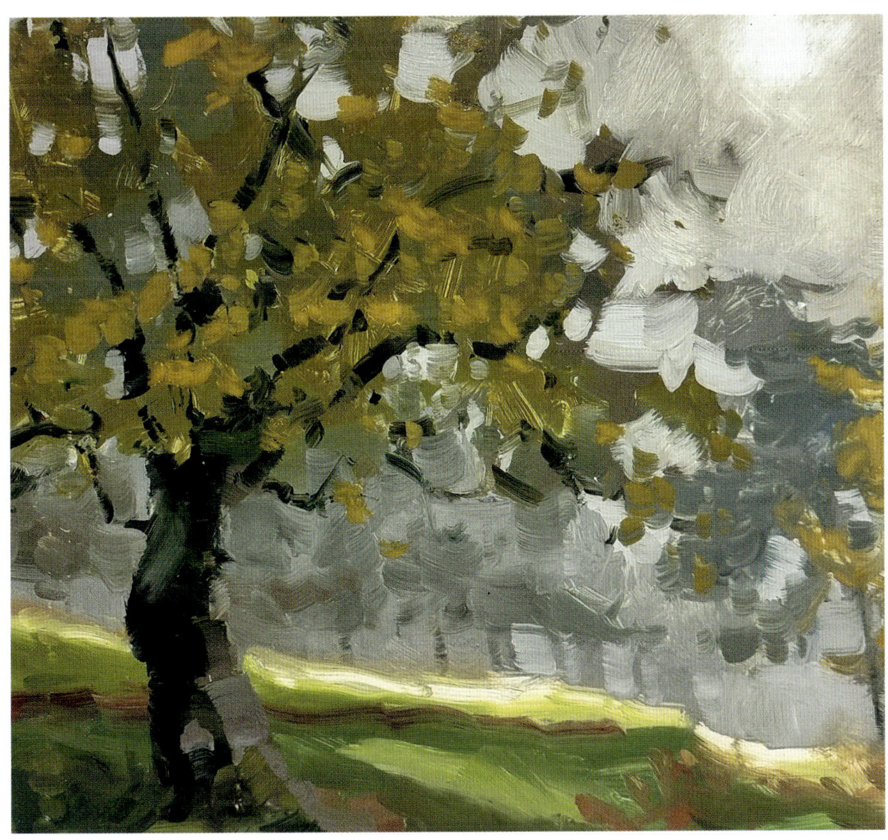

A plein air piece (see page 100) from a breezy autumn day.

There is no need to paint all the leaves – just enough that the eye feels convinced. To do this, I first brushed in a solid canopy shape in a shadow colour, then laid individual strokes in a warmer, more saturated tone on top.

Next, I added the blobby leaves that are in full light (in orange, in this case) allowing some to be separate and blurring others for movement. I dissected the tree by adding the branches last of all, using a rigger and the end of a brush for some scratchy texture.

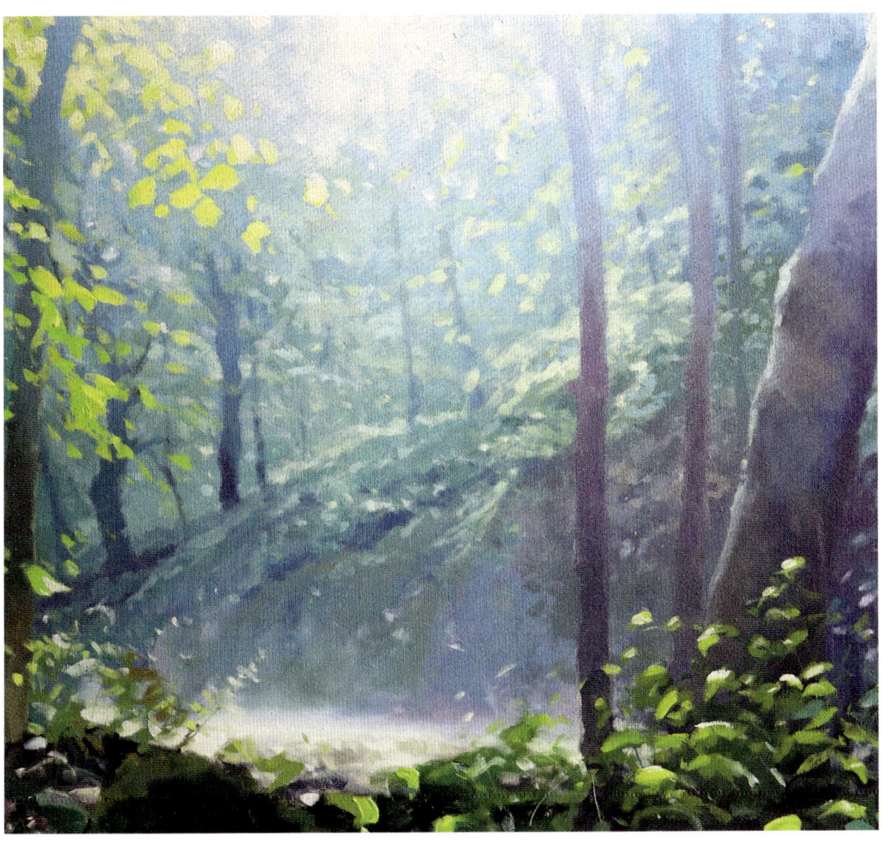

When trees are lost in the light like this, I always paint them as a solid mass – defining them by adding the white sunlight (the negative space) on top.

This approach is true to what is actually happening. You aren't painting trees, you are painting the light coming through. As the trees come away from the direct sun, they become less hazy and more distinct.

Go big: resisting the urge for detail

My work is heavily based in realism and accurate depiction of light, but I always want this end result to emerge from looser beginnings. A simplified impression can be just as descriptive as a drawing – but it will convey far more information about atmosphere, movement and texture. That human urge to tidy everything up, reduce it and make sense of it, can work against us. It is so easy to fall into edging every branch, twig and leaf, feeling duty-bound to reproduce it in paint, when all most of us want is to get the lighting right.

When painting woodlands, I recommend using larger brushes for as long as possible. As soon as you notice yourself reaching for a smaller brush, question yourself. Is that area worth the sharp detail? Will it pull the attention away from the eye path? Does it really need a small brush to say what needs to be said?

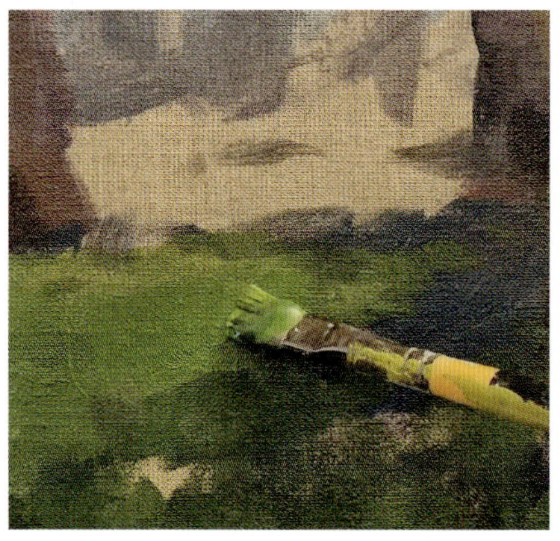 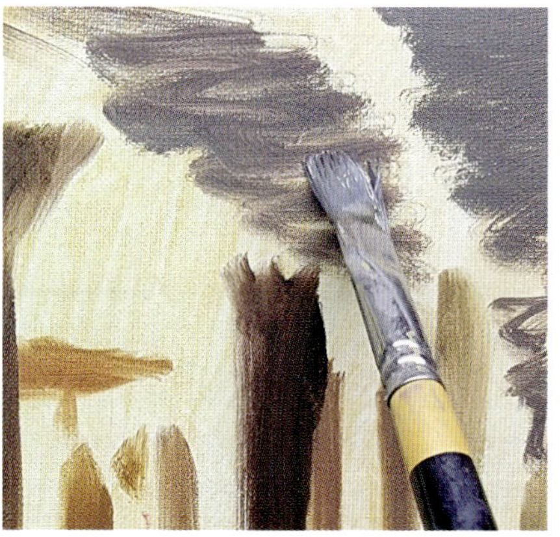 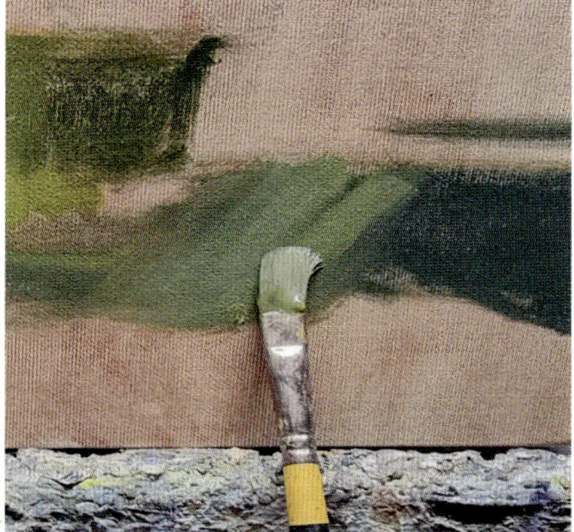

Flat brush flair

My 12mm (½in) flat brush is such a workhorse! It's great for laying down textureless areas of light, squiggled horizontals and subtle angles. Try using the corner and side edge for fine details before you reach for a smaller brush – it will do everything!

SCALING UP

Large brushwork is especially useful when working on bigger canvases or boards. It allows for different gestures and marks, partly because the larger surface means you are more likely to work from the shoulder rather than the elbow or wrist. Using larger brushes will also help you to see and think in a larger format – and feel less overwhelmed by all that white canvas to cover!

Whenever I paint on surfaces larger than 76 × 101cm (30 × 40in), I'll use larger brushes, such as a 20mm (¾in) or 25mm (1in) flat. Scaling up the brush when I scale up the canvas helps to ensure that I get the same movement and atmosphere across all my paintings. If you stick to smaller brushes, you can end up completely bogged down in tiny detail.

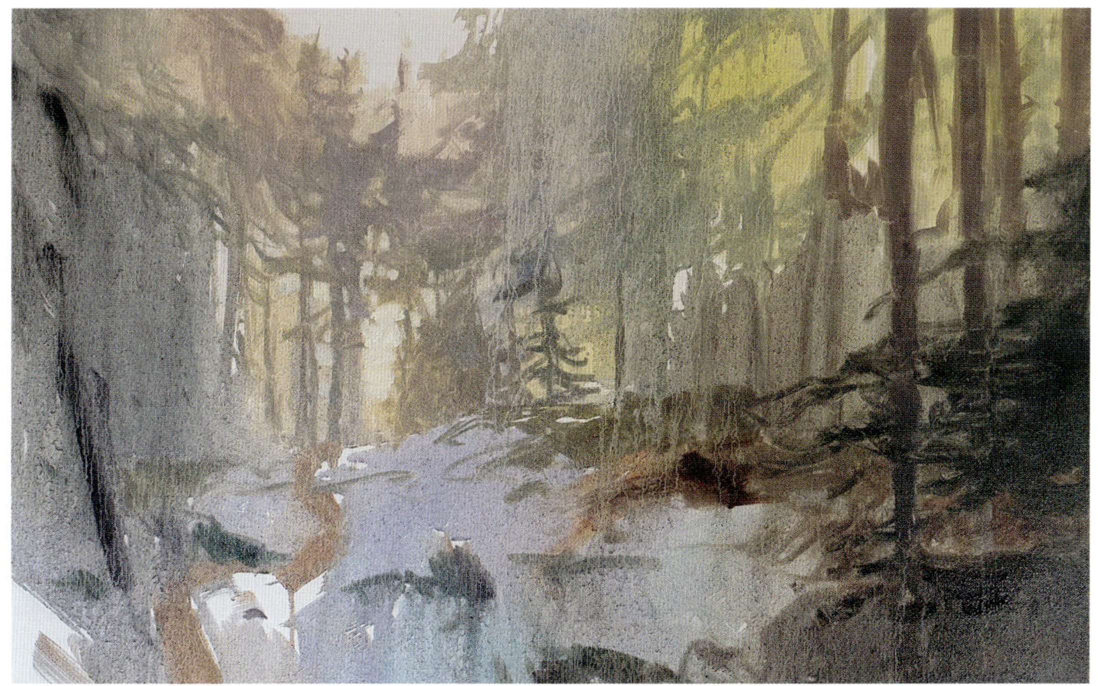

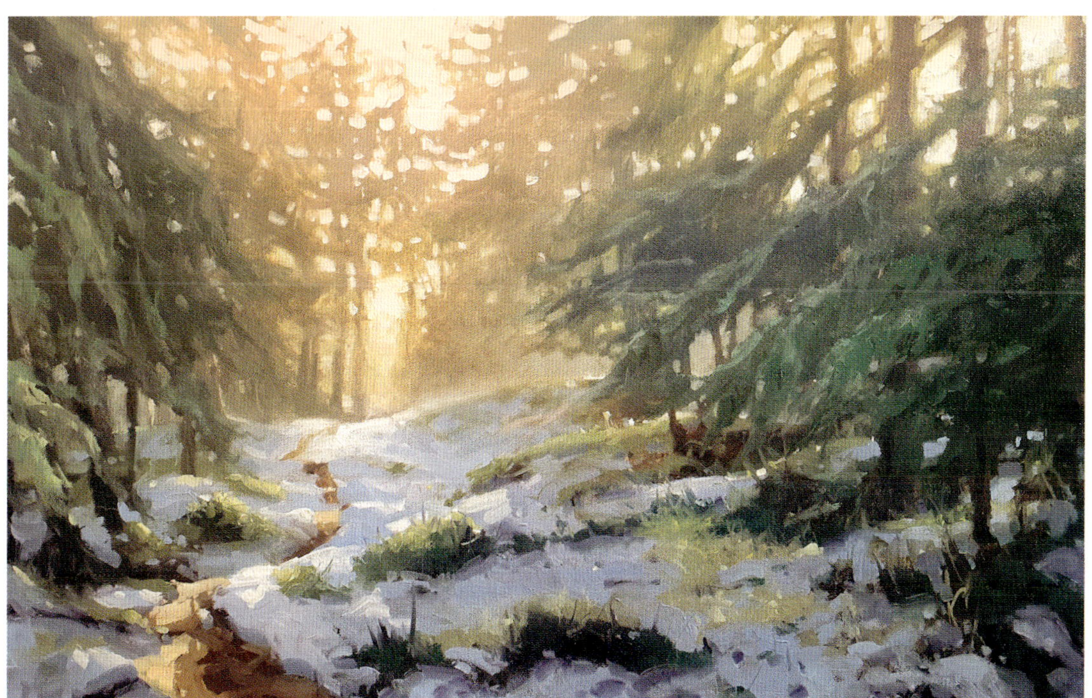

Winter Walk, Cairngorms

76 × 50cm (30 × 19¾in)

With an eye to the colours, I washed the first stage (top) in with a 25mm (1in) flat brush (a size 12 flat from Rosemary & Co.'s Ivory range), using the corner for tree trunks and any branch detail. This just sets the tone for the way I want to paint – freely and with a bit of abandon!

I swapped to my 12mm (½in) flat for more careful placement later on in the process (bottom), but there wasn't much finer work needed. A lot of this transparent underpainting remains visible in the finished work, brought to life through contrast with lighting and thicker paint.

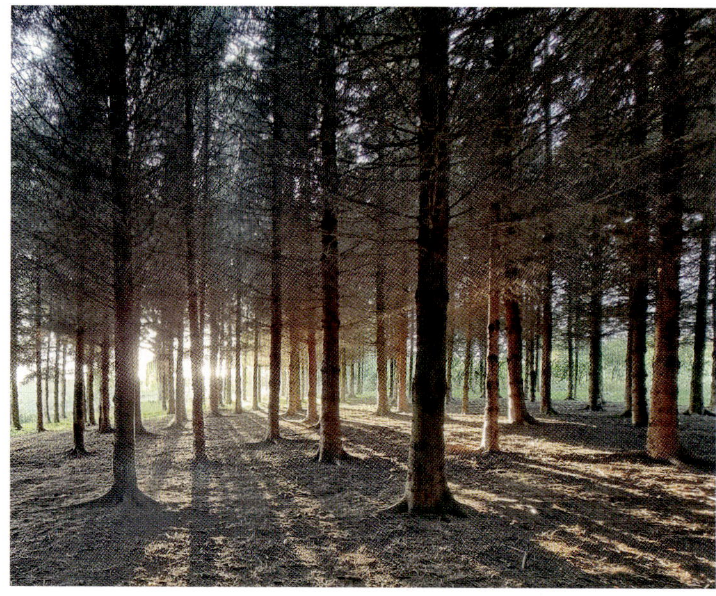

WOODLAND

'If a painting of a tree was only the exact representation of the original[...], there would be no reason for making it; we might as well look at the tree itself. But the painting, if it is of the right sort, gives something that neither a photograph nor a view of the tree conveys. [...] We catch a vision of the grandeur and beauty of a king of the forest.' **Calvin Coolidge**

This project looks at simplifying woodland – a subject of potentially infinite detail. When painting scenes like this, lots of summarizing is necessary to avoid overwhelming the eye.

We are looking for patterns in both colour and shape; exploring brushwork to convey foliage and angle of growth, and using tone to define depth.

You will need

30 × 24cm (11¾ × 9½in) canvas board

Brushes: two 12mm (½in) flat brushes, small filbert, small rigger

Paints: titanium white, bright yellow lake, scarlet lake, deep purple, ultramarine blue, sap green, phthalo green

Low-odour solvent

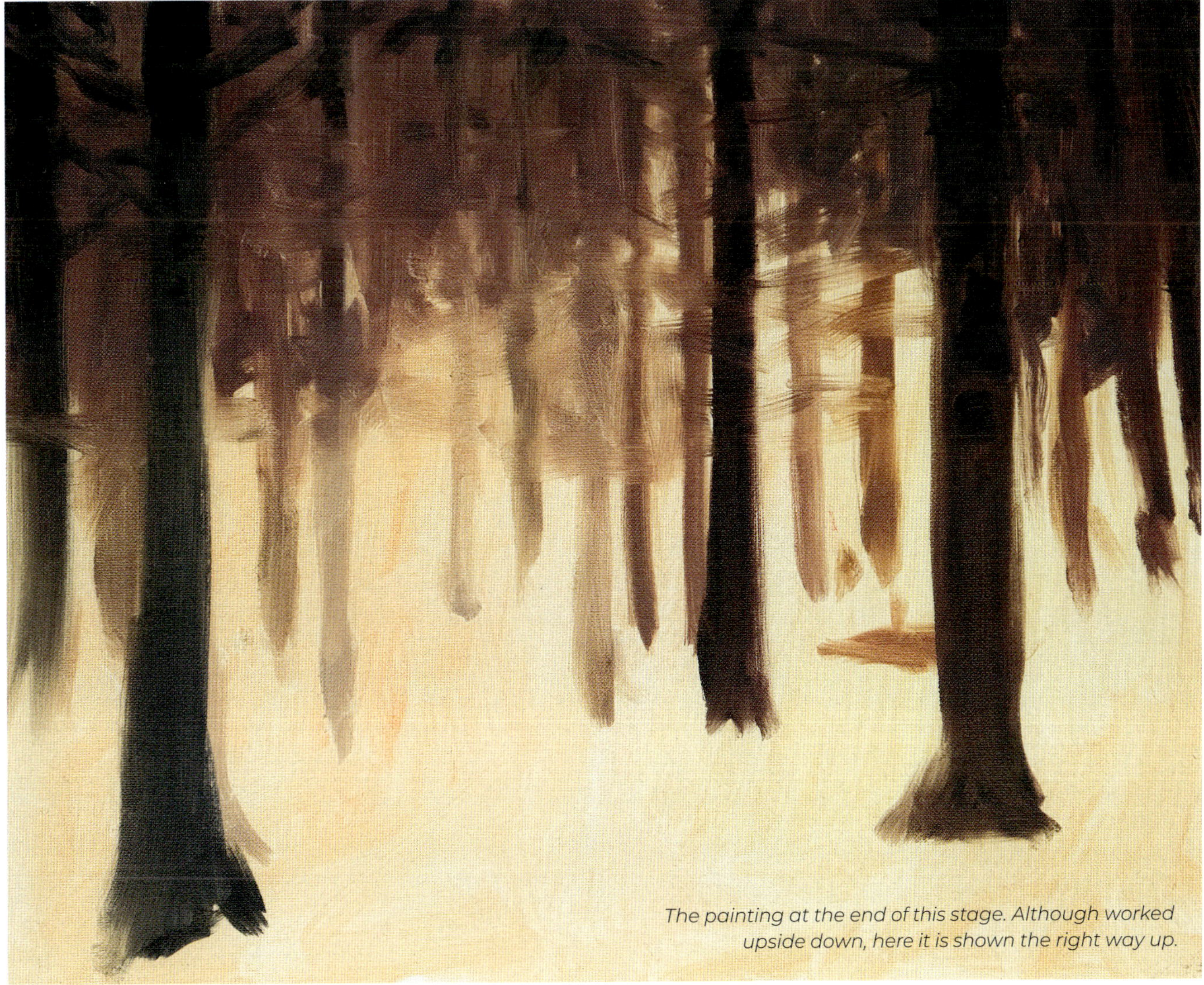

FIRST STAGE

*I really wanted to retain some of
the transparent initial marks in this
painting, for the contrast of glowing,
transparent colour with opaque light.*

*Work this stage with both the
reference photograph and canvas
board upside down, to help you avoid
thinking 'tree'. Aim to paint what you
actually see, not what you expect a
woodland to look like.*

- Use the 12mm (½in) flat to mix bright yellow lake with a touch of scarlet lake and use it to thinly cover the board.
- Lay down the distant trees with bright yellow lake, muting it slightly with a touch of deep purple.
- Add scarlet lake to the mix for the mid-ground trees, then add deep purple and sap green where the trees get darker. For those nearest, add a bit of ultramarine blue to the mix. Throughout, keep the paint thin, but not drippy.
- For foliage, mix scarlet lake and sap green with a touch of titanium white. Scrub this in with the filbert brush, almost dry brushing the lower branches. Pay attention to the angles of the branches you are adding.

Brushwork and the woodland

Observation is key. Trees are one of those subjects we all think we know – but are continually surprising when you come to look at them with an eye to paint.

Having a mind to the nature and movement of your subject can make all the difference to the way you apply the paint. If you think of it as a flat picture, then you will paint a flat painting. Instead, try to think of how the object grows and moves. Think of its texture, how it feels to touch.

Much of your initial brushwork will be lost as you continue to work, but keeping it loose and expressive at this stage can result in some beautiful underpainting that is worth retaining for contrast with later layers.

Once you've applied paint, sit back and try to read what the brushwork itself is saying. Here are some brushstrokes I would use for particular areas or aspects of the woodland:

Young tree trunks Use a flat brush and flowing paint, applied with vertical strokes.

Large tree trunks Flat brush and vertical strokes again, but followed by horizontal flat brush marks all the way up the trunk. This gives a three-dimensional, rounded feel. It's a very good way of painting silver birches in particular.

Branches I generally use a filbert to loosely lay these in, scrubbing them a bit in the distance. However, the marks you make will depend on the type of tree. Have a closer look – do they gently curve down from the trunk like an oak tree, or are the angles hard, as with a fir?

Distant winter trees Fan brushes are great for scrubbing in the impression of all those twigs and branches. Turn the brush on its side for smaller marks.

Distant summer trees I use the side of a filbert to scrub in leafy trees and bushes.

Fir trees It is tempting to brush these on like a child's Christmas tree; but for me, this belies their needled texture. I scrub them in with the side of a filbert, paying attention to their angles and shape.

Twigs, grasses and sticks A small rigger, loaded with flowing paint, is excellent for all these. Scraping out with a knife or the end of a brush is also great for some scratchy highlights. Again, observe the angles and growth patterns, so that your few marks say exactly what is happening.

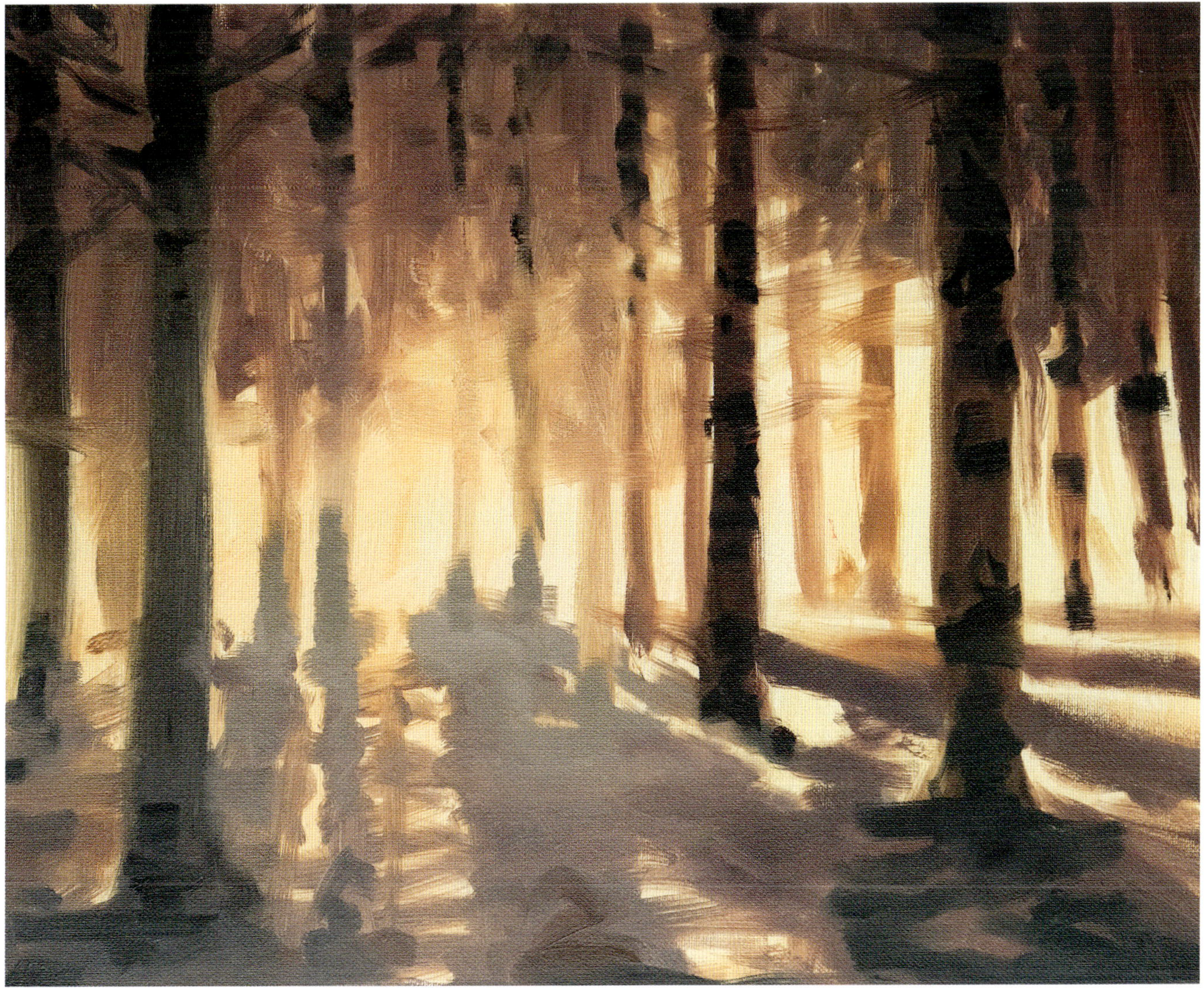

SECOND STAGE

The angles of the shadows in the foreground show how the light radiates out from the sun. It's important for them all to lead towards the same light source for the painting to be a convincing illusion.

- Keeping the painting upside down, mix the forest floor shadows – warmer and lighter nearer the sun (a combination of bright yellow lake, deep purple and titanium white with a touch of ultramarine blue), cooler and darker when further away (the same combination, but with more blue and less white).
- Scrub these colours in with horizontal movements of the 12mm (½in) flat brush, while keeping an eye on the angles of the shadows of the trees.
- Use a mix of phthalo green and scarlet lake for the darkest areas of the foreground trees and shadows.
- Turn the painting the right way up, to engage your interpretation and make sure the shadow angles are all working.

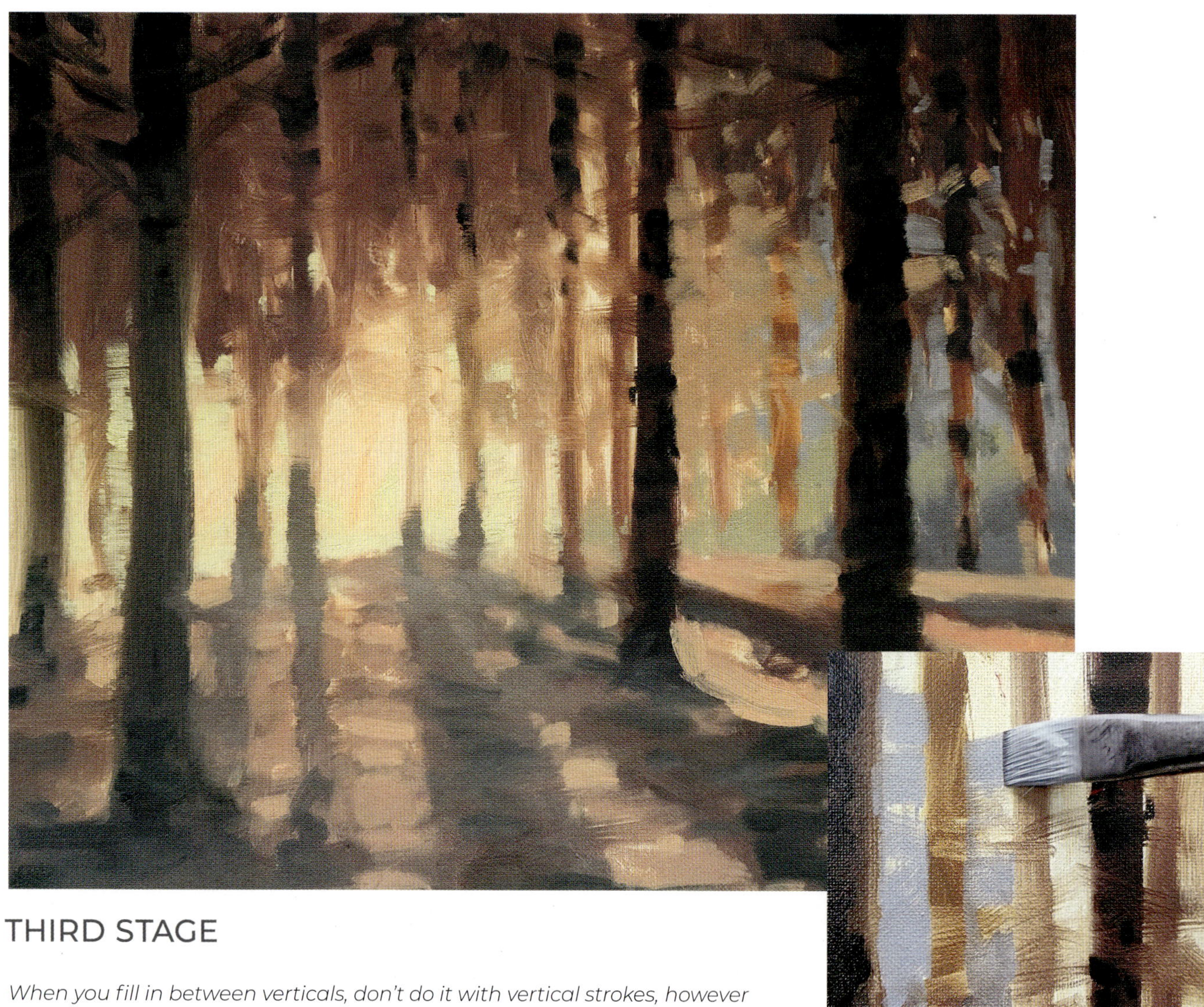

THIRD STAGE

When you fill in between verticals, don't do it with vertical strokes, however tempting. The direction of the brushstroke will make it look like an object next door, rather than a background.

If you instead use a flat (think painting an internal wall in your home) or opposing direction of movement – as shown in the detail – the difference will instead emphasize space.

- If necessary, adjust the angles of the shadows with thicker horizontal strokes placed on the forest floor: a pinky-yellow mix of bright yellow lake, scarlet lake and titanium white for the light areas, and a dark mix of phthalo green, scarlet lake and titanium white for the shade.
- Use criss-crossing strokes of the 12mm (½in) flat brush to apply a little of the pinky-yellow mix into the mid branches, too, in order to add more opacity and light where needed.
- Use the dark mix to thicken the dark areas on the foreground trees, at both top and bottom.
- Still using the flat brush, fill in the blue and green background on the right-hand side. I kept these colours a little warm with a touch of red in each mix, and light.

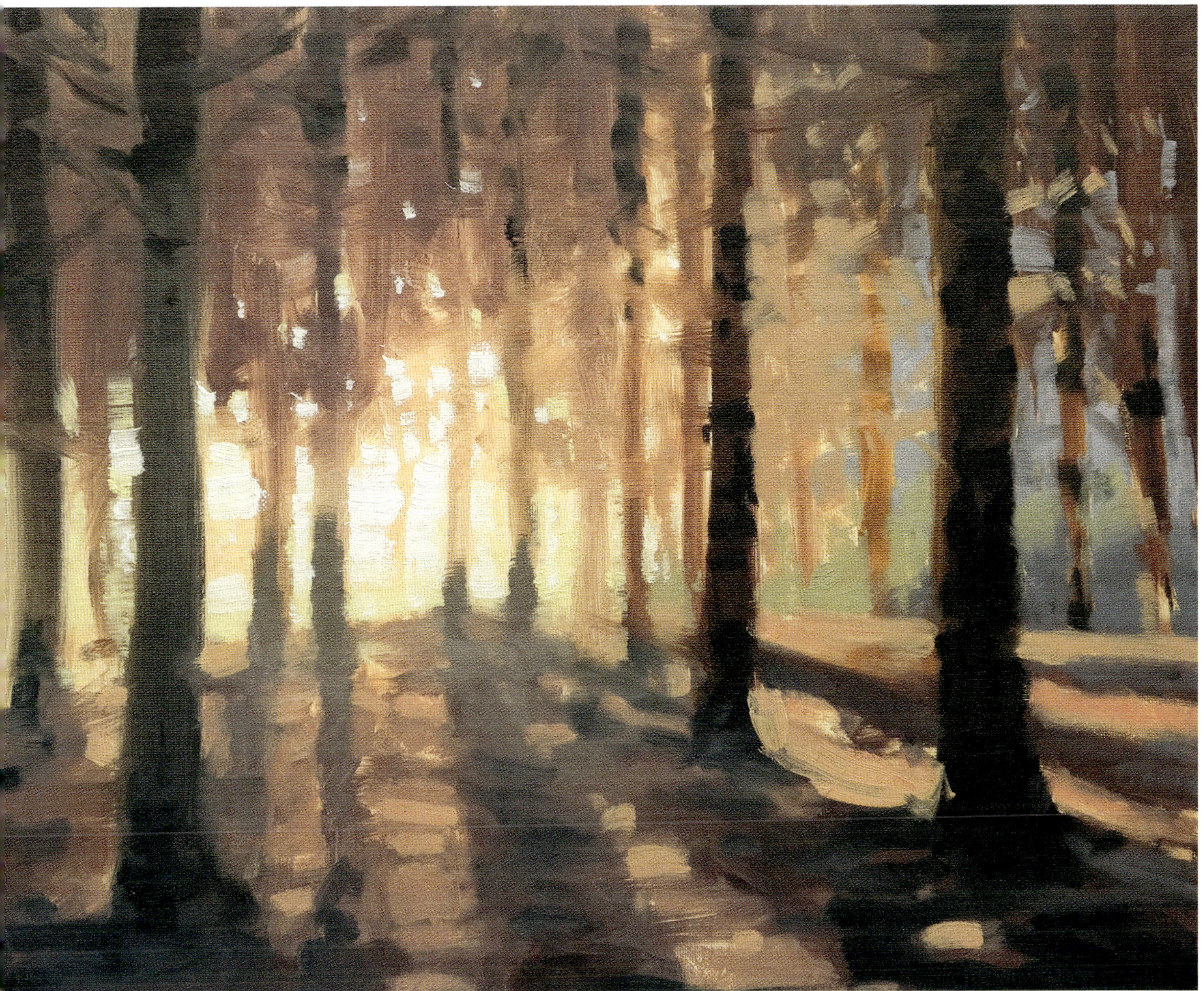

FOURTH STAGE

Now it's time to add the first lights – and as you'll see from the picture above, of the finished stage, this gives the painting immediate and obvious impact.

- With a completely clean flat, mix the tiniest touch of bright yellow lake into titanium white and lay on some light blobs for the sun. Apply the paint using the brush in the same way as for filling in the gaps between the trees (see opposite), to ensure the sense of distance in the light.

- Add a little more yellow as you work on areas further away from the sun's centre, to make the brightest whites there really glow.

FIFTH STAGE – REFINING

Time to go to town on the lighting! Once the initial strokes from the fourth stage complete the value range, it is time to play with atmosphere within the wood itself. There is a balance to be struck here, between showing the effects of the light and losing the mystery of the wood.

When you come to line the edge of the trees with the rigger brush, think about your perspective against the light: if a tree is directly between you and the sun, both edges will have highlights. If the tree is on the right of the sun, the highlights will be on its left-hand side. It sounds obvious but is easily forgotten when you're in full highlight flow!

- With the flat brush, lay some touches of a thick bright yellow lake, scarlet lake and titanium white mix on the floor, and on some of the edges of the distant trees.
- Use a similar mix with less titanium white to paint the orange-tinged areas in the lit shadows.
- In the trees nearest the sun, where they are blocking bright light, use the flat brush and a mix of scarlet lake, titanium white and bright yellow lake, greyed with a touch of deep purple to add a pink haze to create the illusion that your eye is being affected by the sun.
- Switch to the rigger brush and use a flowing mix of titanium white tinted with bright yellow lake and scarlet lake to line the edge of the trees.
- If you feel the foreground trees needed a little more branch definition, you can use a warm dark mix (scarlet lake, bright yellow lake and deep purple) to loosely criss-cross in a few twiggy branches. Avoid being too precise: using too much control here will risk losing the sense of movement.
- Make any further adjustments you feel necessary – but don't overwork things. Once you're happy, step away and the painting is finished.

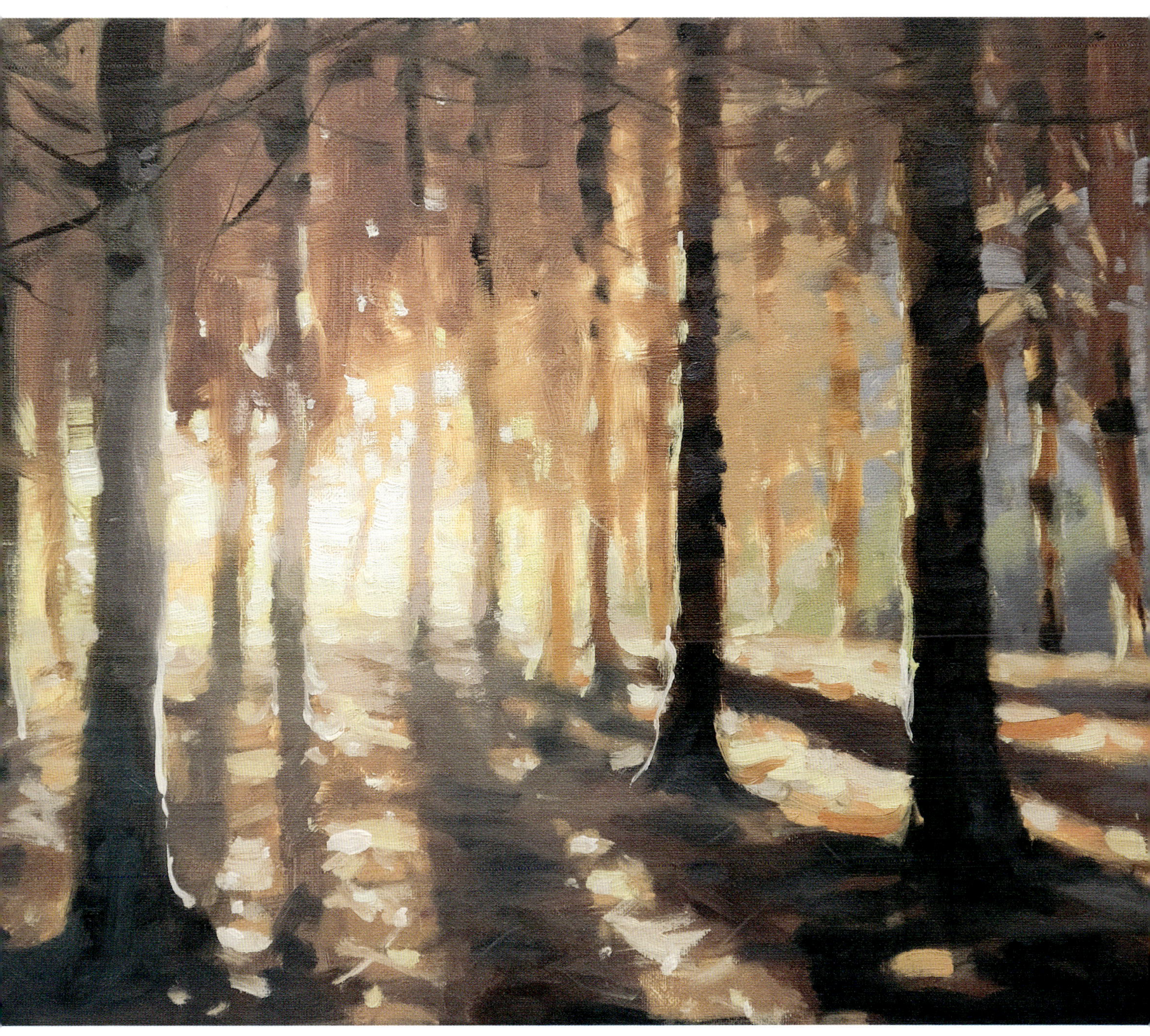

As noted, there's a fine line needed for the right balance of lights and darks here – I'll leave the final judgement on the success of this example in your hands!

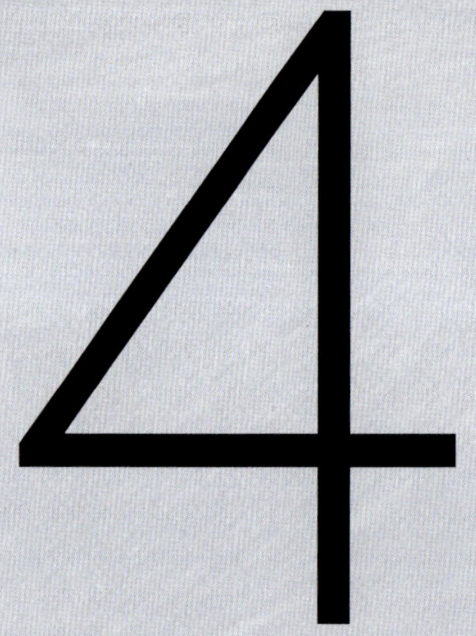

PAINTING *EN PLEIN AIR*

*'I could not paint at all if I had to paint slowly.
Every effect is so transient, it must be
rapidly painted.'* **Joaquin Sorolla**

The challenge of painting outdoors, *en plein air*, can almost feel too great
at first – especially if you take your studio expectations out on the trip.
Painting directly from the landscape takes a different mindset to working
indoors – I think it is almost like switching mediums, where you are
required to think differently for every part of the painting process. No
matter how good you are in the studio, painting from life requires different
skills which will need to be learned through focused practice. Remember
this when you are thinking you can't paint! It is an acquired skill distinct
from studio work; and as such, it feeds into studio work in the richest way.

It's important to know that there will be inevitable disappointment,
but also wonderful opportunities impossible to find indoors.
Fixing a focus on the world before you is a thrilling undertaking.
There is nowhere better to develop your skills than while
painting *en plein air*, in the ever-changing landscape.

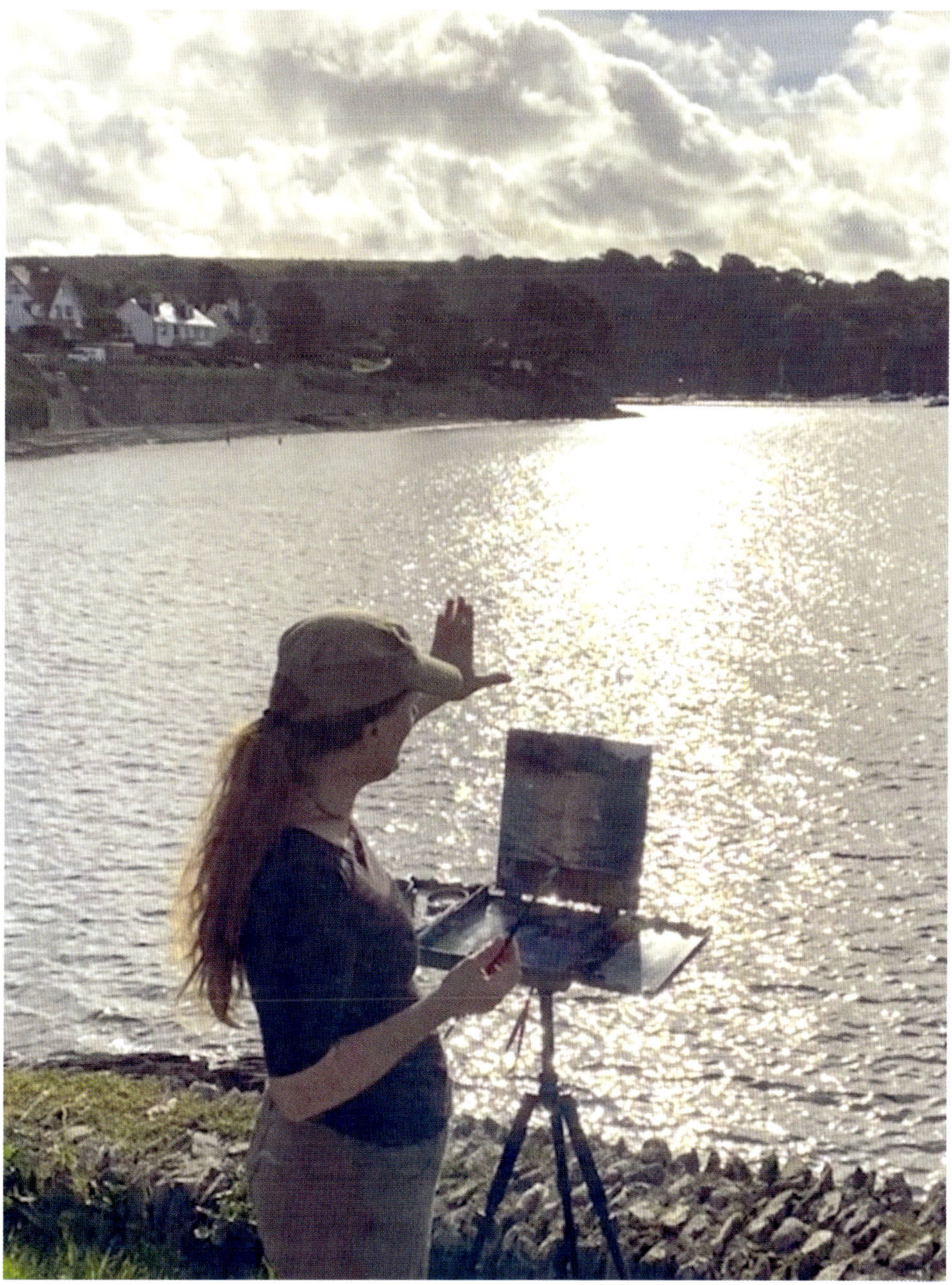

Painting into the morning light

It is obviously vital not to stare into the sun or its reflection on water, so I block the main glare with my hand, use peripheral vision, and exercise quick, careful observation. You don't want to end up with a headache, or worse, retinal burning!

As well as direct observation, I use what I know: any subject in the path of the direct sunlight will be a warmer, lighter colour than it would elsewhere. This includes dark shadows and solid objects blocking the light. Accentuating the coolness of colours elsewhere in the painting will help create the illusion of real light on the canvas.

Painting into the sun outdoors isn't an easy subject to study but much can be learned in a short time – and the painterly rewards are worth it.

FINDING YOUR SPOT

You need somewhere that provides a good composition, and finding that can take a long time. I entered a *plein air* competition once and my search for the perfect view took twice as long as the painting itself! The more variables you can control, the more you can concentrate on painting outdoors, so it is always worth taking time to pick your spot.

We've already looked at what makes a good composition, but painting directly from the landscape can blow all that knowledge out of the water and feel overwhelming. Photographs have a contained viewpoint, whereas outside we have as big or small an angle as we choose. To help assess a potential landscape composition, make a viewfinder with your fingers and thumbs, in the approximate dimensions of your canvas. Look for a strong foreground, mid-ground and background. Keep the strongest sunlight and focal point off-centre. Once you have that, look for ways to draw the eye in and zigzag through. And that is enough to think about!

Make sure you know where the sun is. This may sound obvious but if you end up the wrong side of a hill for whatever shot you're after, it can be frustrating. If you head to the coast to get beautiful sparkling water, you need to know which way the beach or cliff faces. Once you know the lighting direction, work out where the sun is on its path through the sky. If you can plot its path, you can set up so that you are painting your chosen view before the sun reaches the optimum position. That gives you the most time to capture the lighting of the scene.

Aim to spend no more than ninety minutes on a painting outdoors. If you spend more time than that, the colours and shadows will have changed drastically from when you started. If you're just finishing and fiddling (always tempting) that is better done in the studio, when you can better judge what you have produced. If time allows, it is better spent painting several studies rather than refining just one.

If you want to work on a larger scale, paint in stages over several visits at the same time of day. That way the lighting stays the same so your painting won't end up muddy and confused.

PAINTING TOGETHER

Find another painter or a group to go out with. There are outdoor painting groups everywhere, who will have plenty of knowledge to share on the area and the process. Having other painters alongside you helps for many reasons, not least the motivation to keep going when it feels a bit desperate! You soon discover that everyone has the same hurdles, doubts and tricky moments, which can be extremely encouraging when you're struggling to remember how to paint. Don't be afraid that you're not good enough, either – everyone painting outside is there to improve their practice, whatever their experience level.

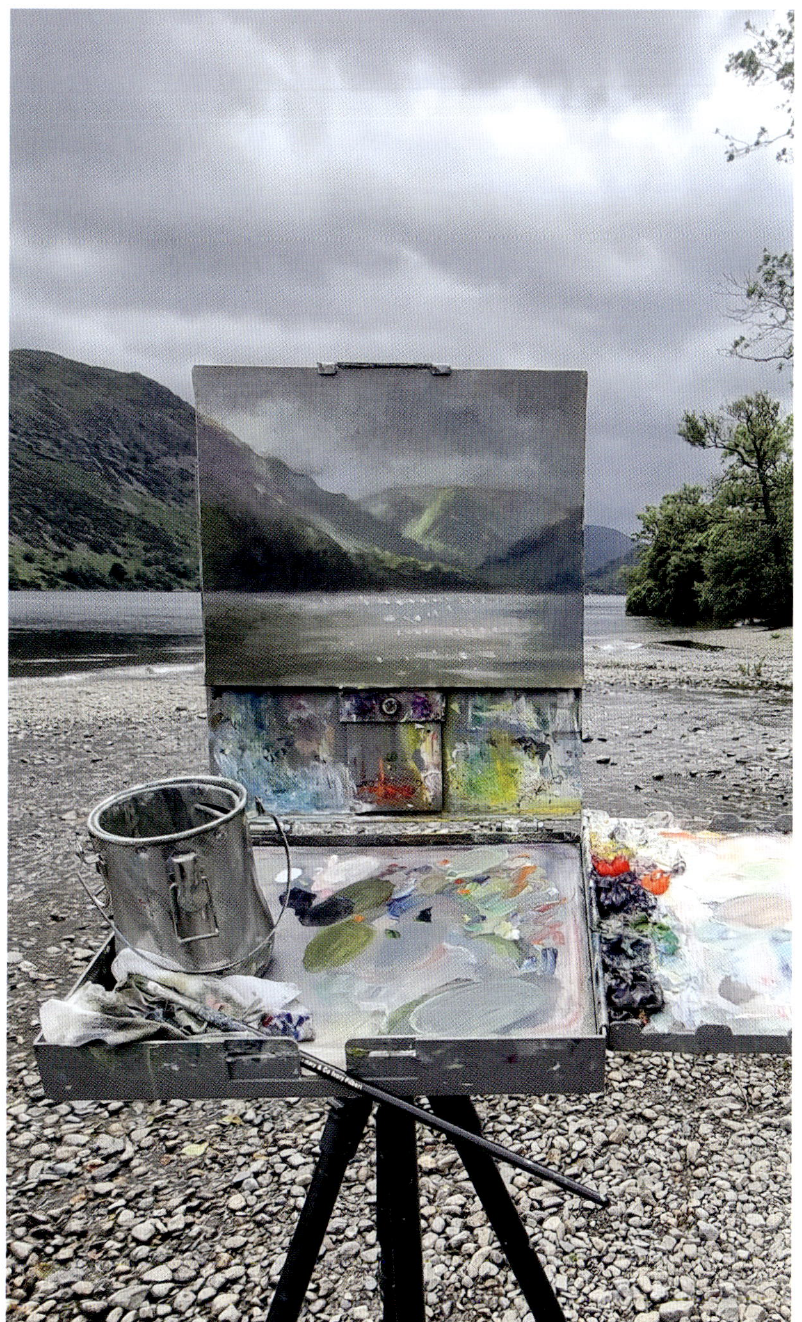

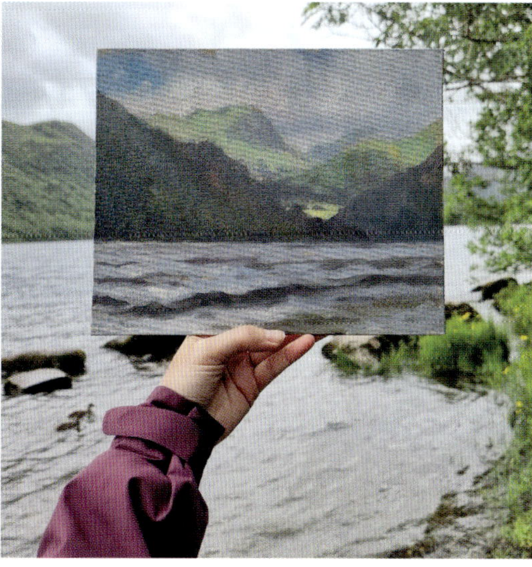

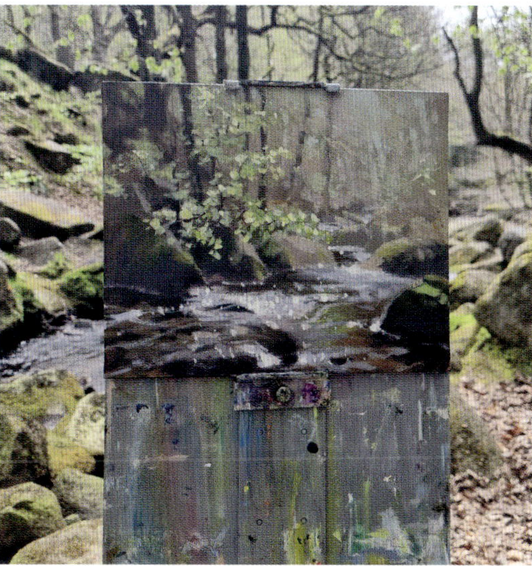

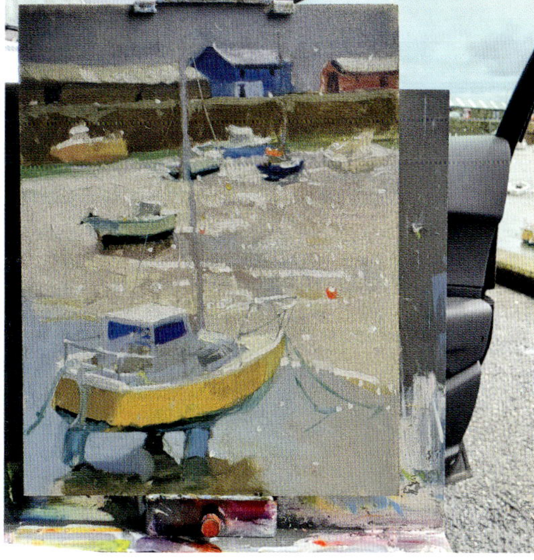

IN ALL WEATHERS!

Don't be put off by turbulent weather. I've painted from my car in between showers and caught the most fantastic lighting effects I just wouldn't have seen if I hadn't been out. All the above paintings were completed in stormy, inclement weather, and they are some of my favourite *plein air* moments so far.

SPEED

I almost always start work *en plein air* with a warm wash over the whole surface, then paint in a basic structure. I usually use a 10mm (⅜in) filbert for this, then switch to a 12mm (½in) flat for building up areas of colour and shape. My preferred surface is a fine canvas or linen board, where any texture is from the paint rather than a prominent canvas weave. I tend to stick to manageable sizes, too: 24 × 30cm (9½ × 11¾in) or 30 × 40cm (11¾ × 15¾in) – though there are exceptions, as the painting below demonstrates.

The way I think of it is to prioritize the painting in terms of how quickly each element will change with the light. Usually my focal point is the strongest area of sunlight – so I get those colours in first without worrying too much about accuracy of form.

QUICK TIPS FOR SPEED

- It is necessary to work quickly, but try to avoid rushing.

- Fully mix the colour you think you see.

- If you are painting a moving subject, like rivers or waves, look for colour information and shape patterns.

- Mix and lay down that paint: there will be time to edit later.

- Don't spend too long on any one area until the surface is covered with the first layer: you will be able to judge better once you can see the painting as a whole.

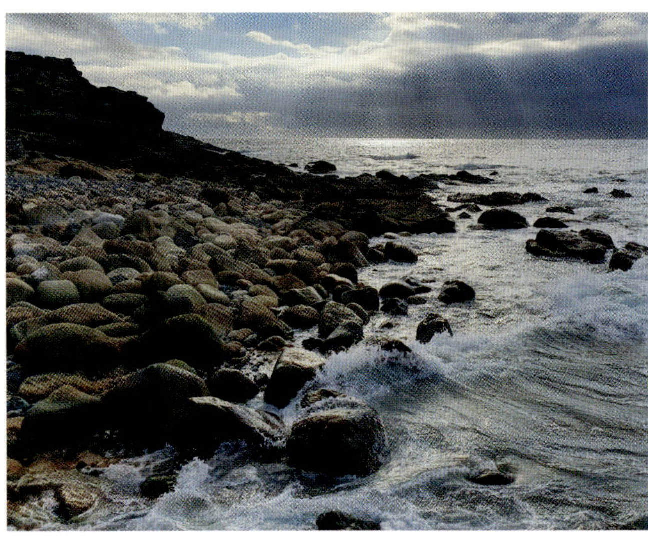

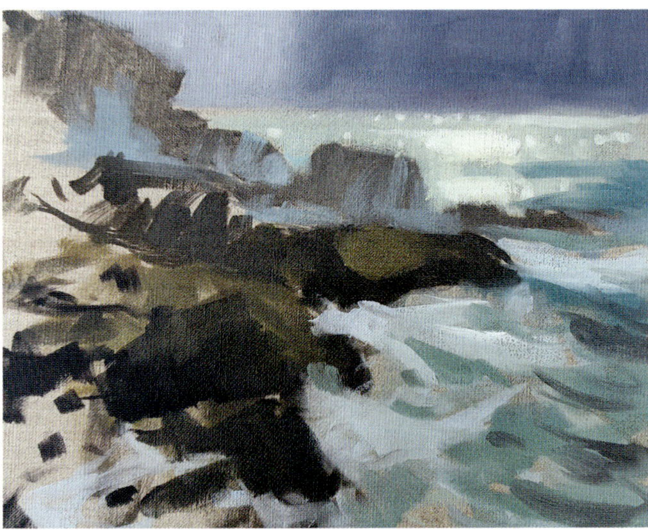

Waves at Sennen Cove
50 × 40cm (19¾ × 15¾in)

I painted this fifteen-minute sketch from the harbour wall, while keeping a close eye on the rising height of the waves! A storm was coming in, so the weather was fickle and dramatic.

I started this sketch with the distant colour of the sea and light, as this was the focal point and the most transient moment to capture. I then built up the rocks, sky and water around it, looking for strong shapes, defining colours and dynamic brushstrokes.

Look how different the colours are in the photograph – the camera has failed to capture the milky green glow of the water or the warmth of the rock. Everything seems colder and more desaturated. You can learn so much about colour through these speedy studies.

Animals *en plein air*

I love painting animals from life, it's so much fun! As they're mobile, you need to work quickly and paint them when they present themselves. I treat them as three-tone shapes – shadow, mid-tone, light. You can add details later, once you've had a chance to work more on the overall painting and become more familiar with them.

Once you study a group of animals in this way, you start to see the repeat shapes and shadows, and it becomes easier to summarize their movements. Don't think of it as drawing, and don't get too fussy – remember, it is *contre-jour*, so too much detail will flatten the light. Tiny highlights and shadows at the end can say everything necessary.

While painting *Early Afternoon in Dovedale, Peak District* (below), an isolated gust of wind took out my easel and sent everything flying – a reminder that that the more variables we can control outside, the better! It is an unpredictable space, which adds to the thrill of it.

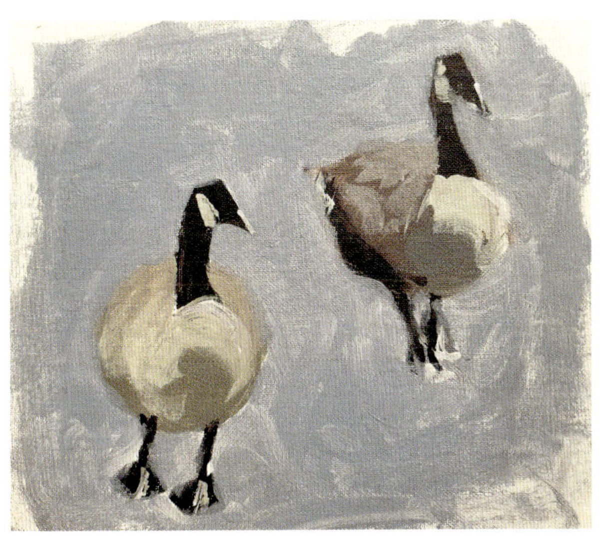

QUICK SKETCHES

Shape and stance – that's all. Simplify the colours to shadow, mid and light and be bold with your brush! Studies like these are so useful for studio paintings, adding to the library of knowledge in your mind.

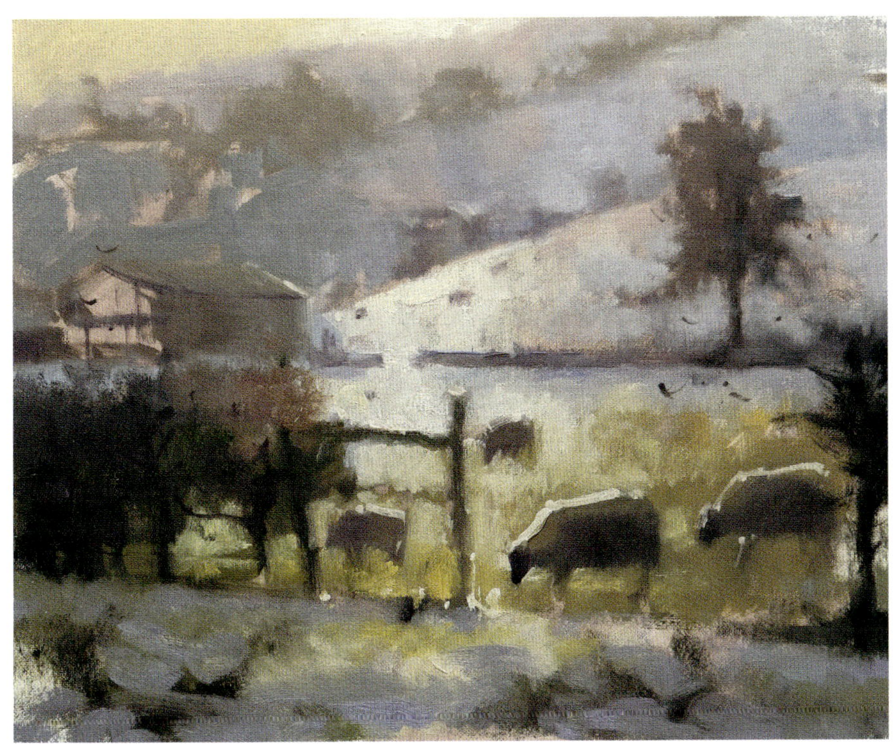

Early Afternoon in Dovedale, Peak District

50 × 40cm (19¾ × 15¾in)

For this painting, I brushed in the foreground sheep early on, painting the main shapes very simply and quickly with a purpley shadow tone, then applied a mid-green colour with a light gold along the top. Later, after studying several sheep milling about, I added a dark face and a highlight in tinted white.

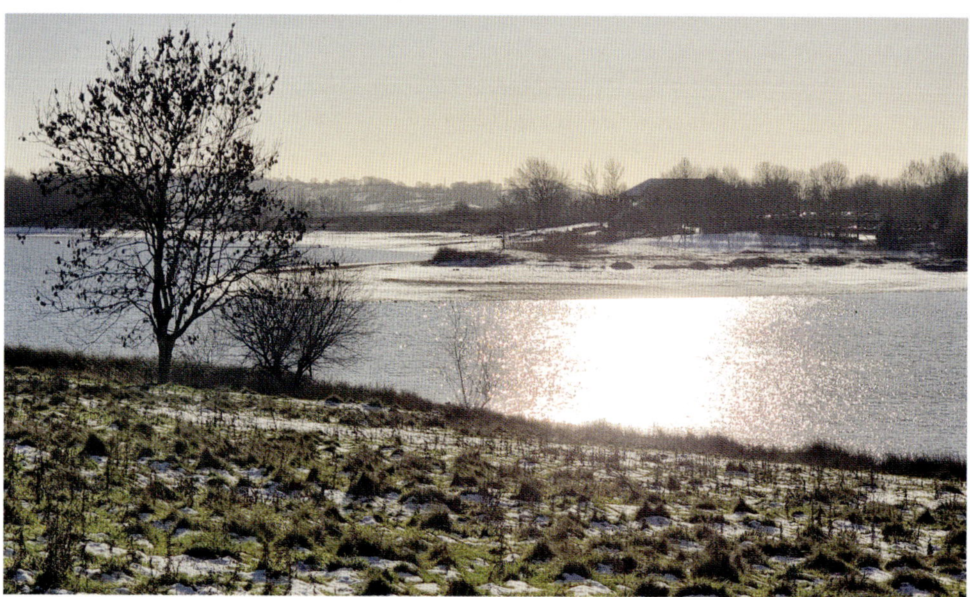

SPARKLE ON WATER

Without a doubt, *contre-jour* on water is easier in the studio!
But it is a rewarding challenge and I'm always excited
by what I have managed to observe in real life.

This project is a little different to the others, as it relies on going
outside and finding a nearby water feature. Rather than asking you
to follow along stage-by-stage, here I have worked through my own
painting and made notes on how I tackled things. If you prefer, of
course, you can simply make your own interpretation of my scene
– but I encourage you to take the plunge and find your own.

I suggest you read all the way through the project before
taking the lessons out into the great outdoors yourself. You
will need to adapt and overcome – but don't worry; the notes
and tips here will give you the best chance of success.

You will need

30 × 24cm (11¾ × 9½in) canvas board

Brushes: 12mm (½in) flat brush, 10mm (⅜in) filbert, small rigger

Paints: titanium white, bright yellow lake, permanent orange,
scarlet lake, deep purple, ultramarine blue, sap green, phthalo green

Low-odour solvent

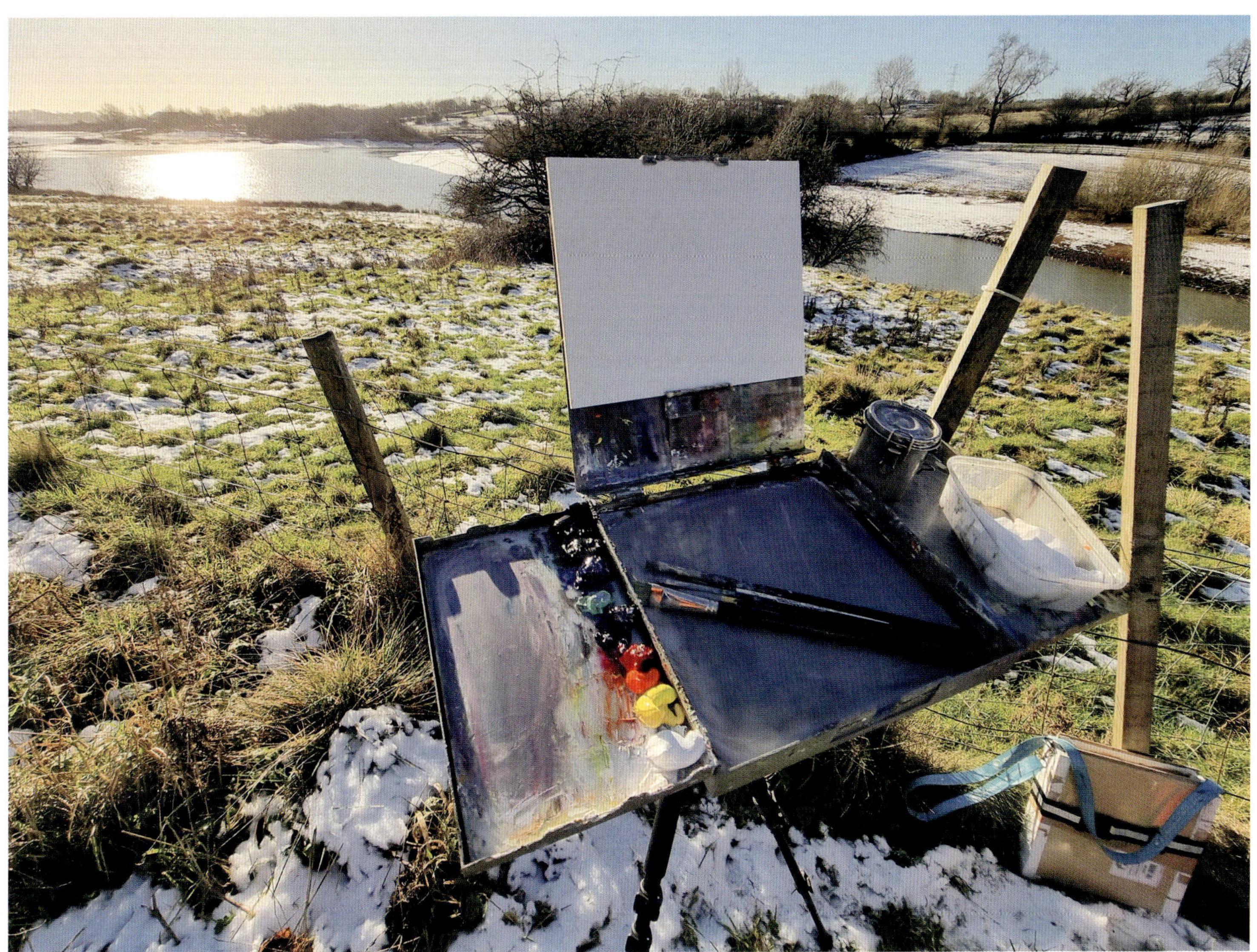

Setting up

I set up facing the view, with the palette and board both in the same light. The water reflection was blindingly bright, so I used my hand to block the sun as much as possible while observing the basic structure of the view.

Remember never to look directly at the sun – squint and use peripheral vision. I look to one side of the brightest light for very short periods – as soon as I've gauged a colour, I mix it.

People ask me if it's possible to paint wearing sunglasses, and while I don't do this, it certainly works, as the colours will still relate to each other on the canvas. Neutral, grey shades are better than colour-tinted lenses. We paint in all sorts of lighting situations, and it is good to experiment. With that said, sunglasses or not, it is still important to avoid looking directly at the sun!

PROPER PREPARATION

The biggest obstacles I have found to my *plein air* painting are discomfort and disorganization.

Appropriate clothing and kit are the most obvious ways to help with this, but taking some time to think about where you will park, the length of the walk in, the nearest amenities, food and drink – all these things need to be factored in so that you can fully concentrate on the actual point of being out: the painting.

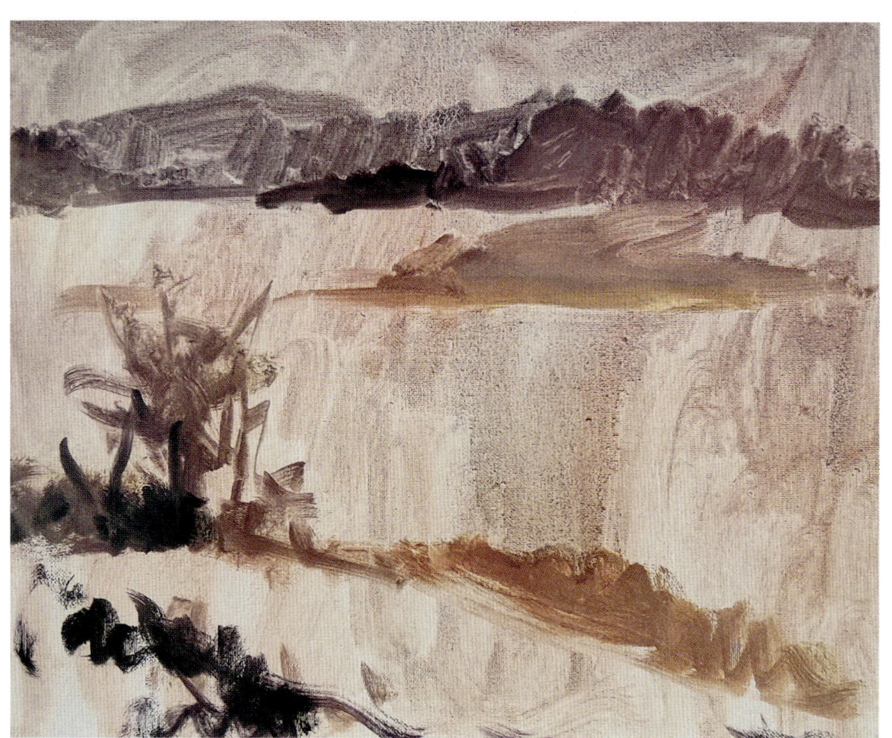

FIRST STAGE

With my 12mm (½in) flat, I washed the board with a thin mix of scarlet lake, bright yellow lake and deep purple. The basic composition was sketched in with a thin mix of bright yellow lake, deep purple and titanium white for the background shadows.

I used the same mix with less white for the nearest headland and less again for the foreground tree. The darkest colours are a mix of deep purple and phthalo green; the warm colours are a mix of scarlet lake, bright yellow lake and titanium white, with a touch of permanent orange. These were placed where the sunlight haze was strongest.

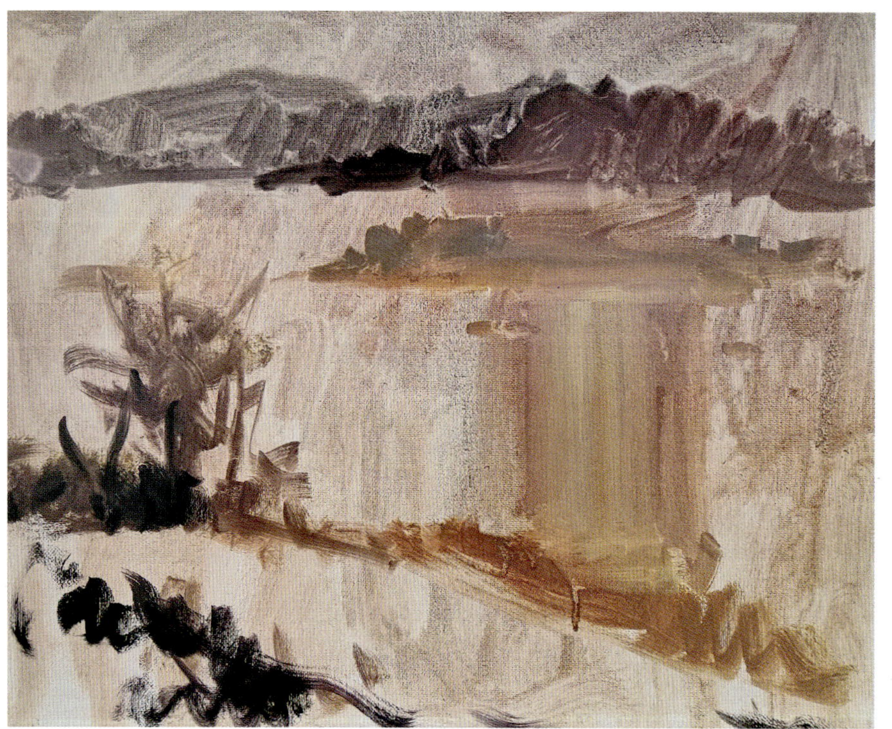

SECOND STAGE

The water haze went on next, a lighter and slightly more opaque mix of bright yellow lake, scarlet lake and titanium white. Although this is a little more opaque than in the first stage, I still kept it quite thin.

In terms of applying the paint, downward strokes of the 12mm (½in) flat brush were important, as these help to build the impression of distance and a reflective surface.

THIRD STAGE

I added deep purple to the bright yellow lake, scarlet lake and titanium white mix from the second stage, and used this to begin adding the water surrounding the reflection.

The addition of purple darkened the mix, and I added ultramarine blue to darken it still more as I worked further away from the light.

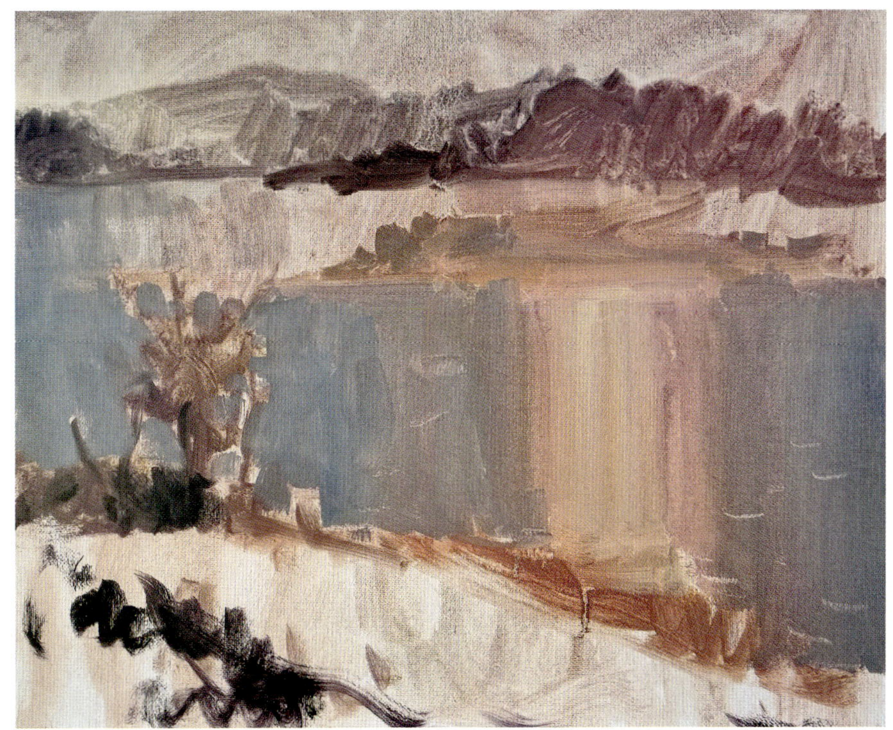

FOURTH STAGE

Having snatched a few more glances, I used a balanced mix of deep purple, bright yellow lake and titanium white, to make a light, warm grey for the background. I mixed a lighter, thicker tone for the haze on the hills, and added a touch more warming scarlet lake and bright yellow lake for the closer headland.

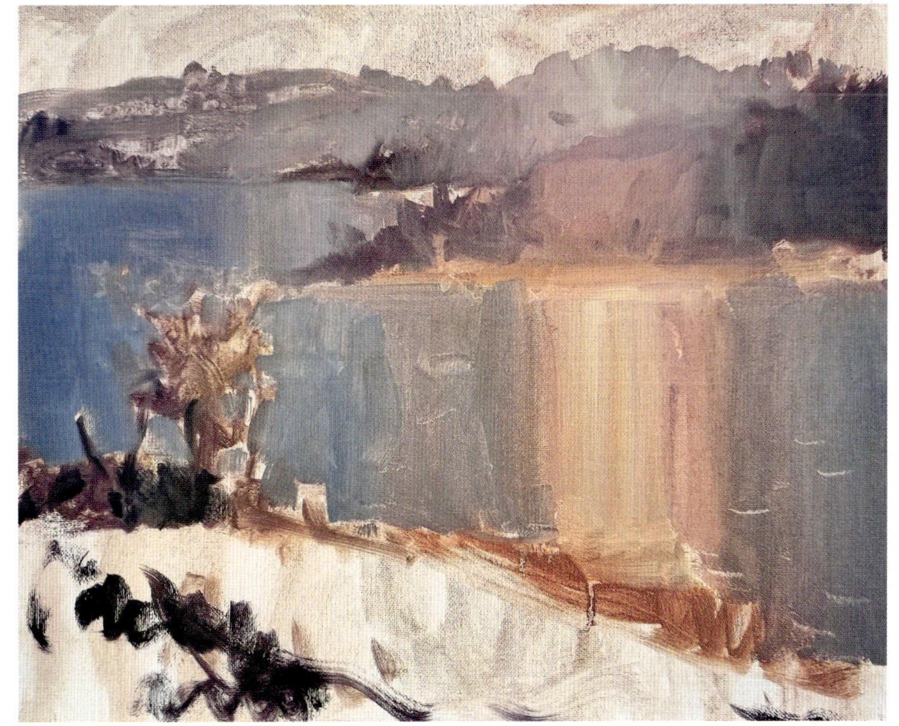

Colour matching and *en plein air*

Photographing your painting *in situ* is not just a gimmick. It shows you how well your mixing has worked, and how well the brushwork is expressing the movement within the scene. You can learn from the photograph, and it's fun!

   In the example painting below, you can see where I have diverged from exact colour representation in order to push the distance a little more. The trees at the river's bend were greener and warmer in real life. Cooling and greying them just strengthens the sense of depth and composition. The area behind the trees on the right contained a lot more tree-life, but bringing some space with a hazy grey-green gives the composition room to breathe.

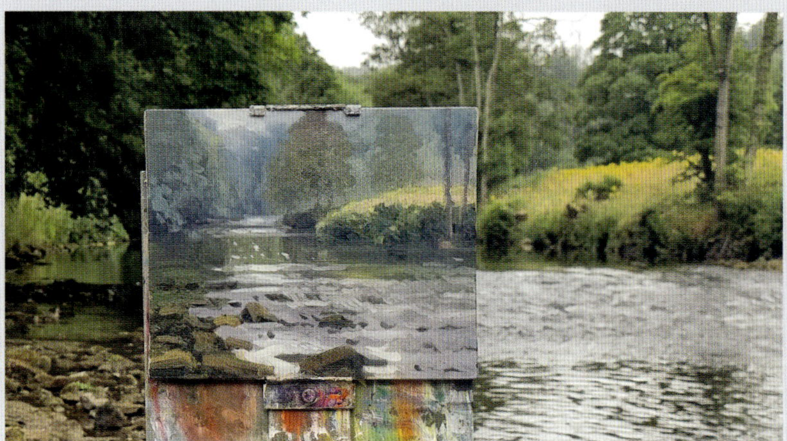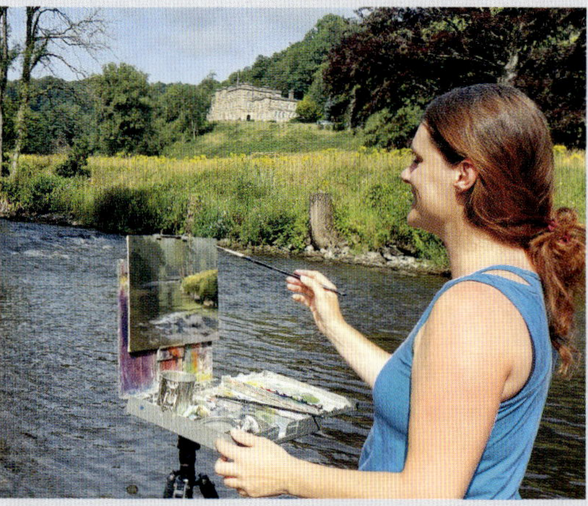

Here are some ideas to help you make sure you can read the colour accurately – after all, you can't adjust for effect unless you can identify the true colour in the first place.

Judging tone Use a tonal scale (see page 29) when you're out – if you hold it up to the colours you're trying to judge, it'll give you some clarity over how dark they are. It is especially useful for judging distant colours, which can seem much stronger than they are.

Judging colour Likewise, try holding up your colour wheel (see page 27) to your scene. I guarantee that most of the colours you see will be greys! Still, it definitely helps show the way the colours are leaning, and can stop you from using over-saturated colour.

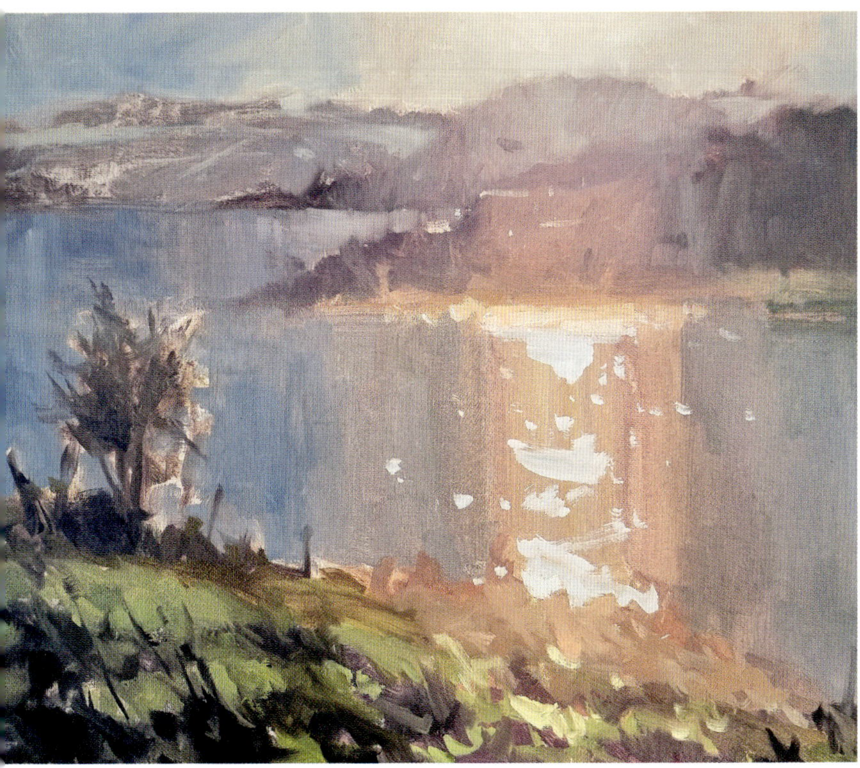

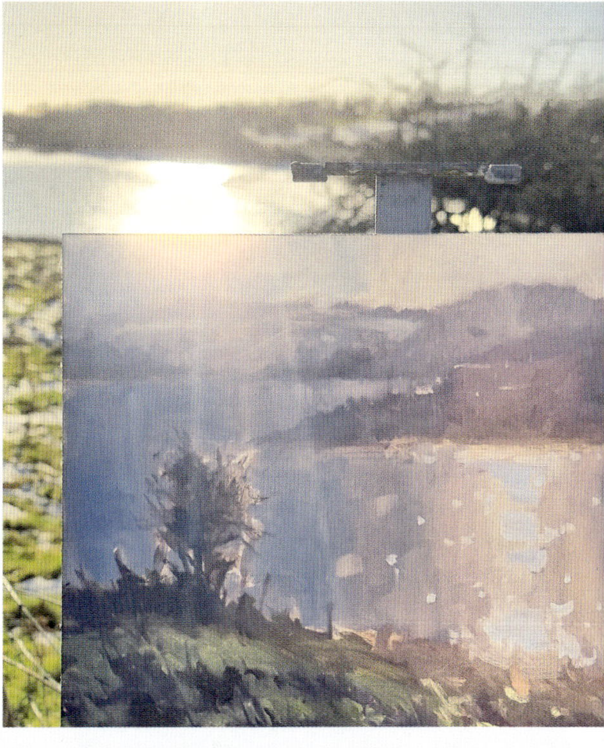

FIFTH STAGE

Time for the foreground, which I was slightly dreading as I wasn't sure how that green would look alongside my exaggerated warmth in the haze. First, I added the grassy shadows – a warm purple mix of deep purple and bright yellow lake for those in the light, and a mix of phthalo green and deep purple for those in the shadow. That strong difference in shadow colour really helps the lighting illusion. If I had made the shadows cold in the path of sunlight, the warm orange would just look odd. Everything has to work together!

The greens of the grass in the sun are bright yellow lake with a touch of deep purple; the highlights just a bright yellow lake and titanium white mix. On the left, there is bright yellow lake with touches of sap green, permanent orange and titanium white; and a bright yellow lake, sap green and titanium white mix for the far left. I used my 12mm (½in) flat brush throughout. Since I was not using that much paint, it was easy to wipe and wash between colours.

Towards the end of this stage, I added white blobs on the water, then realized I needed lighter, thicker tones to support them, so wiped them back off again!

Looking into that light

This should help you imagine how it feels to be painting this view, looking (or avoiding looking) into that glare!

Gauge the colours on either side of the lit area then simply warm and lighten those in the path of the light. You can edit as you progress through the painting.

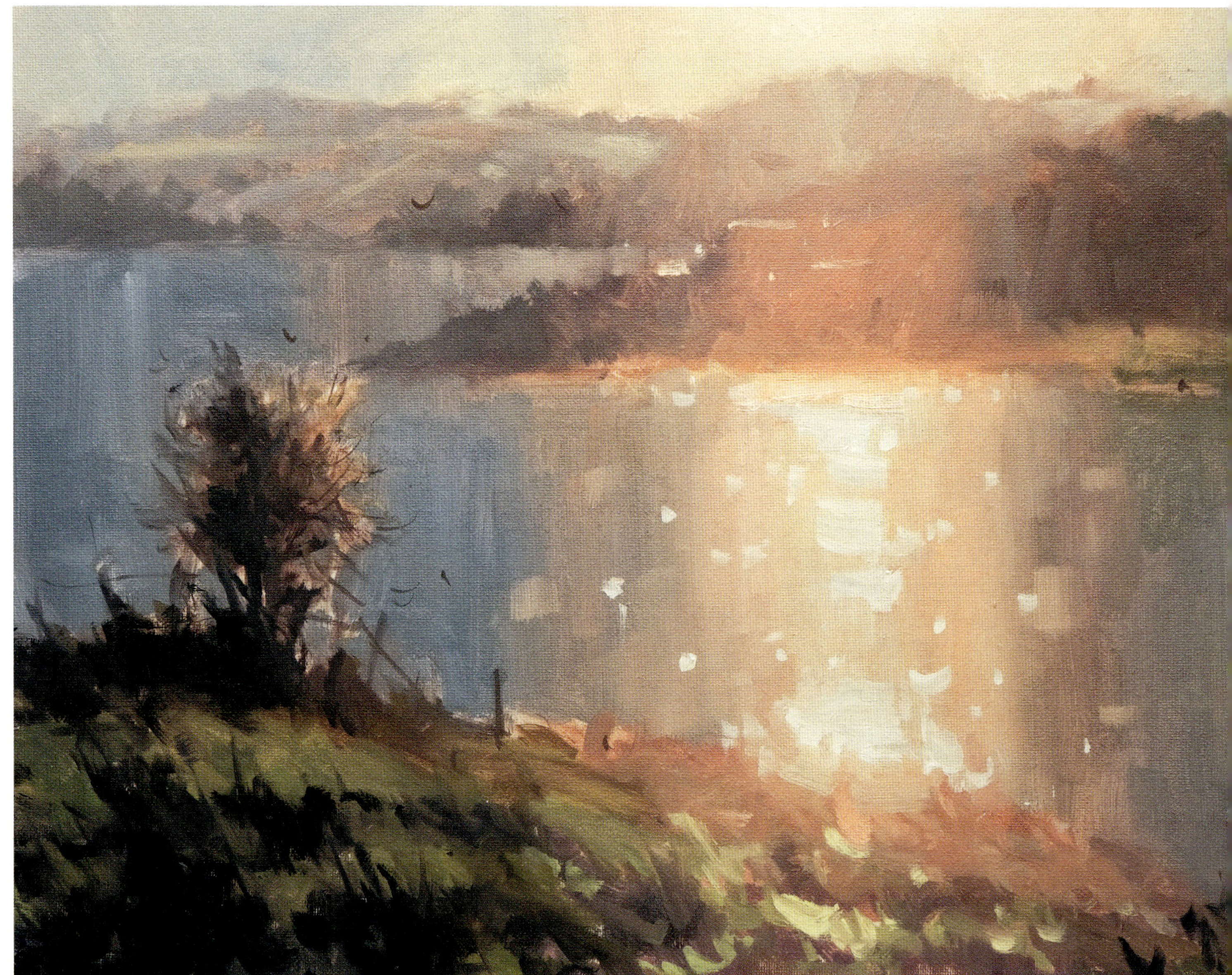

SIXTH STAGE – REFINING

I went back into the path of light with some lighter, yellower tones – again using flat, blobby marks and downstrokes – before replacing the shapes of tinted white for the sun reflection. I lightened and thickened the background in the light path to strengthen the effect of the sun. With a rigger and a thin mix of deep purple and permanent orange, I added that touch of 'noise' for the finish: little marks to suggest birds, errant dots and a bit more detail around the tree.

You might notice the increased warmth of the finished painting, above, when compared with the previous stage. The picture of the final painting was taken in my studio, where the lighting is neutral, as opposed to cold, bright sun. If you are trying to match to colours, as I do, you will notice that unless you adjust, you consequently use a lot less cold colour when painting outside.

Evaluating *plein air* work

So, you've brought your painting home and discovered that it looks completely different in studio/indoor lighting... welcome to the club!

I find bringing a *plein air* artwork indoors both exciting and informative. Work can appear much more blue outdoors – this is because natural outdoor light is rich in the blue end of the spectrum, so blues appear to be more vivid. As a result, once inside, paintings can look duller and warmer than you realized. Adjusting for this comes with practice – but you will immediately notice, when matching tones outside, that you are mixing colours you wouldn't normally go for while in the studio.

WHAT NEXT?

What to do with the *plein air* sketches you've brought home? My plein air work falls fairly evenly into four categories:

Keeper, for framing It's so exciting when a painting works from start to finish, with everything resolved and complete. These are ready to frame and display.

Keeper, for reference Often I love these when I first complete them, then, on evaluation, I see that they don't quite make the grade. I try to discern what it was that attracted me to the composition, and recreate these paintings in the studio with more finesse.

Part-finished Many paintings fall into this category, and I finish them off in the studio. I only go back to the photograph if need a particular detail, so I'm not tempted to completely repaint the image using the photographic colour. Instead, I trust my memory and my knowledge to work out what will finish the painting well. It doesn't always work, but I would rather have a painting I am happy with than ten stored on the shelf that I'm not.

Scraper This happens fairly often – I find that using a knife to scrape away the paint is the best way to deal with irreparable composition or too much paint. Don't see it as a negative – it is not a cliché to see it as a learning process! Don't be afraid to do it, either. I've never regretted scraping one yet. Always scrape it at home once you've had time to evaluate, however. That way you can trust that it isn't just frustration controlling that knife!

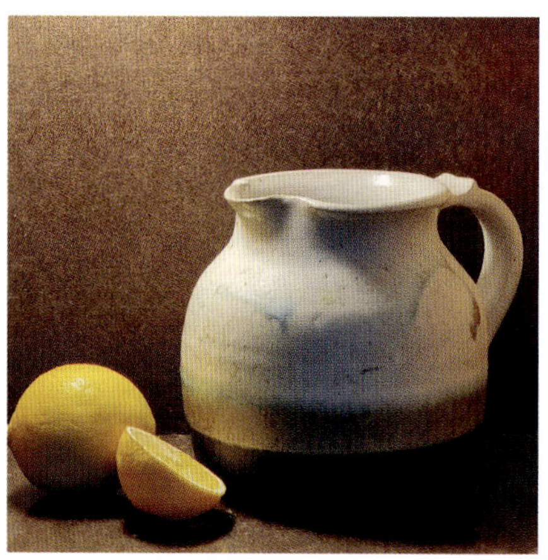

STILL LIFE

'Still life is the touchstone of painting.' **Édouard Manet**

There are few better ways to see the benefits and drawback of a painting method than by contrasting it with its complete opposite – and at the other end of the scale to the unpredictability of working *plein air* is still life. In still life painting, everything can be controlled and there is no rush whatsoever. After the enjoyable pressure of working *en plein air*, this still life painting project will be a peaceful contrast – with the added bonus that you won't be far from the kettle.

Constructed still life, where you have full control, is a great excuse for experimentation, visual poetry and textural contrast. Once you have your set-up with lighting and subject matter, don't be afraid to repeat it multiple times. Just as with *plein air*, the study of light, colour and form from life is excellent practice in all the aspects of successful painting: composition, colour analysis, brushwork, and mixing.

You will need

30 × 24cm (11¾ × 9½in) canvas board

Brushes: 12mm (½in) flat, 6mm (¼in) filbert, small rigger, 10mm (⅜in) flat

Paints: titanium white, bright yellow lake, scarlet lake, deep purple, permanent orange, ultramarine blue, sap green

Low-odour solvent

Wet wipes or cloth

Large cardboard box – about 30 × 40cm (11¾ × 15¾in); clip-on light with daylight bulb; dark, unprimed canvas board; clear Perspex sheet; an odd number of items for the subject – I used a pottery jug and lemons.

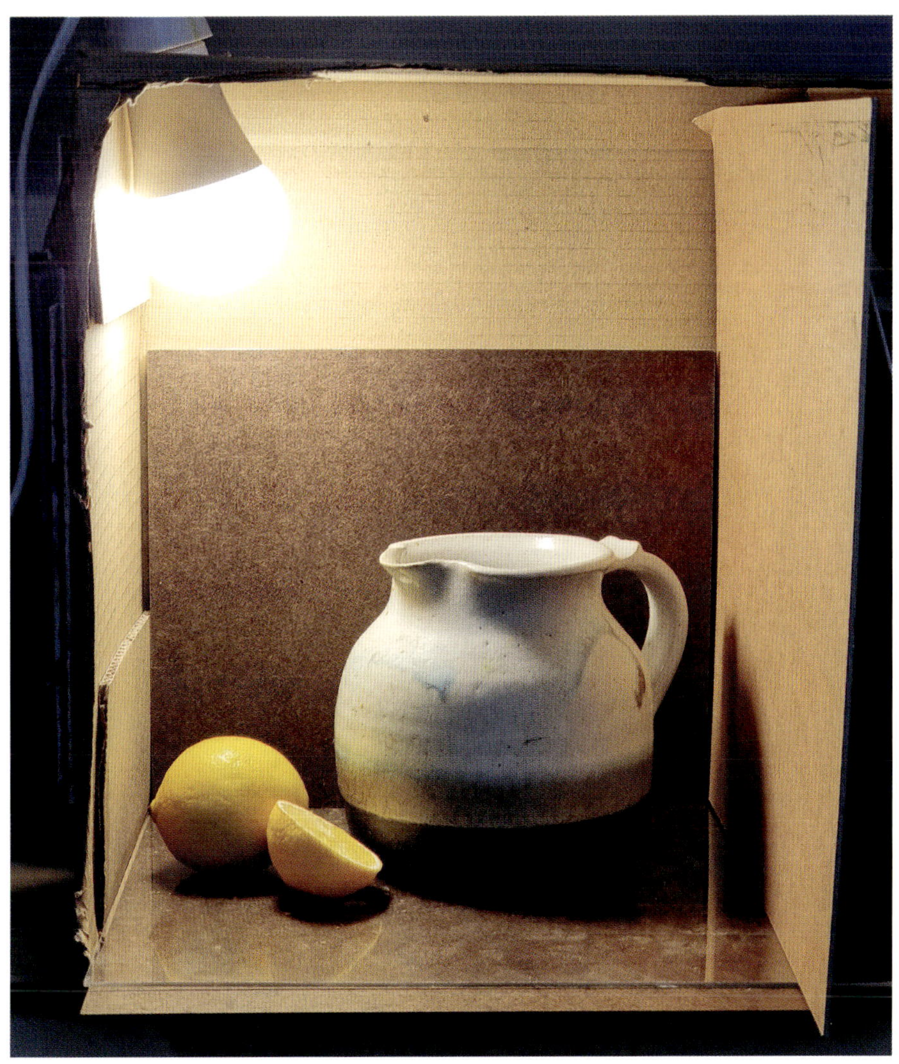

Getting set up

My still life set-up is very basic, but it allows me to control colours and lighting conditions. I removed the lid then cut a hole in the top left corner of a large cardboard box. A clip-on light with a daylight bulb was then fixed through the hole, so that the light is both in my eyes as I look at the subject and at a slight angle for interest. A dark board is placed at the back, and a Perspex board on the floor to give a bit of reflection.

Once the box is ready, it is then a case of fiddling around with your items until you arrive at something you like. Take photographs of each potential set-up, so you can see them two-dimensionally and judge whether the composition works.

For a small composition like this, three or five items, with one dominating the others, works well. Here I have chosen a hand-thrown pottery jug – its subtle turquoise notes work with the warm brown surround – and lemons, because lemons are fun! The reflected light from the lemon onto the jug also creates a lovely glow.

Composition in still life

What to paint is often the most difficult question. From our *contre-jour* perspective, however, almost anything works! Here are my tips for a successful still life:

Keep an eye out The best subjects are often stumbled upon: unassuming, unexpected little tableaux, momentarily lit by the passing light through the window. Look out for hazy light, colourful accents, highlights and a wide value range. The usual compositional rules always apply but well-lit scenarios can usually be altered or edited slightly.

Be odd I use either the cardboard box set-up or natural window light for my still life work. If I'm just setting up a few objects to paint, I find that an odd number works best, compositionally – although that is a very breakable rule.

Tell a story Most importantly, think of what it is you want to say with the image. What connects the objects you have chosen? Colour, use, shape: what is the narrative?

Solo objects A single item can make an excellent subject for still life. As with any other painting, you just want the eye to move around the canvas. In the absence of other objects, you can use the brushwork itself.

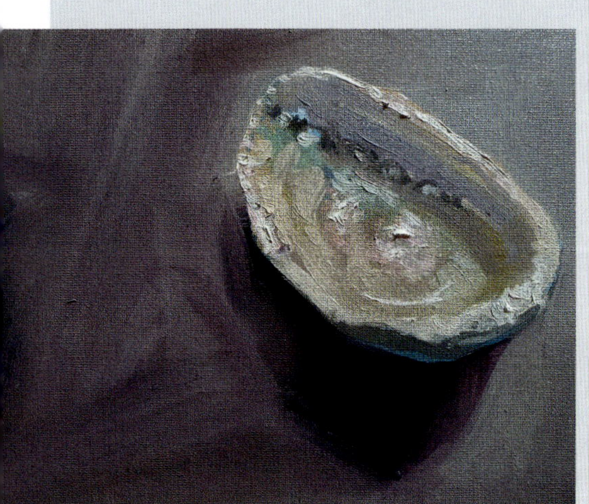

In the painting here, I positioned the ormer shell in front of the light through the window, for strong shadows and lights. The shell is off-centre, so I needed something on the left to keep the eye moving. I tried several different objects in this space – but the focal shell lost impact with all of them.

In the end, two or three chunky brush marks in the background paint were enough to fill the stage. The consequent sense of movement is vital to the success of the painting.

Several contrasts are in play: here transparent/opaque, saturated/grey, cold/warm, busy/calm, big brush/detail. As artists, we give life to these inanimate objects through the visual poetry we create in paint. Use all the tools available to you with this in mind!

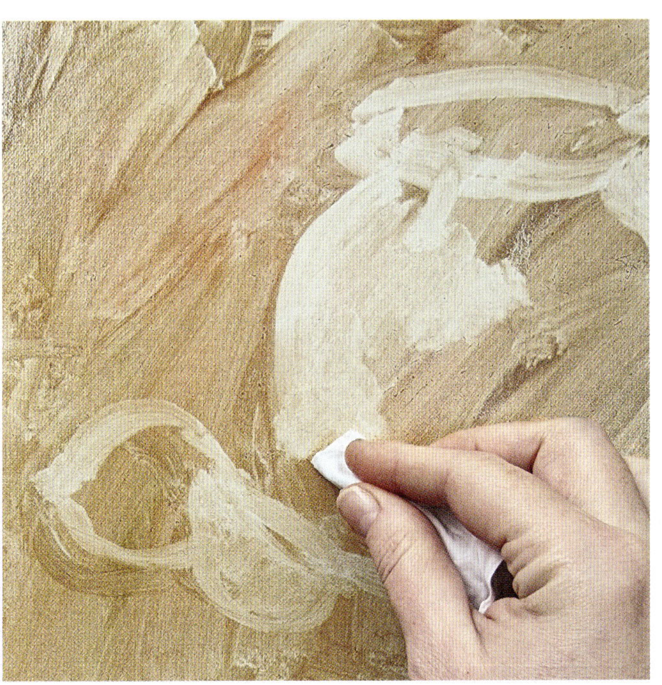 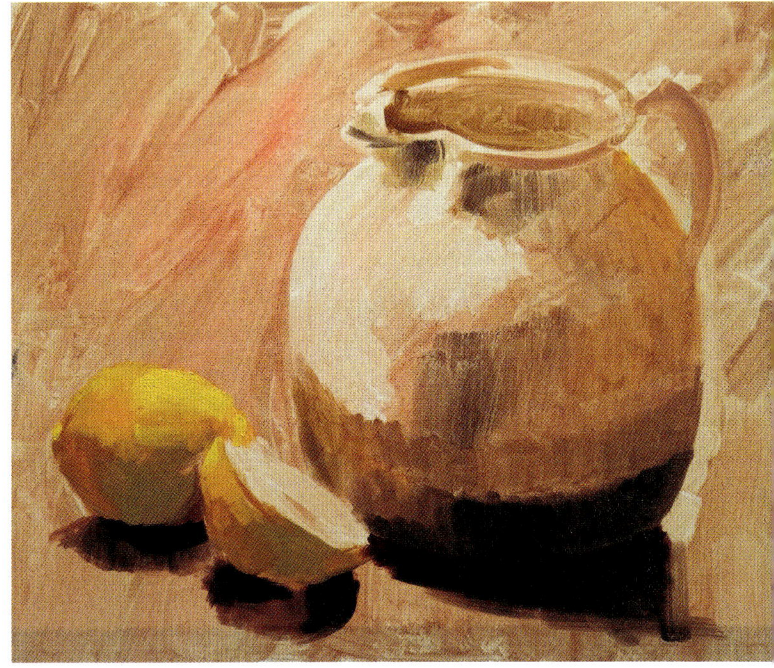

FIRST STAGE

We start by creating a ground, or underpainting, then exploring the shapes through negatives – that is, by rubbing away the paint from the ground in the shapes that you want.

I find that this method, as opposed to trying to draw the objects directly, helps me to see and develop shapes more effectively.

- Prepare a thin warm mix of bright yellow lake, scarlet lake and deep purple.
- Cover the board with a thin warm ground of the mix, using the 12mm (½in) flat brush and loose brushstrokes.
- Use a wet wipe (or cloth dipped in solvent) to lightly rub away the paint in the shapes you want. Look for the shapes of light and shadow on the jug in particular.

SECOND STAGE

Even at this stage, the brushwork is representative of the shape and texture of each object. Brush with a mind to the form, light and general energy of the painting, always looking for that sense of atmospheric movement.

Take note of how the lemons are affected by the warmth of the glowing brown interior, so their yellow is more of an orange in this context. Remember, never assume you know what a colour is or 'should be'!

- Use more of the thin scarlet lake, bright yellow lake and deep purple mix to scrub in the form of mid-tones and shadow with a 10mm (⅜in) flat brush.
- Add more purple to the mix for the shadows.
- Using the 12mm (½in) flat brush, apply a mix of bright yellow lake, permanent orange and touches of both titanium white and sap green to the top left of the lemons.
- Add little more sap green for the lemons' fronts, furthest from the light.

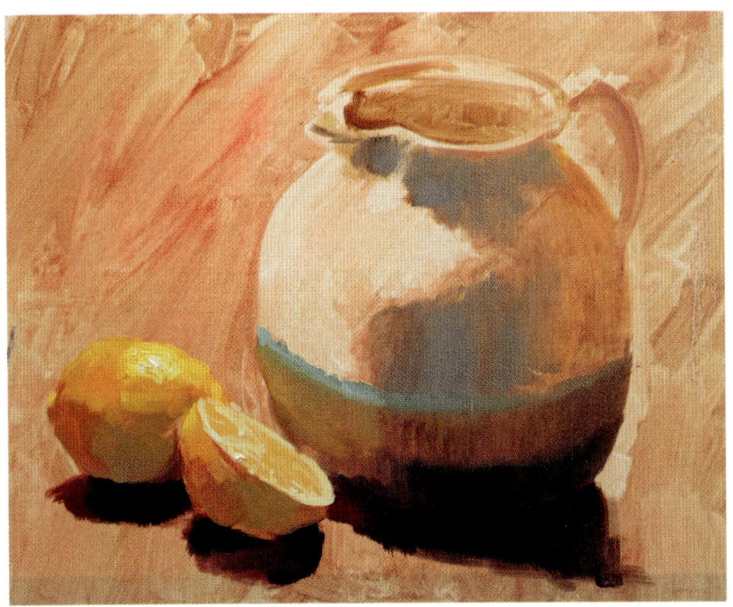

THIRD STAGE

In this stage, we develop the colour on the lemons in context, and add detail. Do bear in mind that the lightest areas should go down last.

- Apply the earlier mix (bright yellow lake, permanent orange and touches of both titanium white and sap green) to the jug, where it reflects the light from the lemons.
- Add more bright yellow lake and permanent orange to the mix for the lower left-hand side of each lemon. Next lay in a thicker sweep of bright yellow lake, with touches of permanent orange and titanium white, for the lit waxy skin of the left-hand lemon. Use a mix of bright yellow lake and titanium white for the highlight.
- Paint the exposed cut surface of the right-hand lemon with a mix of bright yellow lake, permanent orange, a tiny touch of sap green and titanium white. Load the rigger with flowing white tinted with bright yellow lake and permanent orange and add in a few loose notes for the pith and segment marks. A final blob of highlight puts it in the same lighting as the left-hand lemon.
- With the 10mm (⅜in) flat brush, lay in a soft line on the jug using a mix of ultramarine blue, bright yellow lake and titanium white. On the left, this line has more yellow and white in the mix – on the right, I pick up some of the earthy tone of the jug by brushing a little harder.

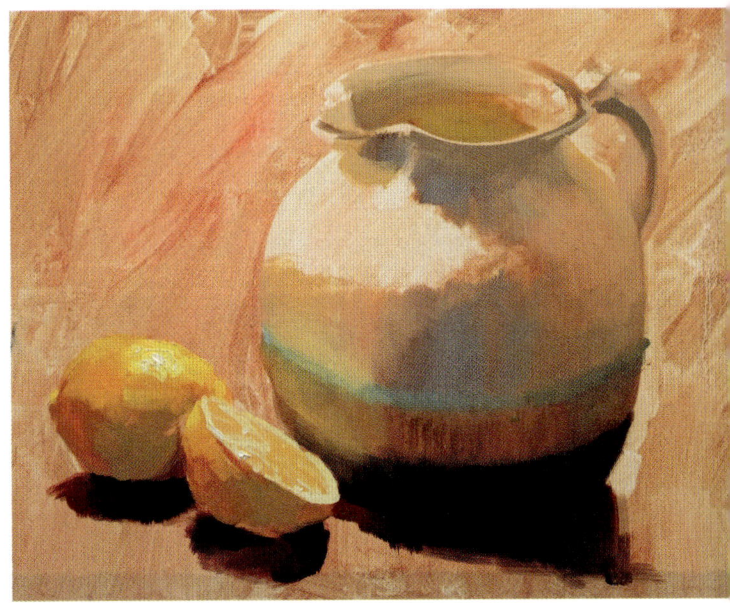

FOURTH STAGE

Each colour mix emerges from a process of guessing, matching and subsequent adjustment.

I will see colours differently to each one of you – the importance is in how the mixes relate to one another, for subtlety and credibility in lighting.

- Use the greeny yellow of the lemon (bright yellow lake, permanent orange, plus tiny touches of sap green and titanium white) to blend in for a reflection at the front of the jug, and for the inside of the jug.
- Fill in the midtones using a mix of bright yellow lake, deep purple, scarlet lake and titanium white. Keep your brushwork soft and force yourself to stay aware of shape.
- Add a little ultramarine blue to the mix for shadows along the rim of the jug and handle; and a little more blue for the cool shadow in the centre of the jug, where the light is lowest.
- Thicken the shadows with a mix of scarlet lake, bright yellow lake and deep purple. This is the same shadow mix used earlier, but with a higher paint to solvent ratio – it should be fairly thick at this point.

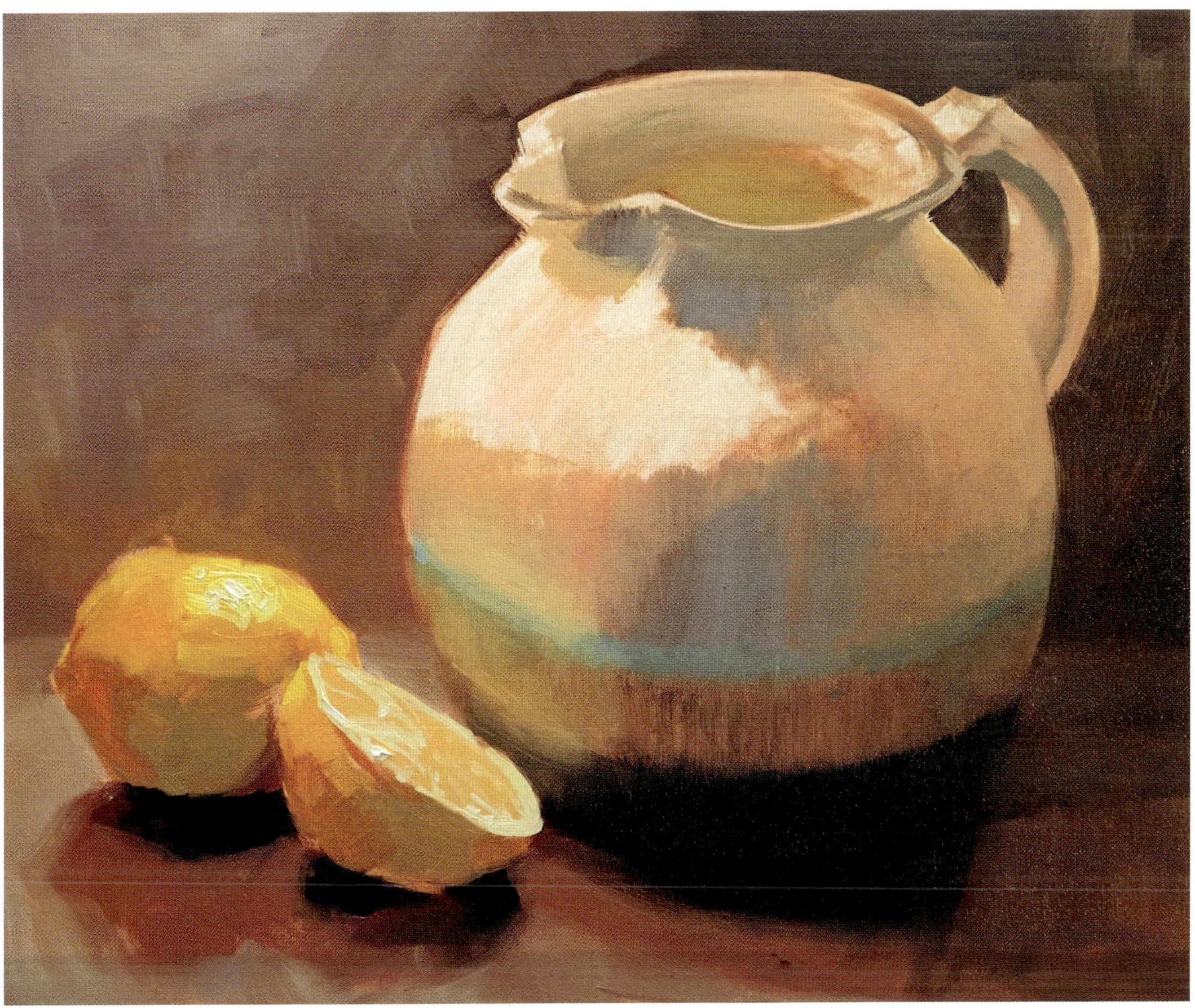

FIFTH STAGE

Time to cut in. Here we'll fill in the background and paint slightly over the edge of the subject to develop and refine the jug.

- Mix deep purple, bright yellow lake and scarlet lake with a bit of ultramarine blue for the darker areas on the right. Use the 12mm (½in) flat to carefully refine the edges and fill in the background.
- Allow a little of the warm underpainting to stay visible on the left side of the jug, as a nice little contrast.
- Define the surface from the background using directional brushwork – verticals for the surface, flat and angled for the background.
- Add more titanium white, bright yellow lake and scarlet lake to the mix for the area on the left where the light is strongest, and reflect this on the surface.
- Around the lemon, strengthen the bright yellow lake and permanent orange mix from the third stage to create the illusion of a glow.

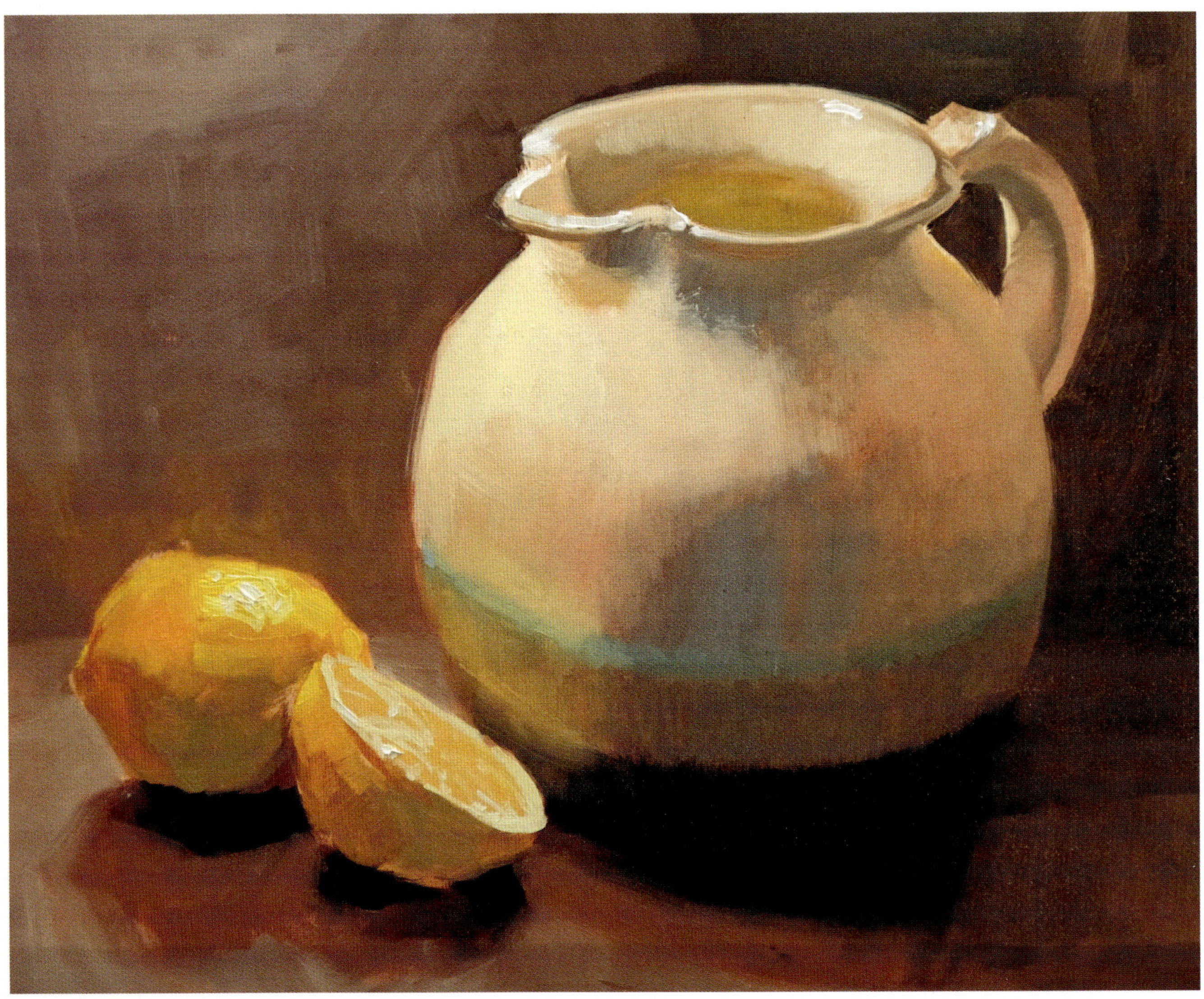

SIXTH STAGE

We're now nearing the finish. This is the stage in a painting when I stare a lot more than I paint. The surface is covered, and the values and colours are there. The question becomes 'how to finish'?

At this point, I think the painting has become a little dull. It needs some special effects and lighting to brighten it up!

- Apply an opaque layer of titanium white, mixed with a touch of bright yellow lake and permanent orange, to soften the lighter areas of the jug. Use soft downstrokes for a blurry feel, blending with any edges.
- To make the lip and rim of the jug stand out, use the rigger to apply some blobs of titanium white mixed with a little bright yellow lake.

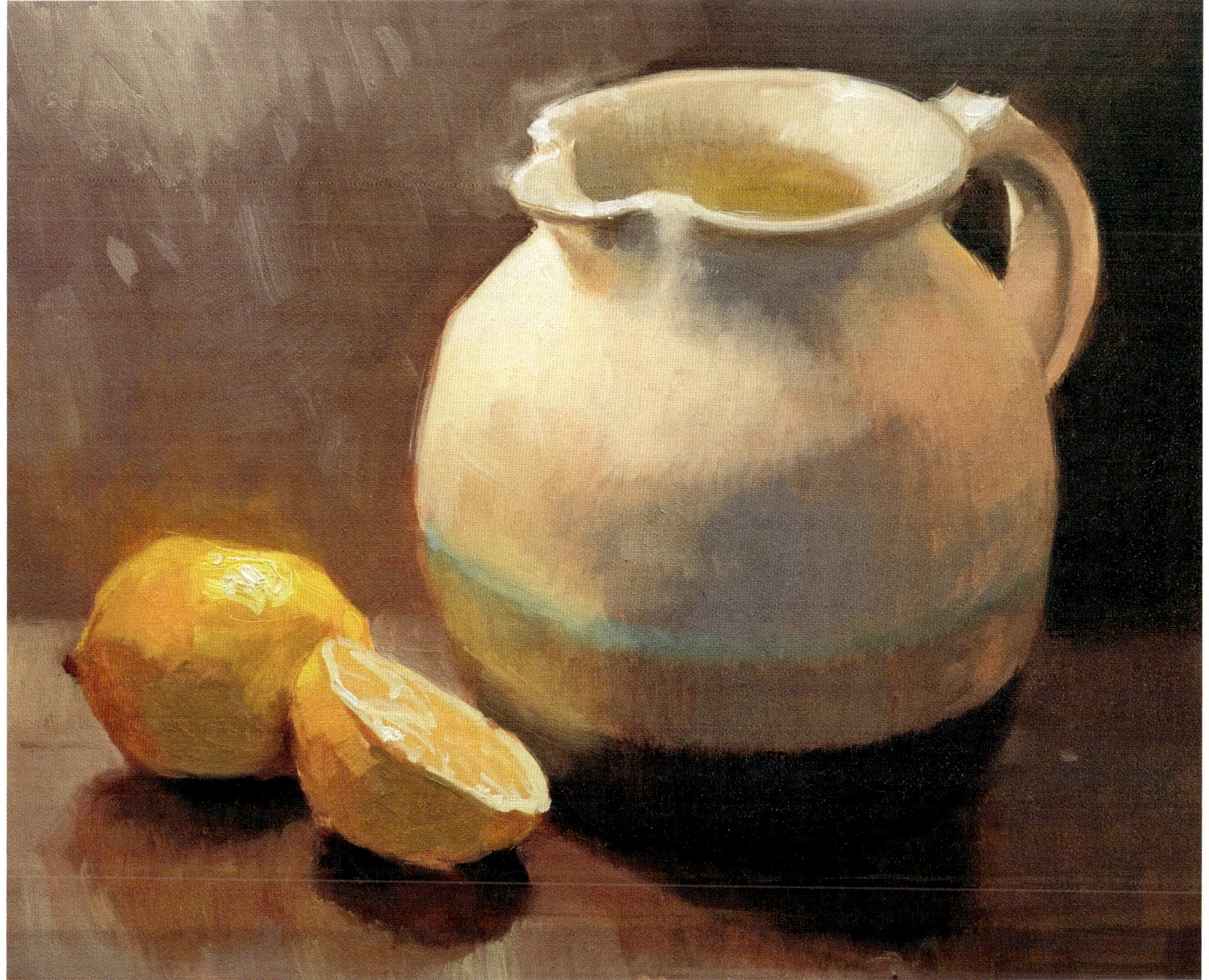

SEVENTH STAGE – REFINING

The finished painting

Sitting back from a near-finished painting and evaluating is such a valuable act. Take a break and come back with a cup of tea to sit and stare for a while. Ask whether your intent has been achieved. If not, why not? What does the painting lack? Is it redeemable as-is, or does paint need to be removed? This moment is not a failure – it is a natural part of the painting process and for me, often results in some of my best work.

This very simple subject has to say so much to succeed – the trick, as ever, is to do that in the most minimal way possible. By the end, each individual area needs to stand out in its own right, making the narrative stronger for it.

- If any areas look fussy or flat, rub or scrape off the area and redo it. Here, I removed some paint from the top left, before adding lighter marks with my 10mm (⅜in) flat brush, and echoed them in the reflection on the ground around the lemons and jug with subtle downstrokes.

- I added a glow around the highlights on the jug, with a pinky-white mix of scarlet lake and titanium white.

- Realizing that the background contained no cold colours in the foreground, I added ultramarine blue into the shadow tones on the right to balance the composition and make the oranges and brights sing.

- I also added neutral-toned marks within the jug, using scrubby up-and-down strokes with a 6mm (¼in) filbert. This made the chalky surface stand out against the empty background and reflective surface, for variety in texture.

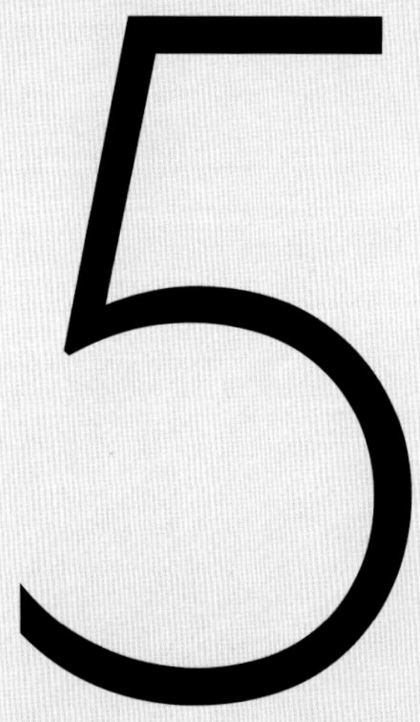

ATMOSPHERE

'The real subject of every painting is light.'
Claude Monet

When painting *contre-jour*, what you are painting is not the scene or subject before you, but light. You are painting the colour of the light between your eye and the subject, in the shape of the subject. As we have seen, this warrants less attention to descriptive detail but more sensitivity to colour and temperature change. The more we try to pick out the detail, the more the desired illusion of light will fade, and the more the atmosphere will be lost.

This elusive quality – atmosphere – is key. When painting *contre-jour* mountains, it really hits home that what I am painting is light, not grass, trees or rock. Mountains have the additional note that the more we define edges and detail, the closer and smaller the mountain will appear. Since a strong foreground is needed to provide reference for size and depth and lead the eye into the picture, we need to make sure that we treat the mountains subtly to capture that atmosphere. These qualities make them ideal subjects as we explore atmosphere in general.

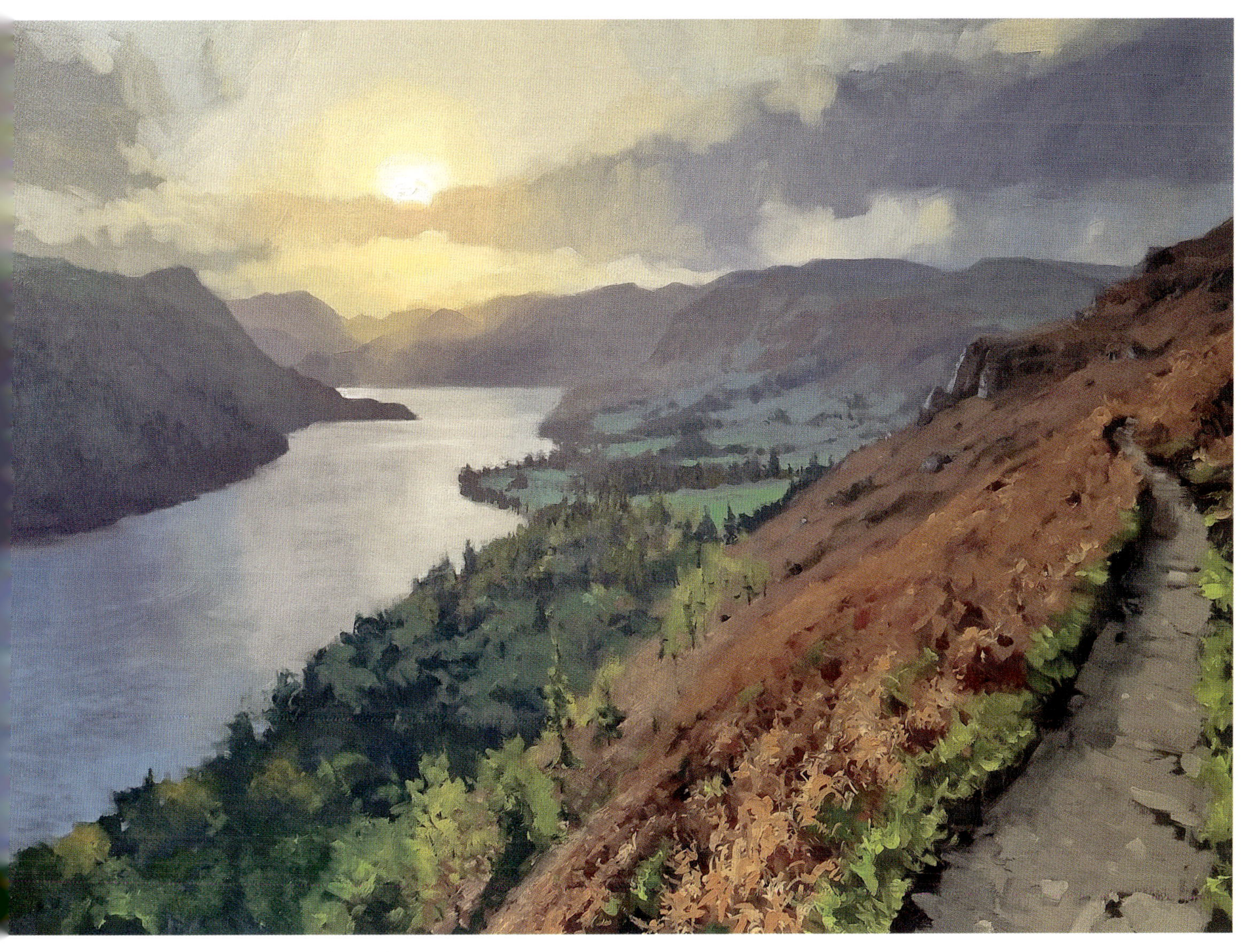

Above Ulswater

100 × 80cm (39½ × 31½in)

A high path in the Lake District, looking west into the sunset. The warm haze around the sun, which contains the only white in the painting, gives it prominence and impact as a light source. The contre-jour mountains are rendered simply as cloud-like planes of tone and flat texture.

MOUNTAINS

Photographs are one of our tools...not the art itself.

Looking through my paintings and photographs of *contre-jour* mountains for the purpose of this book was an education in itself. Mountains are just so... immense! And cameras reduce them, mute the lighting and the colours in a way that can make it unsatisfying to try to paint from photographs in the studio. But we have tools, and we have imagination, so we can forge onwards.

When photographing mountains into the light, we must consider the composition more deeply than other subjects to ensure we capture the right atmosphere. As the sun blinds with light, mountains do similar with grandeur – I cannot tell you the number of times I think I've taken fabulous shots, only to find that there's no strong point of interest, no foreground included or too small a spread of values. Always look for that visual story – the eye path. The mountains, like any other subject, are not enough without it.

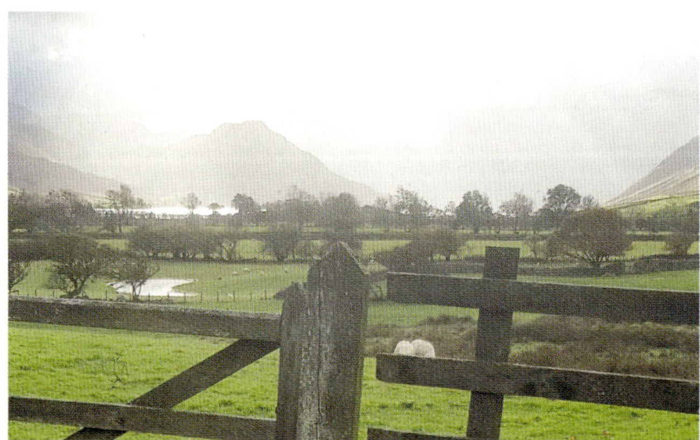

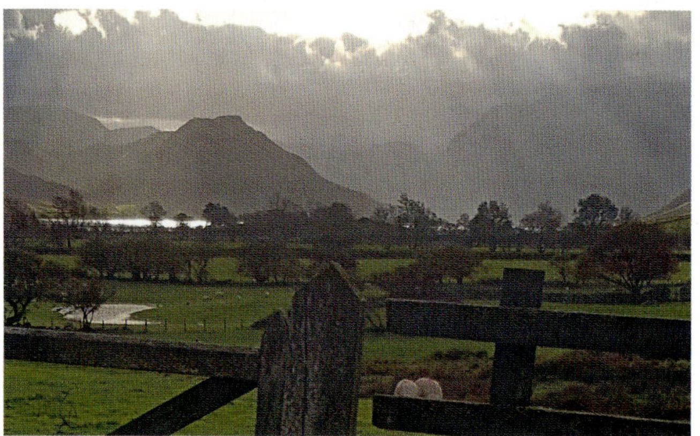

Taking photographs into the light

Remember to think of your photographs as tools. Take several images at a different exposure, to give you a wider spread of values – as in the examples to the left. The first captures the dazzling impact of the light and the freshness of the atmosphere, while the lower one better shows the shapes of the mountains and clouds. You need more than just one quick 'snap' to end up with something usable.

Even on a phone camera, you can usually change the exposure level in your photographs by moving the focal area to the dark or light areas of the scene. It is just a handy way of taking down a bit more information for the studio – along with your colour notes and memory of the place.

Build a mental library

Even if you don't fancy the outdoor painting bit, if you see a view worth painting, don't just snap it and run. It is worth staring for a while and taking mental notes of the colours and atmosphere, too. Your photograph will give you structure, but it's your recollection that will help you use that information to reflect your personal experience. The longer you spend soaking in that view, the deeper and more vivid the memory. Practise accessing that mental library: I'm certain it is good for you and it is an excellent reference tool in itself.

The example *plein air* paintings below are from the Lake District, UK. (Yes, it was absolutely freezing while painting both!), and I've noted my recollections in the captions. At Latrigg, despite the temperature, the colours were all still really warm – as the evening sun came down, the light on the hills flushed rosy-gold, echoed in the fading autumn russets and orange of the foreground trees. Similarly on Ullswater lake, the transparent water revealed green/brown shadows; the distant hills a spread of earthy greens and greys. The sun poked out at me every now and again to gift the light you see in both – but the camera didn't record any of this.

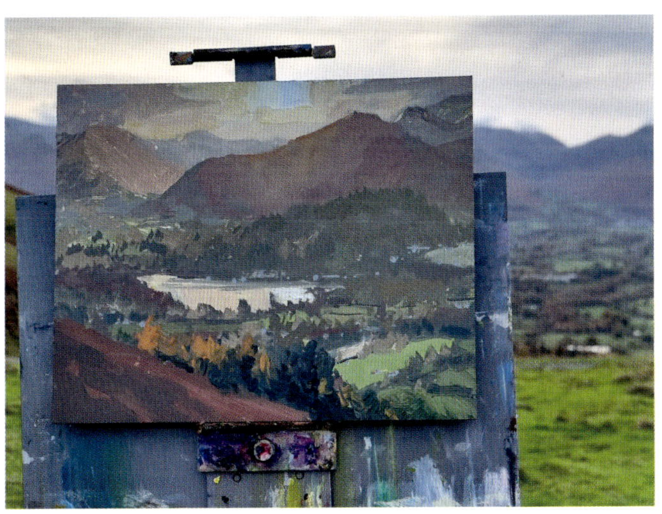

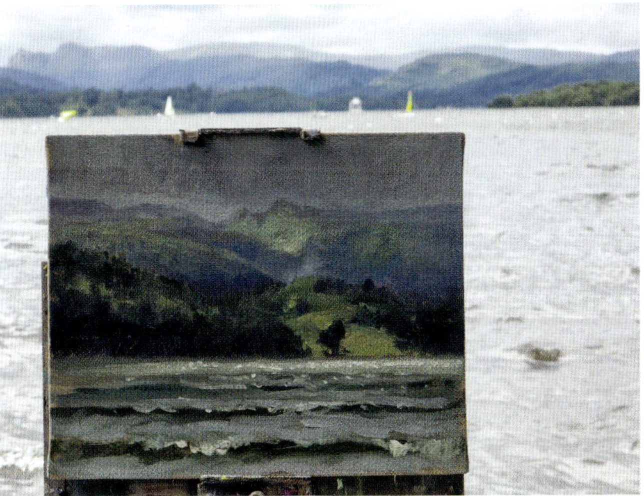

Latrigg viewpoint notes

Weather *Windy and cold: -2°C (28.4°F)!*

Hills *A mix of grey, red, gold*

Sky *Yellow, red and white with purple at the edges*

Mid-ground *Grey warmth and green, earths*

Greens *Sap, orange and blue.*

Ullswater notes

Weather *Cold, wet, stormy, light patches*

Hills *A mix of purple-greys, pastel lime in light*

Trees *Warm, grey-greens, grey-green shadows*

Sky *Neutral grey, blue/umber/white, pink light*

Water *Darker version of sky, shadows green/umber*

Water light *Light cool lime, yellow white sparkle.*

COLD DISTANCE

Cold, unpolluted mountain air can make for the sharpest edges – fantastic for photography, a challenge for painters. Keep in mind two factors: cool background with low contrast – when you hold your brush up and colour match to the supposed 'darks', you will see they are much lighter than you realize. This is key to capturing that crisp atmosphere.

If the foreground colour in your photograph or view is dull, use your license to increase the warmth, saturation and highlights a touch. This will knock the mountains back and increase the sense of hazy distance, to stronger atmospheric effect.

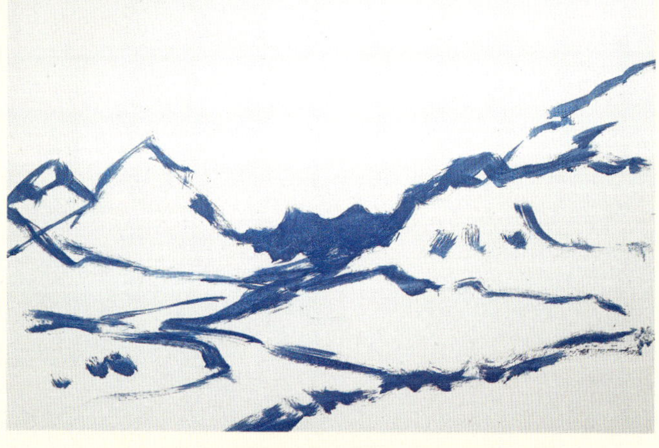

1 Get the mountains in first, loosely and with that slightly less precious energy we all have at the beginning of a painting.

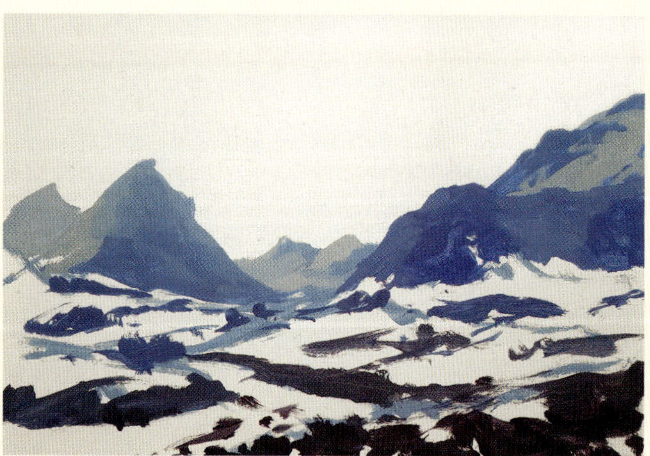

2 You might see dark shadows on the peaks, but in order to portray depth, you need that background to really stay at the back – keep it simple. Add the larger shadow colours in before the colourful, lit areas. This represents what is actually happening when the sky lights a subject.

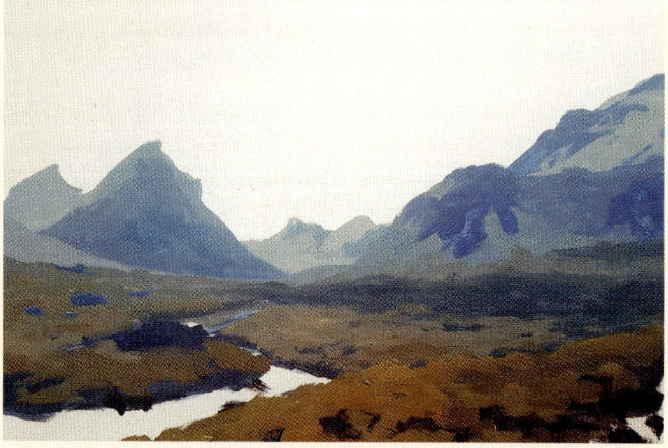

3 Add the colours for the foreground hills. They will be the same as those in the distance – just less faded and cooled further forward.

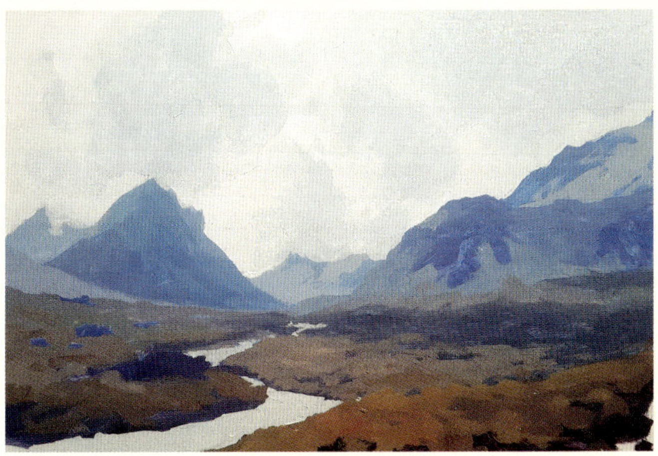

4 Shape the mountains and distant shapes by cutting in the sky. This softens the edges and harmonizes the sky with the distant land.

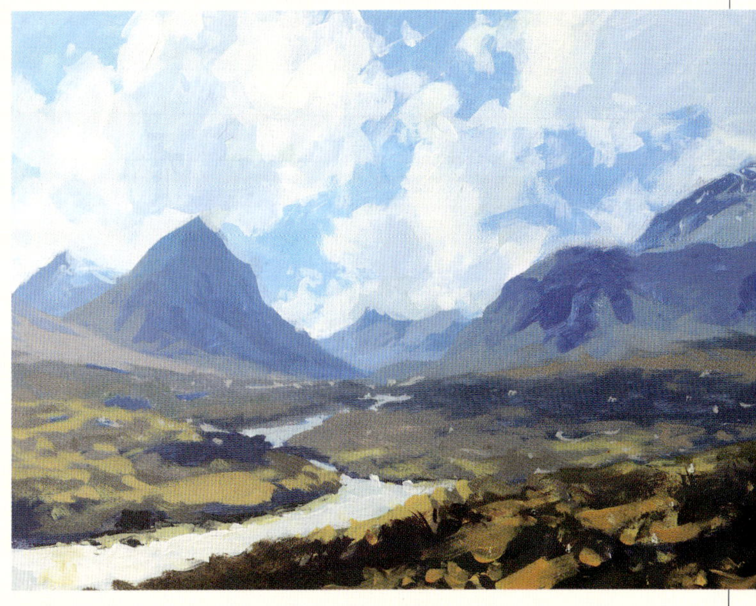

The finished exercise

MIST AND DISTANCE

I love the pastel colours in mountains on a bright and hazy winter's morning. Such colours are still greys – not just a secondary mixed with white – but they are strongly tinted towards a recognizable colour.

This unifies them with the foreground colours, reminding us that they are just a cooled, faded version of the same thing. That background purple is a mix of purple, yellow and white, which ties it in with the golds of the foreground.

The blues of the mountain were made by adding ultramarine blue and more white to the mix. You can see how grey they are in comparison to the more vibrant sky, a secondary mix of ultramarine blue, yellow and white. There was just enough warmth in the sun to burn through and give me sparkles.

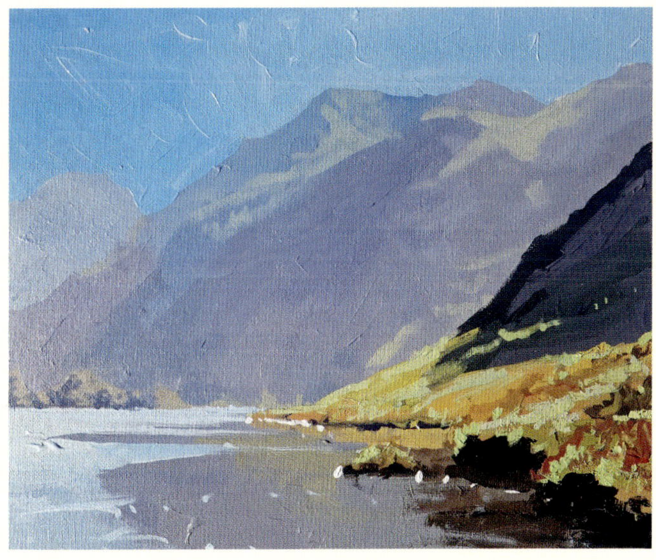

Misty Sparkle, Crummock Water 30 × 24cm (11¾ × 9½in)

SNOW

We can't look at atmosphere and not include the fabulous subject that is snow! It is one of those nouns that goes with a colour: white – but we already know that this knowledge can't be relied upon for colour mixing.

Just like water, snow reflects the wide range of colours and light bouncing around. Even out of the sun, it has tonal variation. The trick is to achieve its texture in paint through soft brushwork and awareness of lighting. As with water, there is never a hard edge between the bright lights and dense darks – there will be mid-tones in between. Keep the substance of it in mind as you paint.

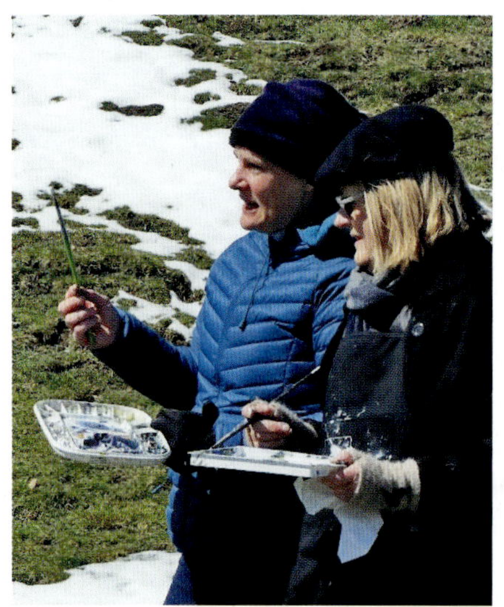

Painting, teaching – and squinting! – above the snow-line in the Pyrenees. Snow has so much colour, which depends upon lighting and surrounding landscape.

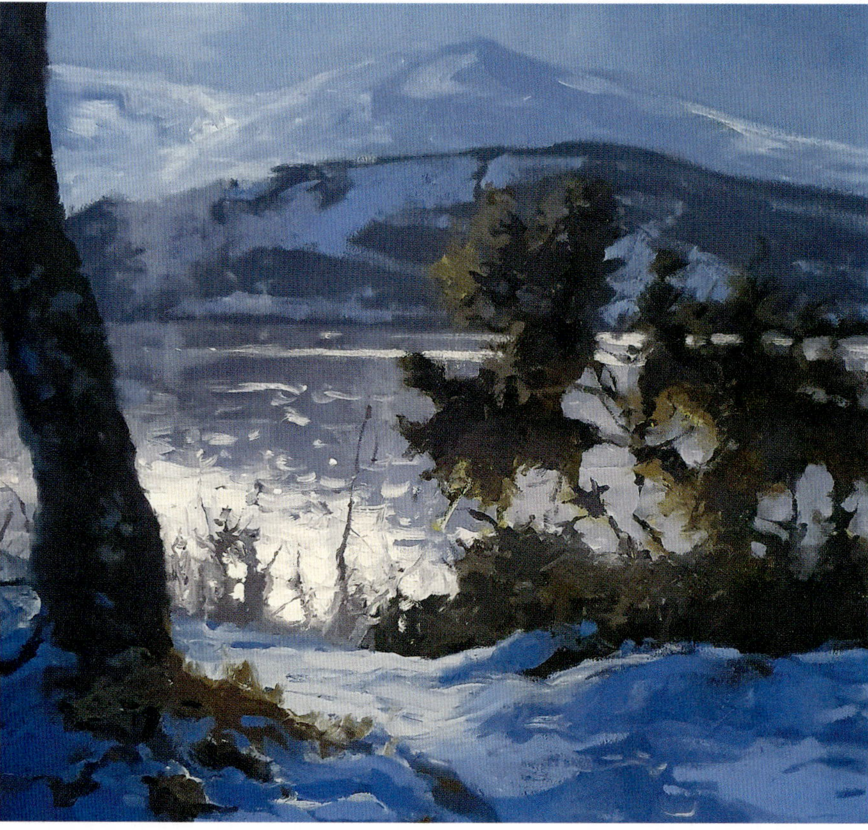

When faced with icy landscapes like this, think how to break up the heavy blue bias. The first thing I did here was to find foreground colour to interrupt the monotone. A gorse bush and scrub by the tree, with a little exaggeration of the browns into gold, gave me a great accent colour. Secondly, each blue area has a different hue and value – the foreground is saturated with a phthalo hue, while the background is based on ultramarine blue, greyed with complementary colours.

The ice is painted in a similar way to water – the way it stands out as a distinct texture is in its reduced reflective quality. The reflection is lighter than the hillside.

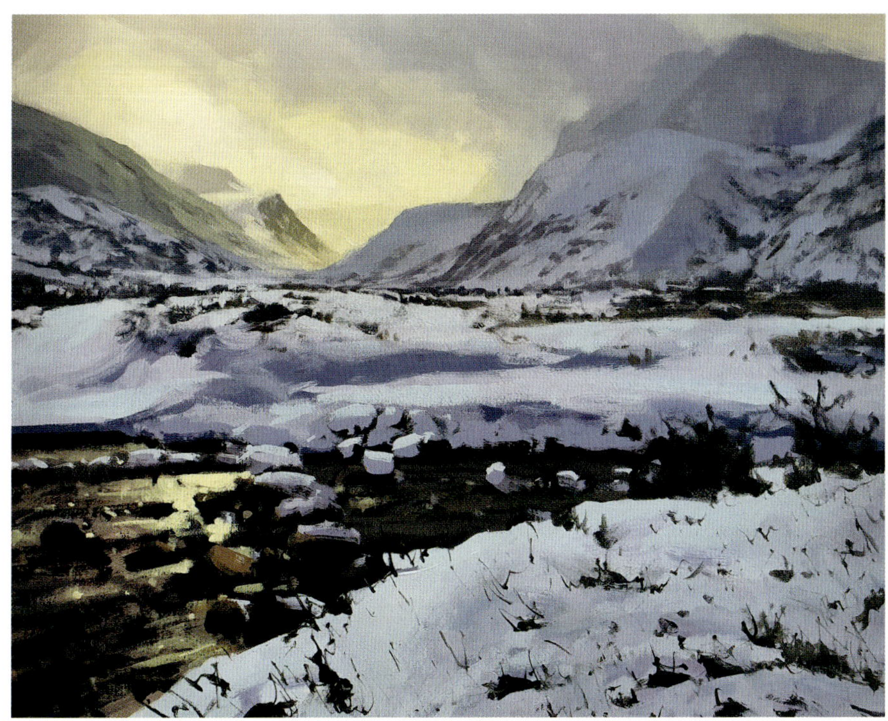

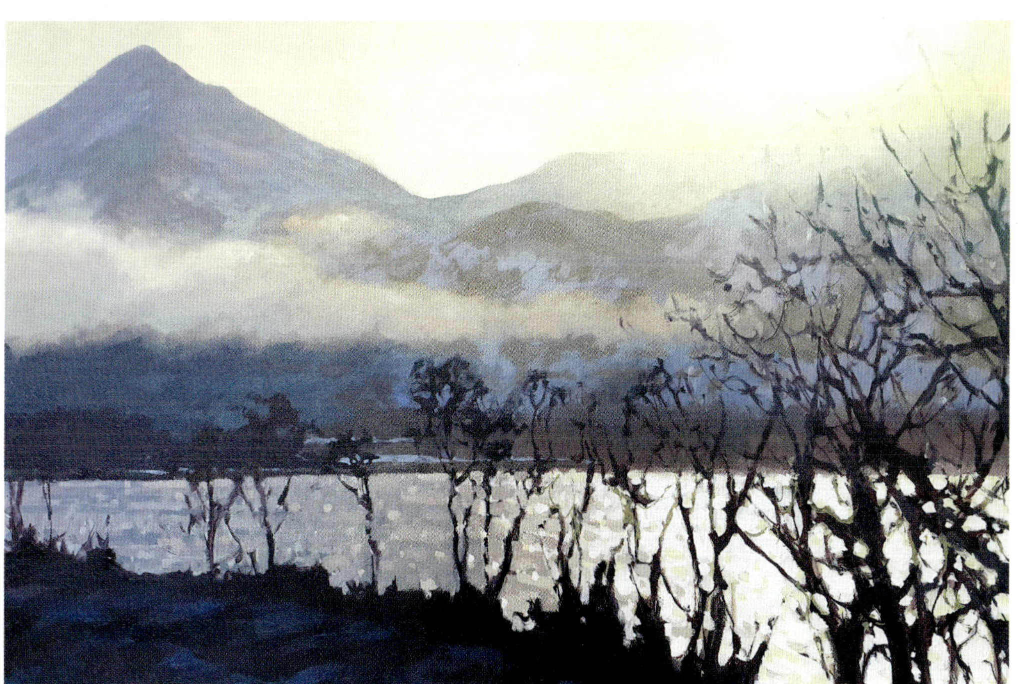

In warmer zones, snow can appear lilac-purple; in the cold, blue and green-greys. Here, the contrast between softly textured snow and bare mountain was achieved through a balance of temperatures and tone: grey-orange against grey-blue. The low cloud was very tricky – it had to vary all the way along with the light to be convincing. The trick was to keep it opaque, but blur its edges a little into the colours beyond. With strong contre-jour lighting comes less contrast. All the cold, snowy colours here turn into a wintry yellow haze. Subtlety will bring authenticity.

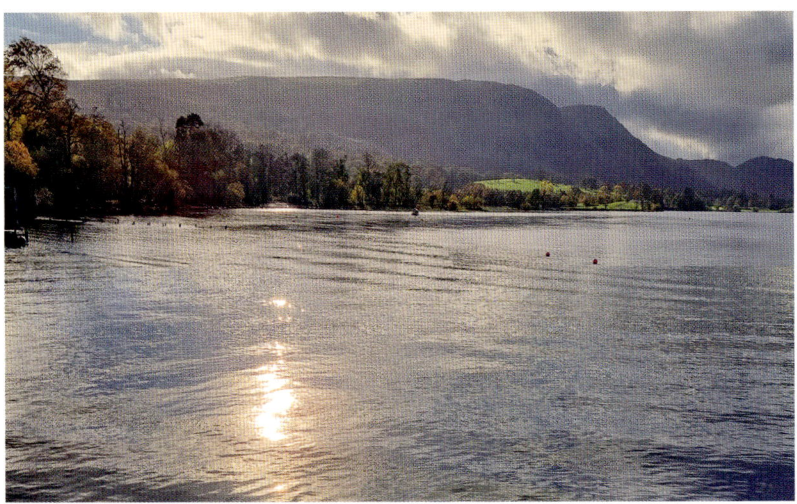

MOUNTAINS

A mountainous vista benefits from a decent foreground and mid-ground to provide a proper sense of scale. Whatever your style, if you desire the illusion of distance and depth, you must balance your interpretation with careful observation of tones, colours and temperature contrast.

The composition, as always, is key to a successful, engaging painting. The eye must be drawn in, over, around and back, with just enough detail along the way to keep it moving. Use rivers, valleys or prominent rocks as anchors and pointers. Influence the eye path with angled, bolder brushwork in the foreground; and keep it flatter and softer for the distance. Keep smaller dots, lines and sharp detail minimal in the background, as they will confuse the illusion of depth – but splash them about in the foreground to imply texture, breeziness and light. Aim for a sense of atmosphere, movement and life – and with a solid composition, you'll be winning.

You will need

100 × 80cm (39½ × 31½in) canvas

Brushes: 25mm (1in) flat, 12mm (½in) filbert, small rigger

Paints: titanium white, bright yellow lake, scarlet lake, deep purple, ultramarine blue, sap green, phthalo green, burnt umber

Low-odour solvent

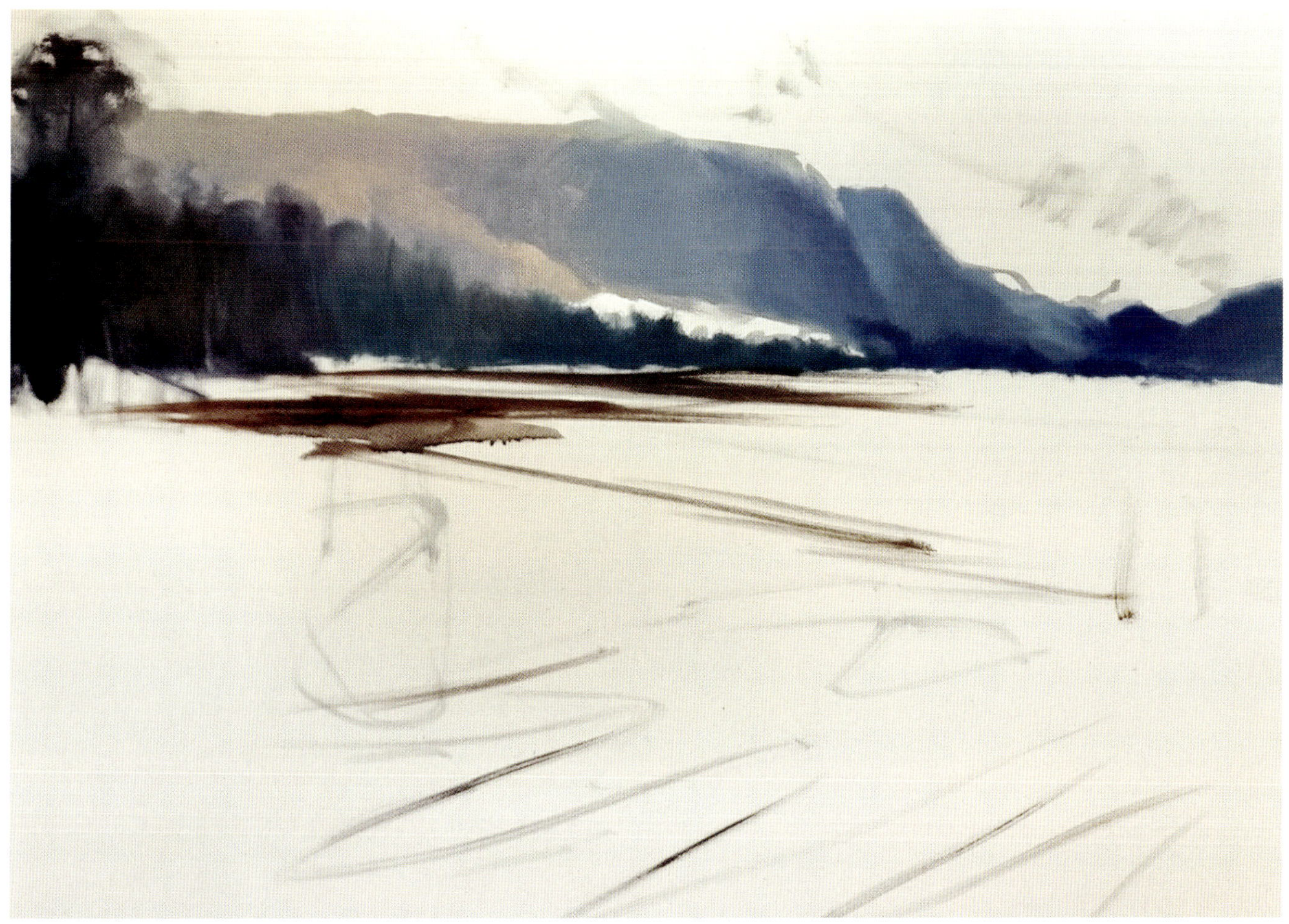

FIRST STAGE

I love a foreground lake. This one is Ullswater in the Lake District, giving a beautiful sense of scale to the hills beyond. A massive canvas calls for a massive subject! Larger paintings need two things: bigger brushes and space to stand back and evaluate. It is largely a case of scaling up – more paint, more mixing space, more room to evaluate. This applies to the brushes, too.

Stand up to paint. Straight lines are easier when you hold the brush up and walk along, rather than moving from the elbow or shoulder.

- This is a large painting, so use a large brush: a 25mm (1in) flat will help to keep the flow of your brushwork dynamic and expressive.
- Get the distant landscape in first. Lay down the mountains using a thin but opaque warm-tinged mix of scarlet lake, bright yellow lake, ultramarine blue and titanium white for the nearer mountains on the left-hand side.
- Add more ultramarine blue to the mix as you work into the more distant mountains, creating cooler, bluer colours.
- Add the tree shadows next using deep purple, burnt umber browns and cold phthalo green as the base for the mixes.
- To avoid the impression of a river flowing from right to left, the marks need to zigzag the eye into the scene in one subtle sweep. Make a few guiding, angled marks with thin burnt umber to help guide you through later brushwork in the water; which will in turn help to quickly draw the eye into the painting, toward the main, mountainous subject.

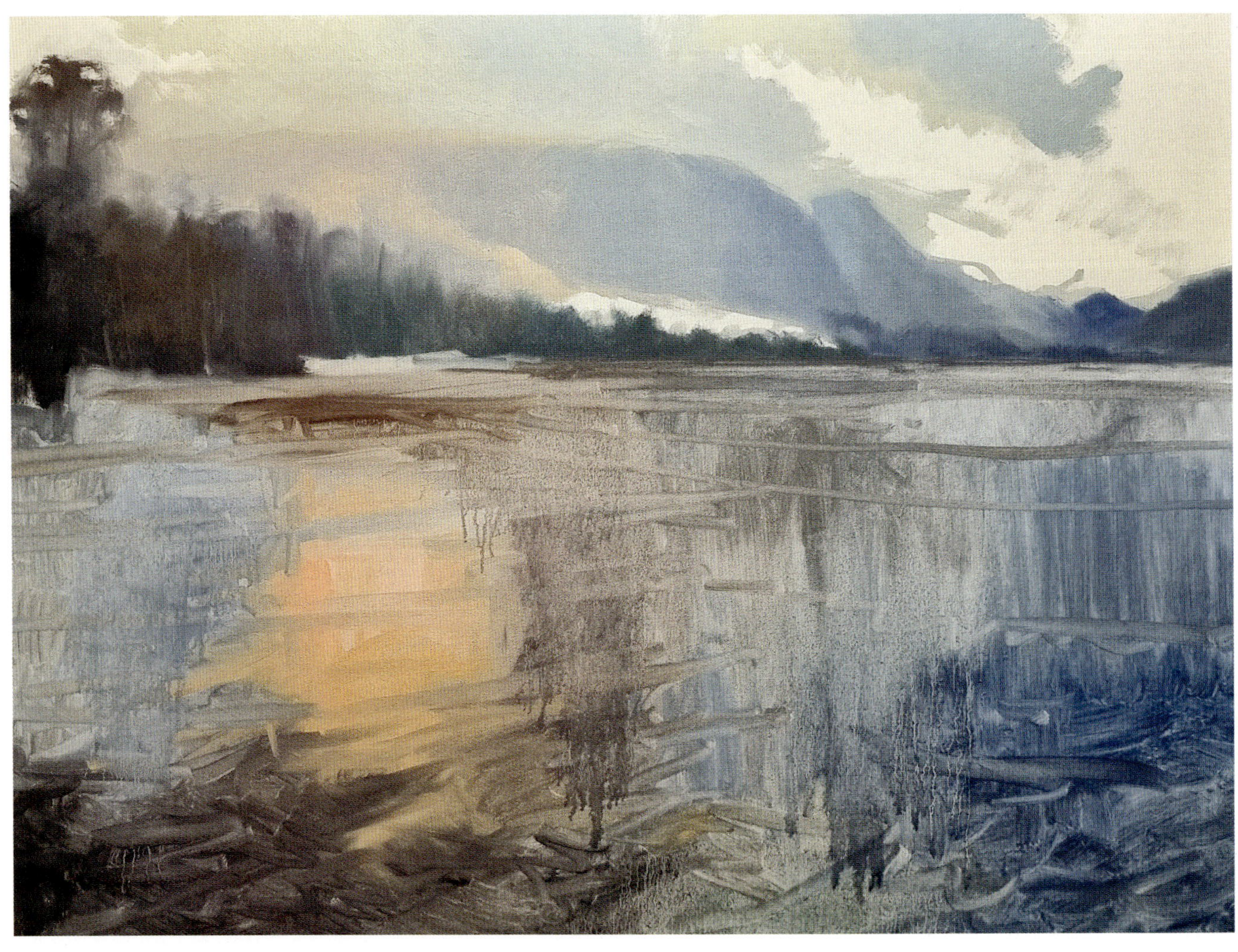

SECOND STAGE

A thin underpainting at this stage will form a nice surface for the thicker paint you will add later. The underpainting is also potentially useful to leave exposed in places, remaining as a textural contrast later on.

Be guided by colours discerned from the photograph when adding the underpainting. We also see here how vertical brushstrokes in the distance help the water look convincing, rather than like a wall.

· Lather on a washy underpainting for the water. The glowing light in the water is pivotal to the eye path and atmospheric light, so start with this area, adding it in with the 25mm (1in) flat brush and a mix of scarlet lake, bright yellow lake and titanium white.

· Apply the brushwork to the water using vertical strokes – you can see above how such strokes represent distance on water by implying reflection of the elements above and beyond, even when they're not that visible.

· Still using the 25mm (1in) flat brush, add a few curving horizontals to suggest subtle waves and currents.

· Cut the yellowy-blue sky in over the edges of the mountains with a mix of titanium white with bright yellow lake and a touch of ultramarine blue and scarlet lake. On the left, the colours are close in value, showing the strength of the direct light.

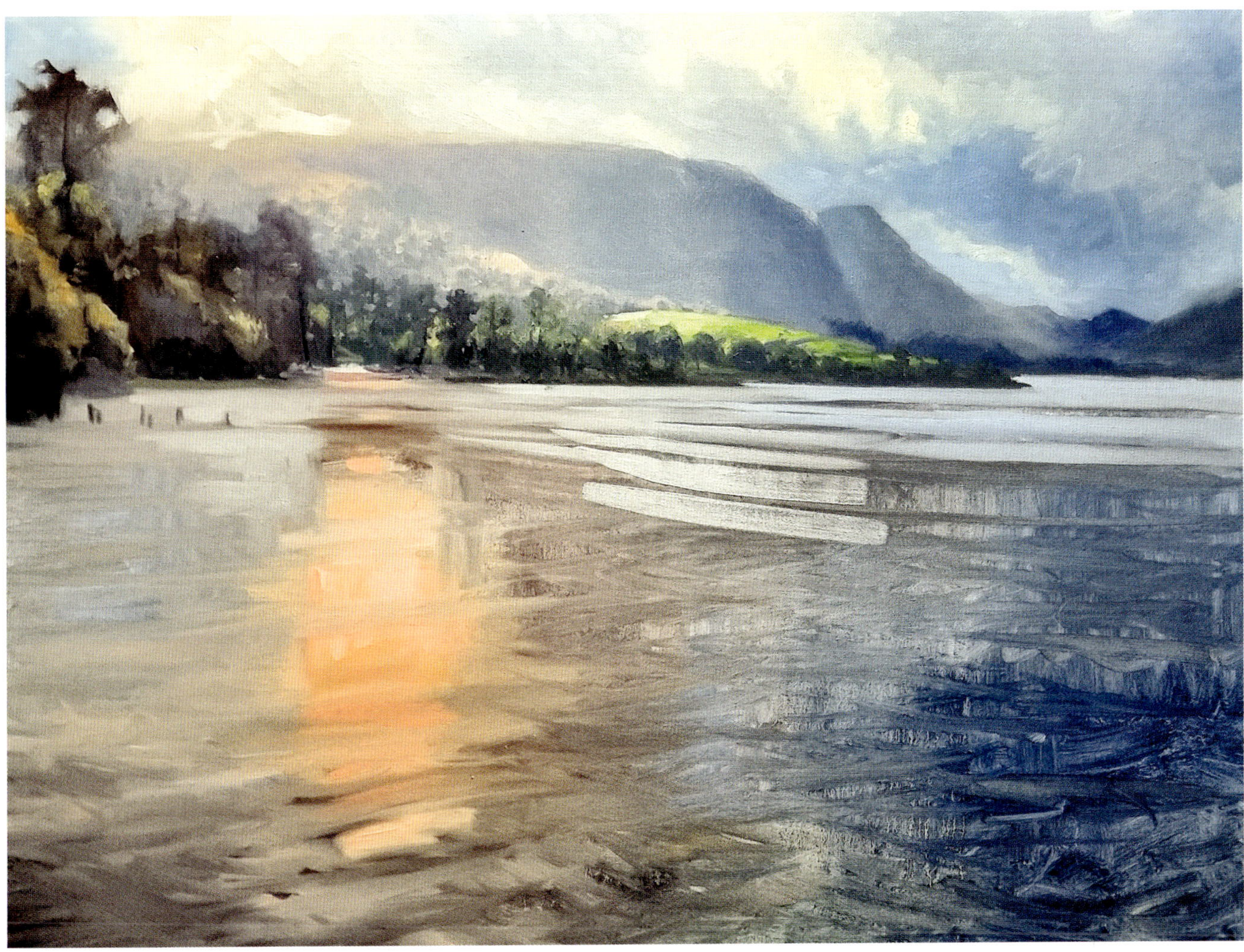

THIRD STAGE

Once the canvas is covered, we can start to work into areas with slightly thicker, opaque paint. I was so excited about that grassy headland, with its beautiful lime-green light. Beware greens however – they are usually warmer and less vibrant than they look!

- Use the 25mm (1in) flat brush to work from the background through to the foreground with thicker mixes of the same colours used in the second stage (see opposite), softening any hard edges as you go.
- For the headland, use a green mix of bright yellow lake and titanium white, adding a tiny touch of ultramarine blue to the mix for shadows.
- Pick out warm whites in the sky using titanium white tinted with scarlet lake and bright yellow lake. This will reserve the brightest white for the reflection of the sun in the water.

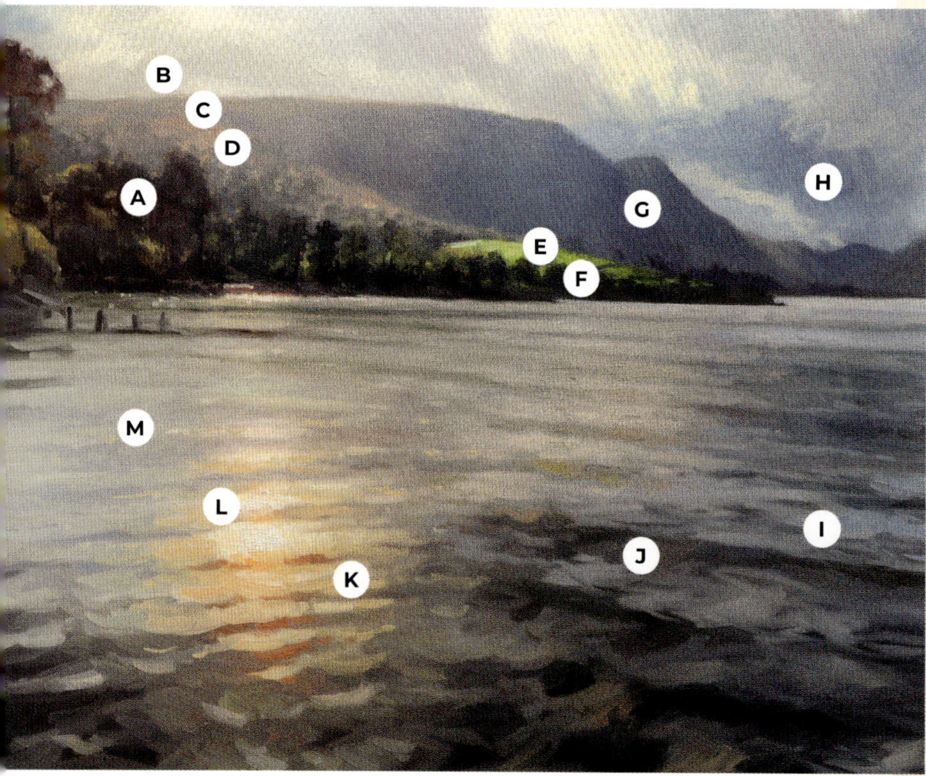

FOURTH STAGE – REFINING

The many greys in this water are the reflections of all that colour in the landscape and sky, as well as the colour of the lake bed itself. If you find yourself painting a big lake with one colour, have a rethink! It acts as a mirror; even when moving, there will be subtle reflection of light and surrounds.

- I've summarized my mixes below, but colour recipes should always be secondary to your interpretation – use these as starting points rather than solutions.
- For the grey mixes, start with either three primaries; or a colour and its complementary, and then tint, warm, cool, darken or lighten it, as the subject dictates.
- Place the final thicker, tinted whites for the sun with a 12mm (½in) filbert, along with the curvy foreground wave shapes. I added the distant sparkles with a rigger, but otherwise kept everything relatively soft.

Trees (A) Deep purple and phthalo green shadows, with scarlet lake, bright yellow lake, sap green and titanium white lights.

Sky (B) Titanium white, scarlet lake and bright yellow lake, a touch of burnt umber added for shadows.

Warm mountain (C) scarlet lake, bright yellow lake, ultramarine blue and titanium white mixes.

Treetops (D) As C, but with more red and yellow in the mix.

Grass (E) Bright yellow lake and titanium white with a tint of ultramarine blue.

Trees (F) Ultramarine blue, bright yellow lake and burnt umber.

Cold mountain (G) Ultramarine blue added to the warmer mix (C), plus burnt umber for shadows.

Sky (H) A cool grey mix of ultramarine blue, scarlet lake, bright yellow lake and titanium white for the clouds. Add a bit more blue into the mix for cool blue-greys for those in shadow.

Sky reflections (I) Same cool and blue greys used in the clouds above (H).

Dark wave shadows (J) Sap green, ultramarine blue and burnt umber.

Light wave shadows (K) Orange-greys: scarlet lake, bright yellow lake and a touch of sap green.

Light reflections (L) Titanium white tinted with a touch of bright yellow lake at its brightest. Add scarlet lake for deeper tones.

Sky reflections (M) Same colour mix as B, with a touch of ultramarine added.

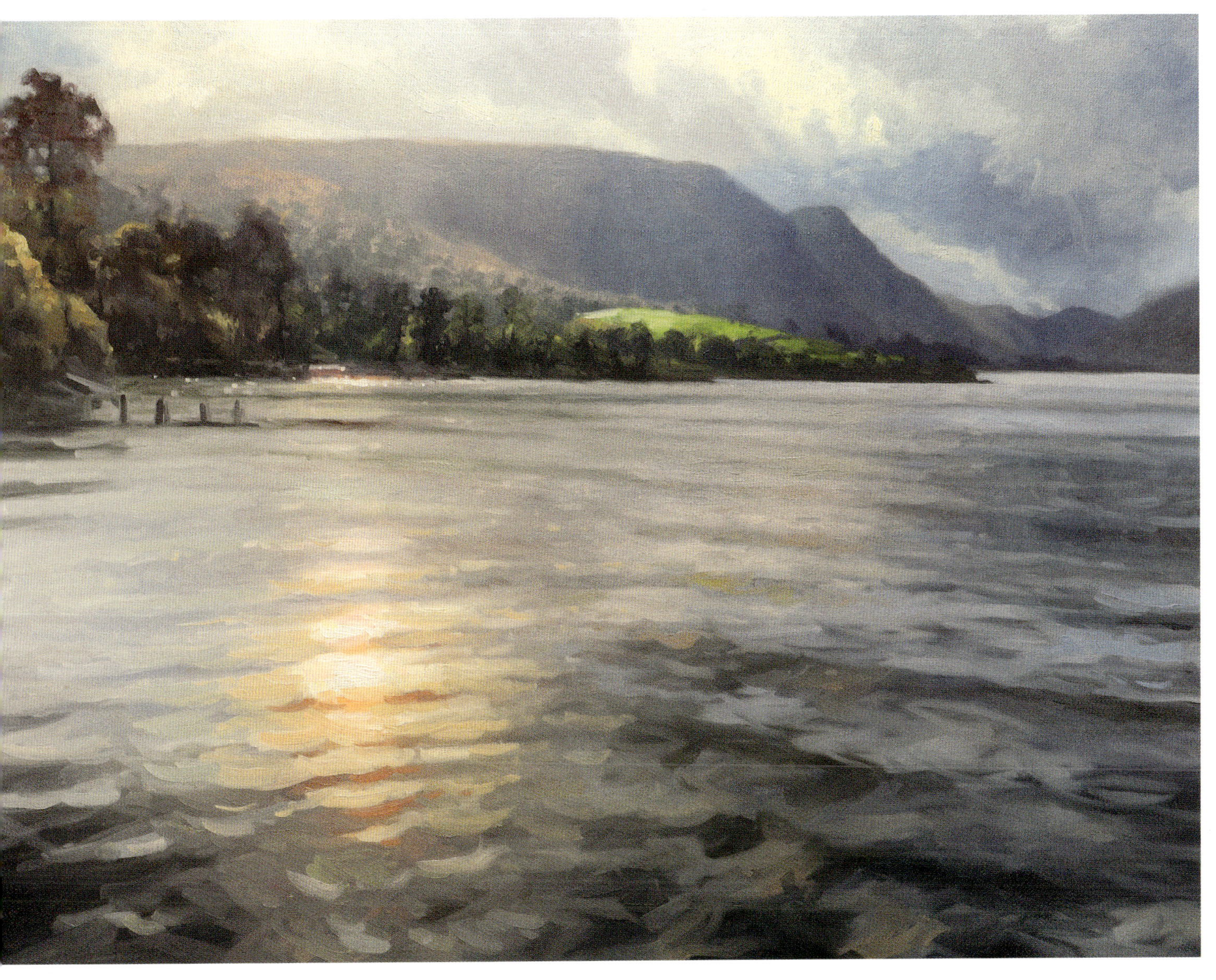

The finished painting

In terms of brushwork, the large flat works in pretty much the same way as the 12mm (½in) brush, and is still capable of the level of detail you need, so don't be afraid of it. For a large painting like this, you don't want to go much smaller than the 25mm (1in) flat, or you will risk losing the dynamism of the strokes.

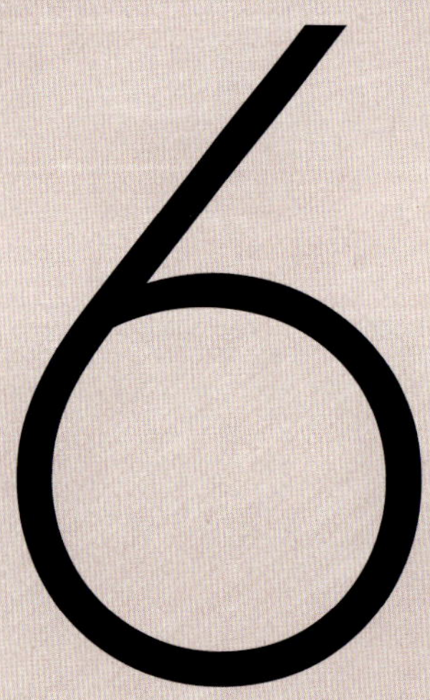

6

———

IMPACT

Almost everything I paint is slave to the light, as for me, that eye-catching
impact is everything. I want to be startled by the light in a painting, not
the accuracy of the drawing. I want a painting to grab you immediately,
then draw you into the intriguing backstory, no matter the subject.

When a scene is complex and busy, it can be challenging to prioritize light
and atmosphere. With scenes like harbours, so joyfully full of painterly
content, you have to decide what to sacrifice for the greater good.
To invest your paintings with impact, keep in mind editing for
better design, and simplification to allow freedom for the eye
to engage. Try to discern the elements that most eloquently
speak the nature of the subject; and remember: the truth of a
subject can be achieved through the loosest of marks.

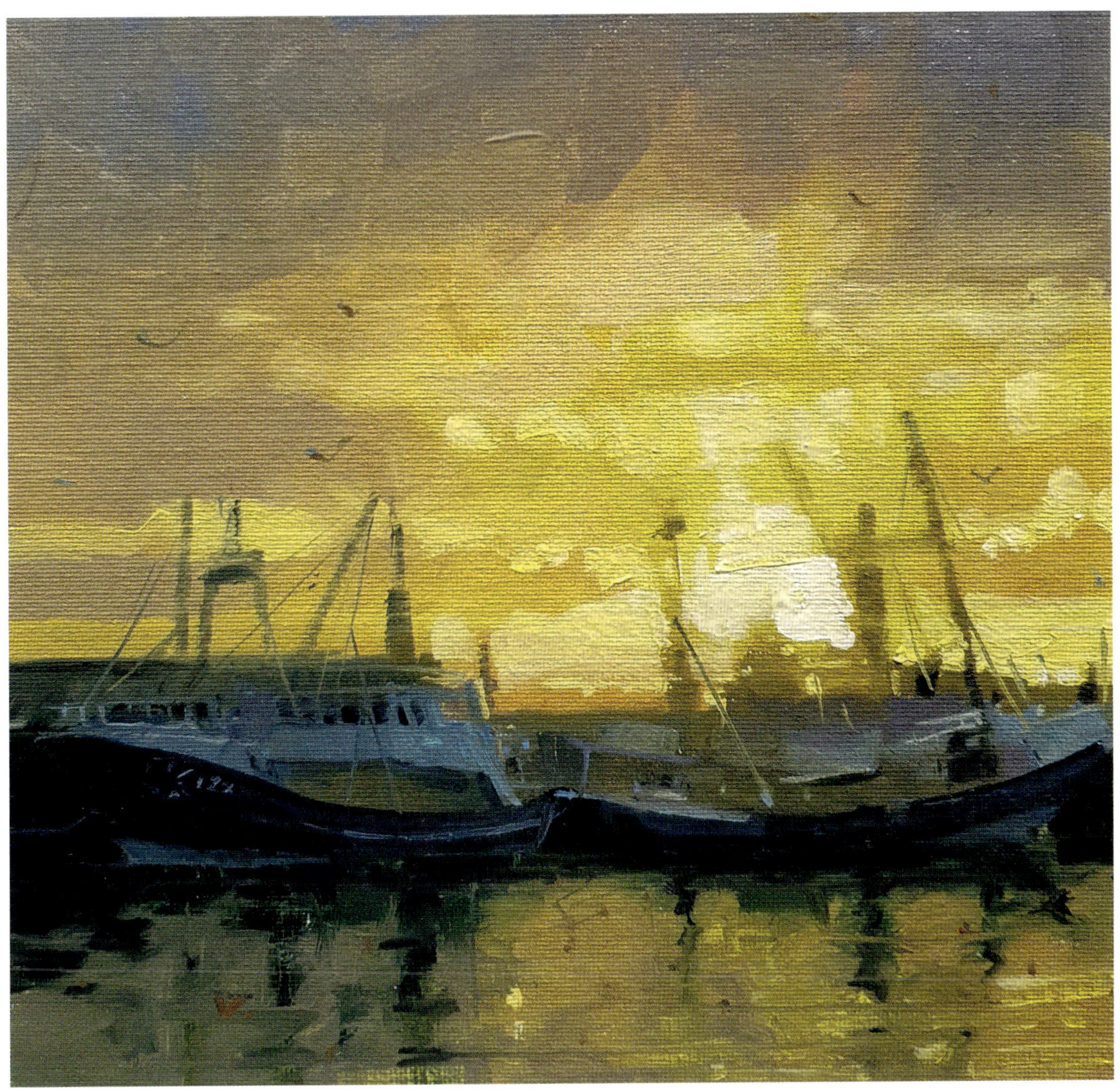

Morning Light, Newlyn Harbour

30 × 30cm (11¾ × 11¾in)

The elements that make this little painting work are the complementary colours of the 'white' turquoise boats and golden sky, and the accurate economy of brushwork.

In studying the photograph, I blurred my eyes to try to see the strongest pattern and theme to the structure. The left-hand boat was important to the composition, zig-zagged across from the focal point of the sun. Convincing angles and shapes, where visible, were a given – but the main subject that stood out was the windows. The first time I put them in, I tried adding loose dashes of dark over the turquoise background. They ended up looking drawn and irregular, inauthentic – which detracted from the lighting impact. I scraped that and instead added a horizontal bar of black, then laid angled verticals with a rigger for the frames. Still loose, but a much more convincing upper deck. Every painting is a brushwork experiment!

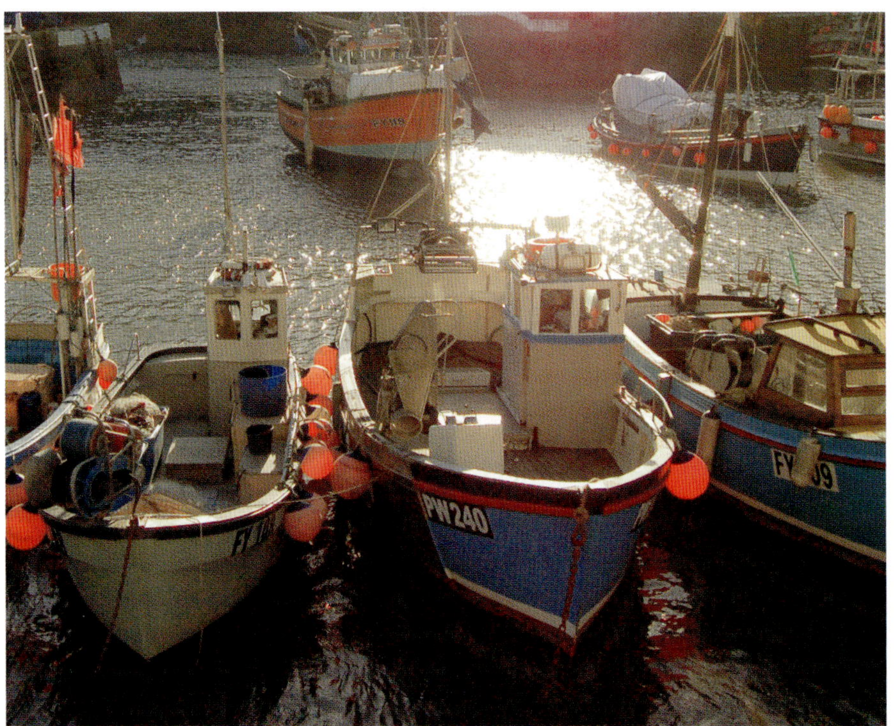

MEVAGISSEY HARBOUR

Whenever scenes require high accuracy, I sketch out a loose drawing in thin paint. This enables a convincing structure to hold all the loose, splashy paint. If you get the bones right, the body of the painting will hold together.

Figure out what needs to be right. Fishing boats are unexpectedly oddly-shaped! This makes it tricky to get them looking loosely right. Careful observation will get you everywhere!

You will need

30 × 24cm (11¾ × 9½in) canvas board

Brushes: 6mm (¼in) flat, 6mm (¼in) filbert, two 12mm (½in) flat brushes, 15mm (¾in) bristle filbert, size 0 rigger

Paints: titanium white, bright yellow lake, scarlet lake, deep purple, ultramarine blue, sap green, phthalo green, burnt umber

Low-odour solvent

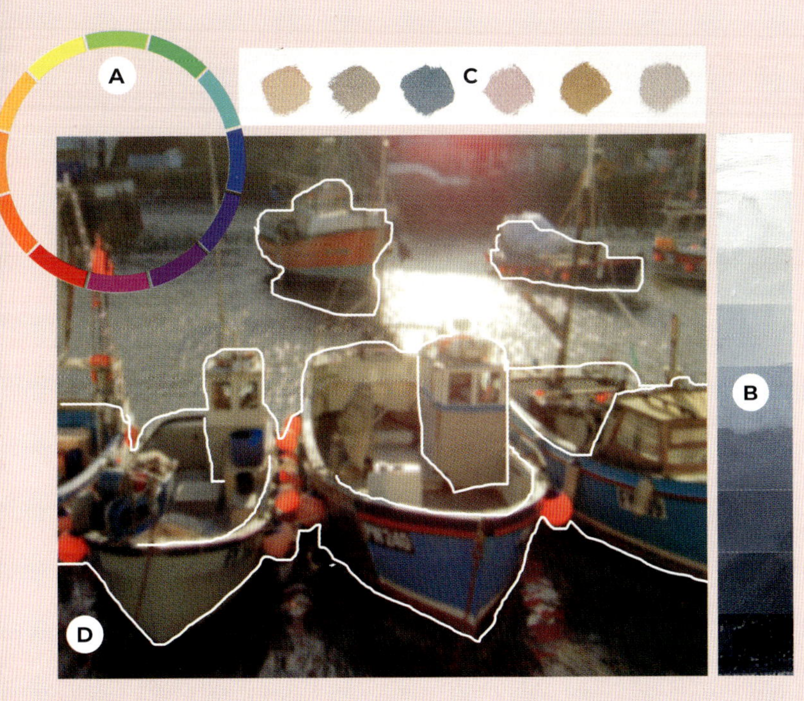

Seeing shapes

Try to block out the noise of the detail, and just see the main themes within the scene.

PROPER PLANNING FOR COMPLEX COLOURS

With busier scenes, don't just launch in. Give yourself that basic map for the journey before you start.

Check colour and tone Hold up a colour wheel (A) and a tonal scale (B) to check where your saturated and darkest colours are.

Make that mixing chart (C) There is a lot going on, colour-wise, but you'll find a reason for every mix when you take the effect of lighting into account. and compare some of those beautiful, subtle colours to those in your image.

Look for shapes (D) Reduce the picture to shapes in your mind – or blur it in a photo app if you have one.

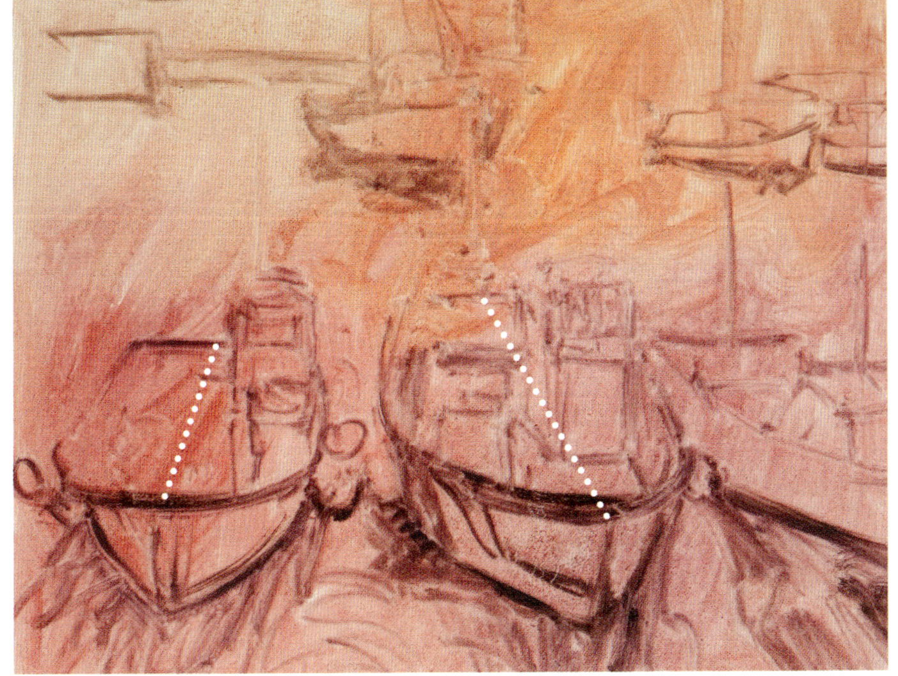

FIRST STAGE

If you are looking head-on at boats, as here, be aware of foreshortening and perspective.

- On a pinky-orange ground, and working upside down, sketch out the boats in thin burnt umber using a small filbert.
- Keep the bow (pointy end) opposite the middle of the back of the boat, in line with your perspective. If this isn't right, they will look ungainly and wrong.

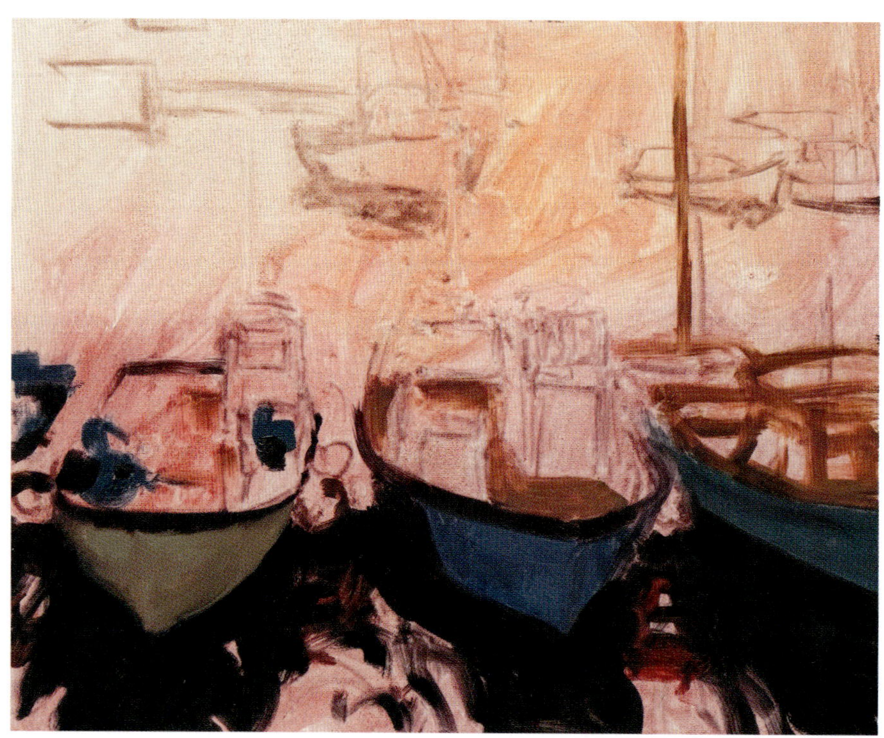

SECOND STAGE

As you start to fill in the various planes of colour and shadow, the colours appear vibrant at first glance, but careful observation will reveal otherwise. Given that they are in shade, there must be an element of grey to them. Only the colours in full light will be saturated.

- With a 6mm (¼in) flat brush, mix ultramarine blue with bright yellow lake for the blue boat, adding a touch of titanium white for the nose.
- Add more yellow to the mix for the right-hand boat.
- For the left-hand boat, use a mix of bright yellow lake and deep purple, with titanium white for the lighter area.
- Use a mix of deep purple and sap green for the shadows, adding scarlet lake for the buoy reflections.

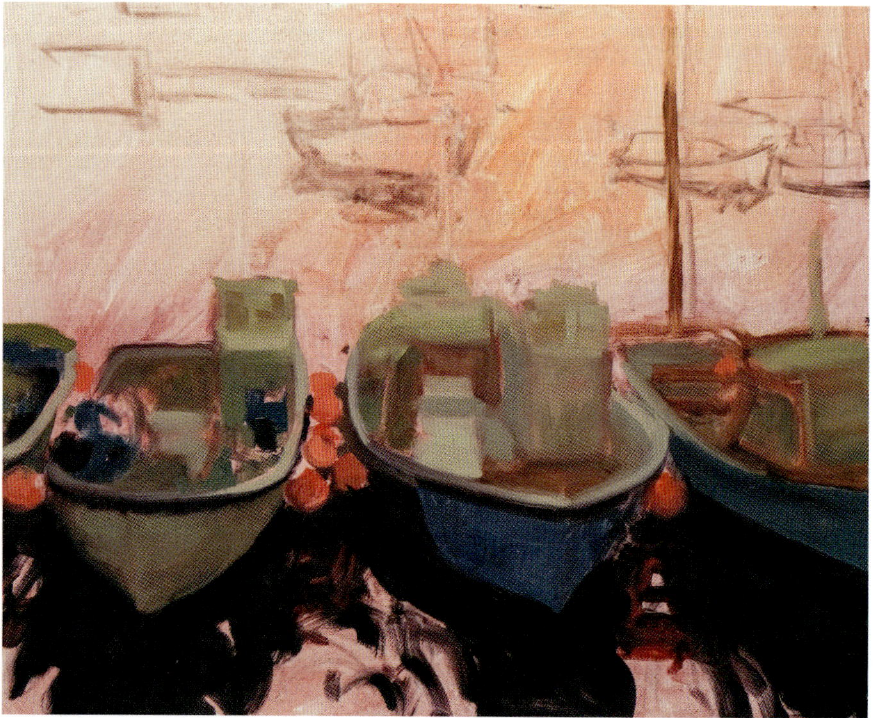

THIRD STAGE

This stage feels a little like putting together a jigsaw, with the knowledge that sense will emerge at some point in the process!

- Continuing with the same 6mm (¼in) flat brush, identify, mix and place shapes of colour.
- Work systematically. Resist the temptation to spread colour around to fill gaps, in a rush to make sense of things. Just keep going, bit by bit.
- Add the buoys using an orange mix of scarlet lake and bright yellow lake plus a little titanium white and a touch of deep purple.

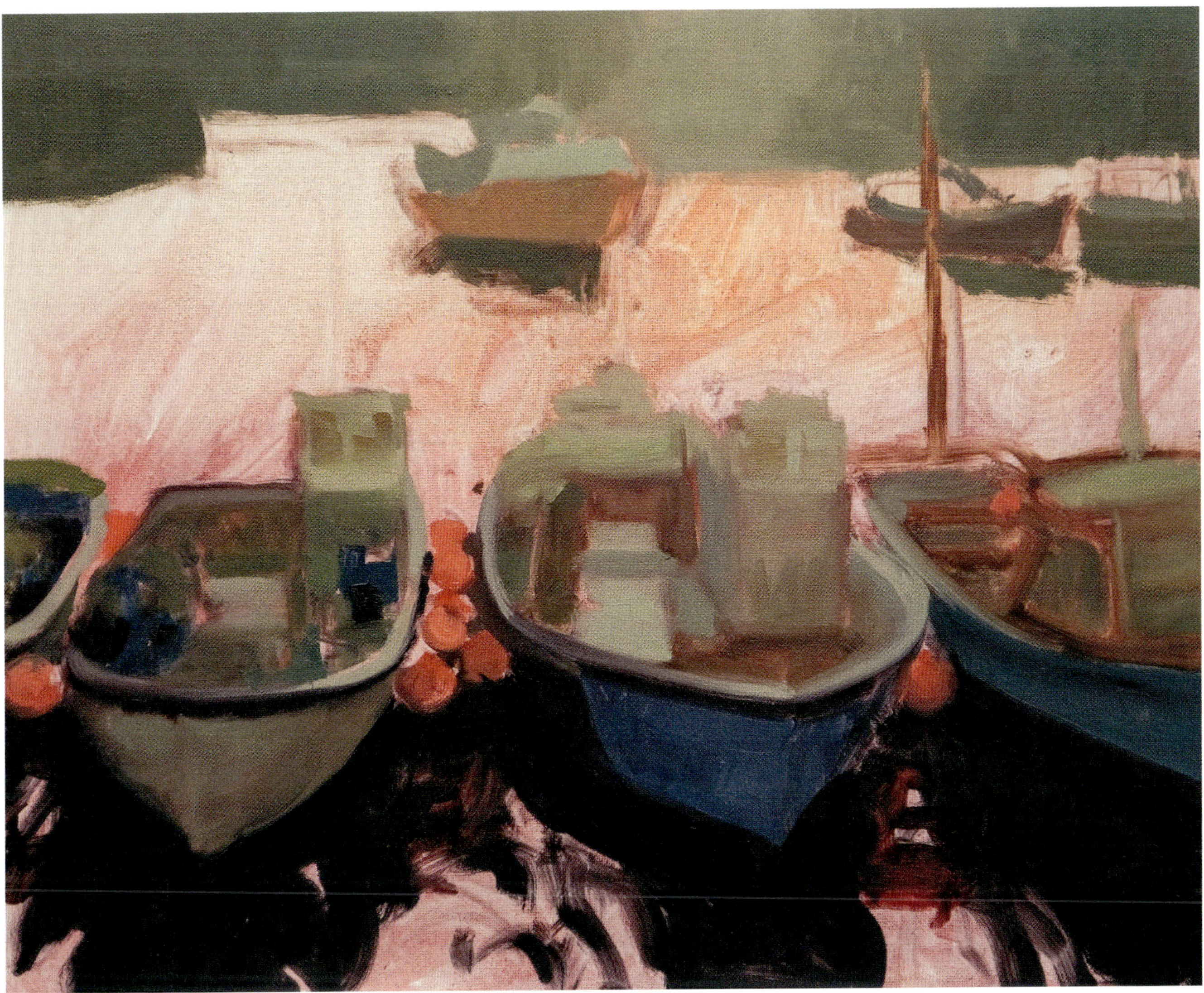

FOURTH STAGE

Gradually it comes together! A fair amount of the neutral colours I've chosen are greyed and lightened greens, pinks and yellows – look for them in your mixing chart!

- For the background shadows, use various combinations of cooler sap green and burnt umber.
- Where the sun falls, gradually add a mix of titanium white, scarlet lake and bright yellow lake to tint these background mixes to a light green-gold.
- For the background colours (including the 'red' boat), use lighter and more muted, greyer mixes. This will give a sense of distance.

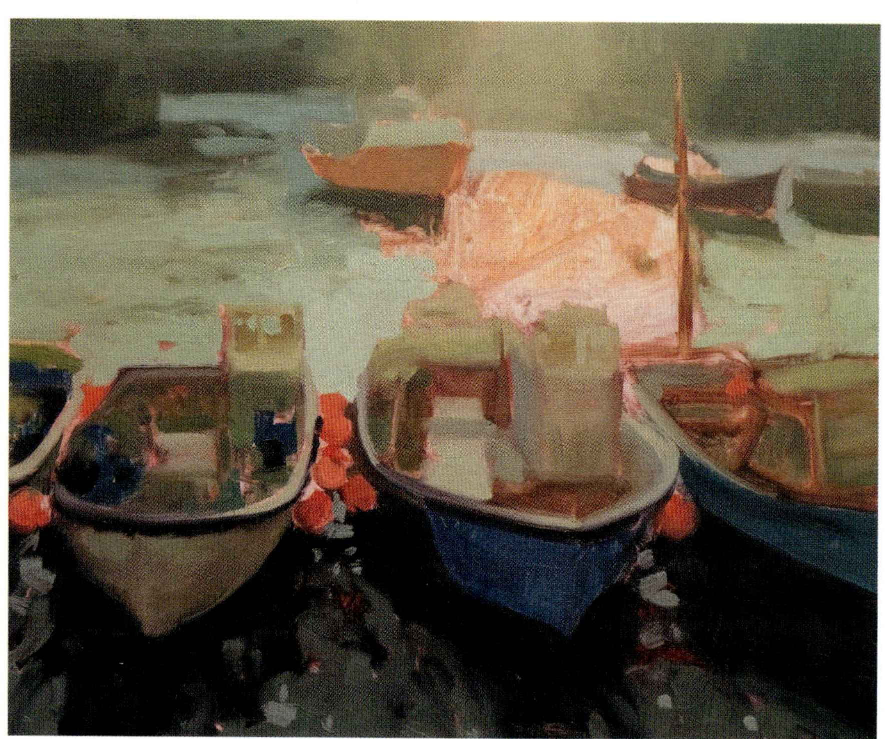

FIFTH STAGE

The satisfying part! At this point, in goes the water, finally connecting it all together and giving the colours context.

· Using a 12mm (½in) flat, apply lighter grey-greens for the background. A mix of sap green and titanium white with a little scarlet lake is a good starting point.

· For the foreground, use a darker grey mix of phthalo green and scarlet lake.

· Use a mix of burnt umber, phthalo green and titanium white for the grey spaces in between the boats, leaving the transparent red reflections as a nice contrast.

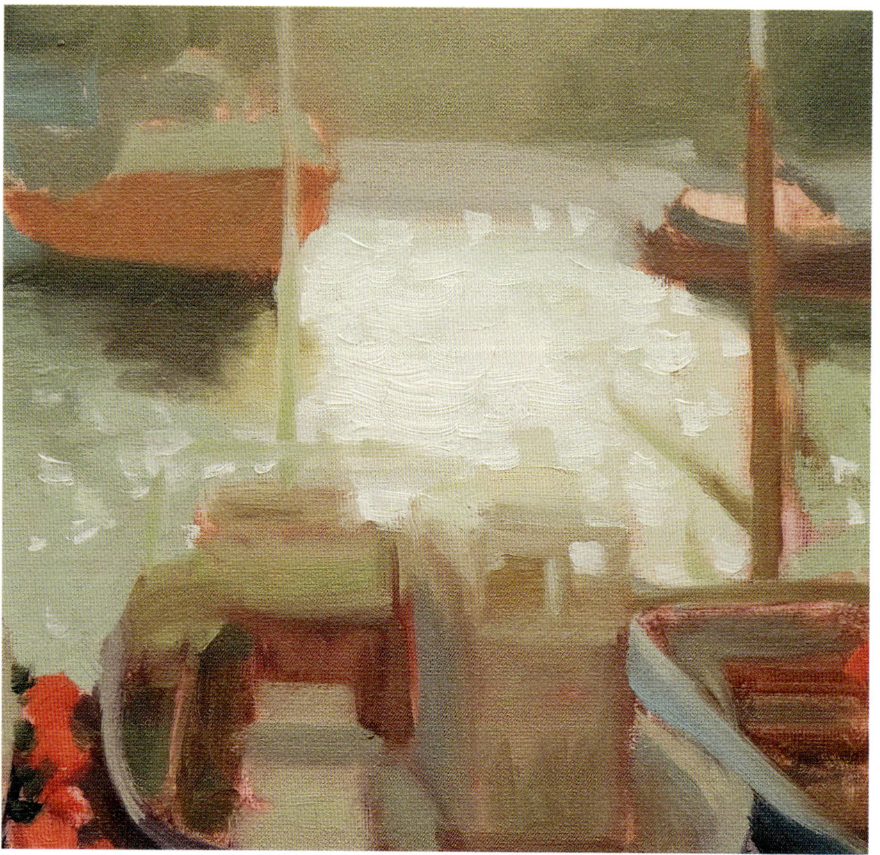

SIXTH STAGE

After the satisfaction of the previous stage, this is the part I find most exciting, as the light goes on.

Using a bristle brush for this is ideal: they are great for letting go of luscious, buttery paint!

· Firstly, create an opaque – but not too thick – mix of titanium white tinted with bright yellow lake and scarlet lake. Dot some of this about on either side of the pool of light, using it to cut into the boats both either side and in front.

· Load up the 15mm (¾in) bristle filbert with some thick titanium white, tinted with the tiniest dot of yellow) and lay it on top. Being thick and clean, the white really stands out against the surrounding texture and colour.

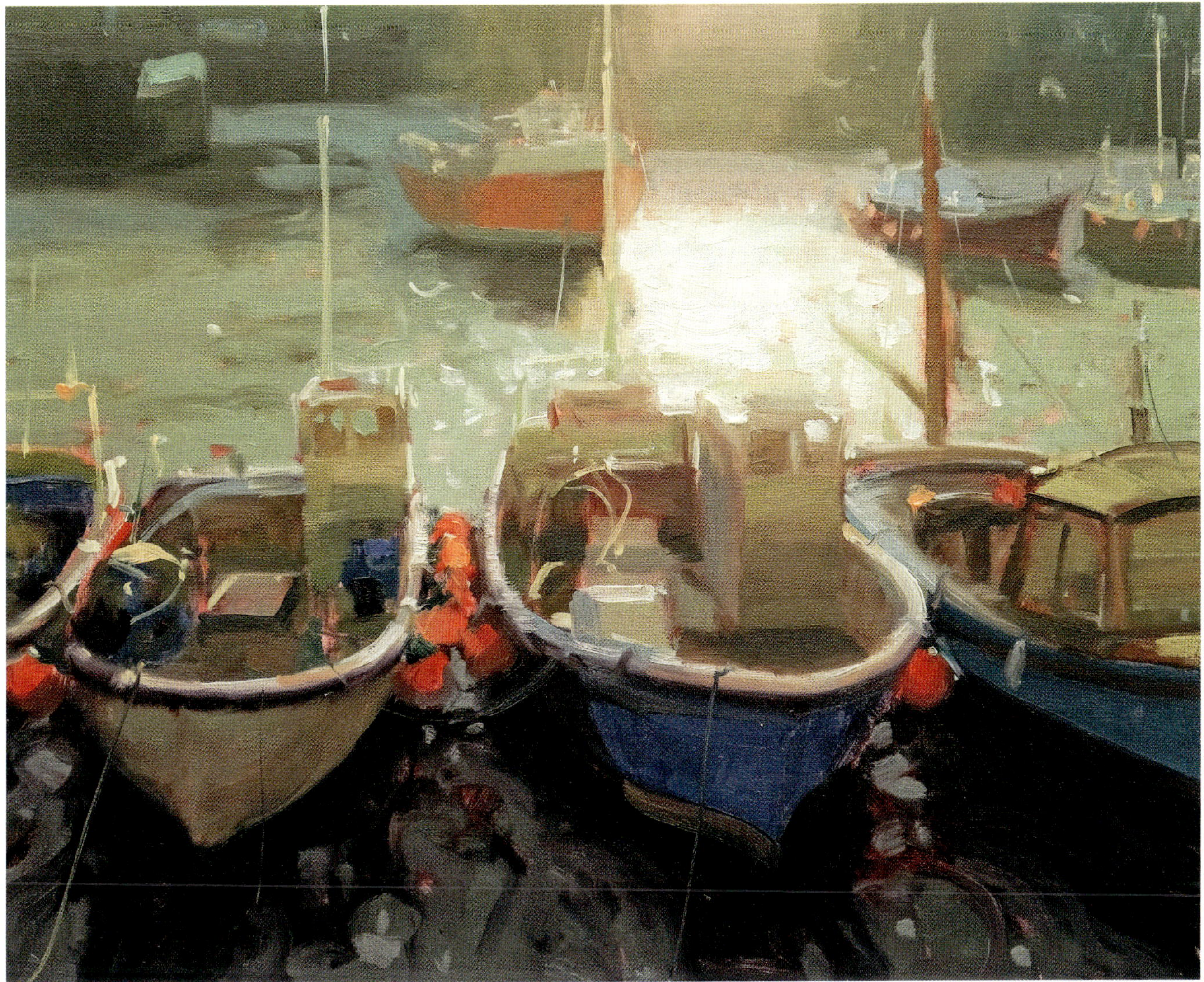

SEVENTH STAGE – REFINING

Finishing a highly detailed painting like this needs careful work. The feel of my painting is soft and atmospheric, with the focus on the light; as ever, I am after movement and a sense of the place.

Don't be tempted into drawing, or adding too many small, hard edges, or you risk the detail looking like it is sitting on top of the painting. The final details and highlights must be placed with the overall impression in mind.

- Use a clean 6mm (¼in) flat brush to lighten the area above the brightest light.
- Swap to a 6mm (¼in) filbert and paint the masts, holding the brush against a ruler for stability.
- Use the same brush to add some soft highlights and details to the boats. Use your finger or a dry brush to smudge anything that starts to become too detailed and refined.
- Finally, use a rigger with flowing paint for the smaller marks: highlights on the buoys and within the boats, along with ropes and splashy visual noise.

SAILBOATS

I think that the harder a subject seems to us, the harder we try to paint the detail – when, as with the birds and figures, the most effective way is often to reduce subjects to shapes. You can build up to as much detail as you like.

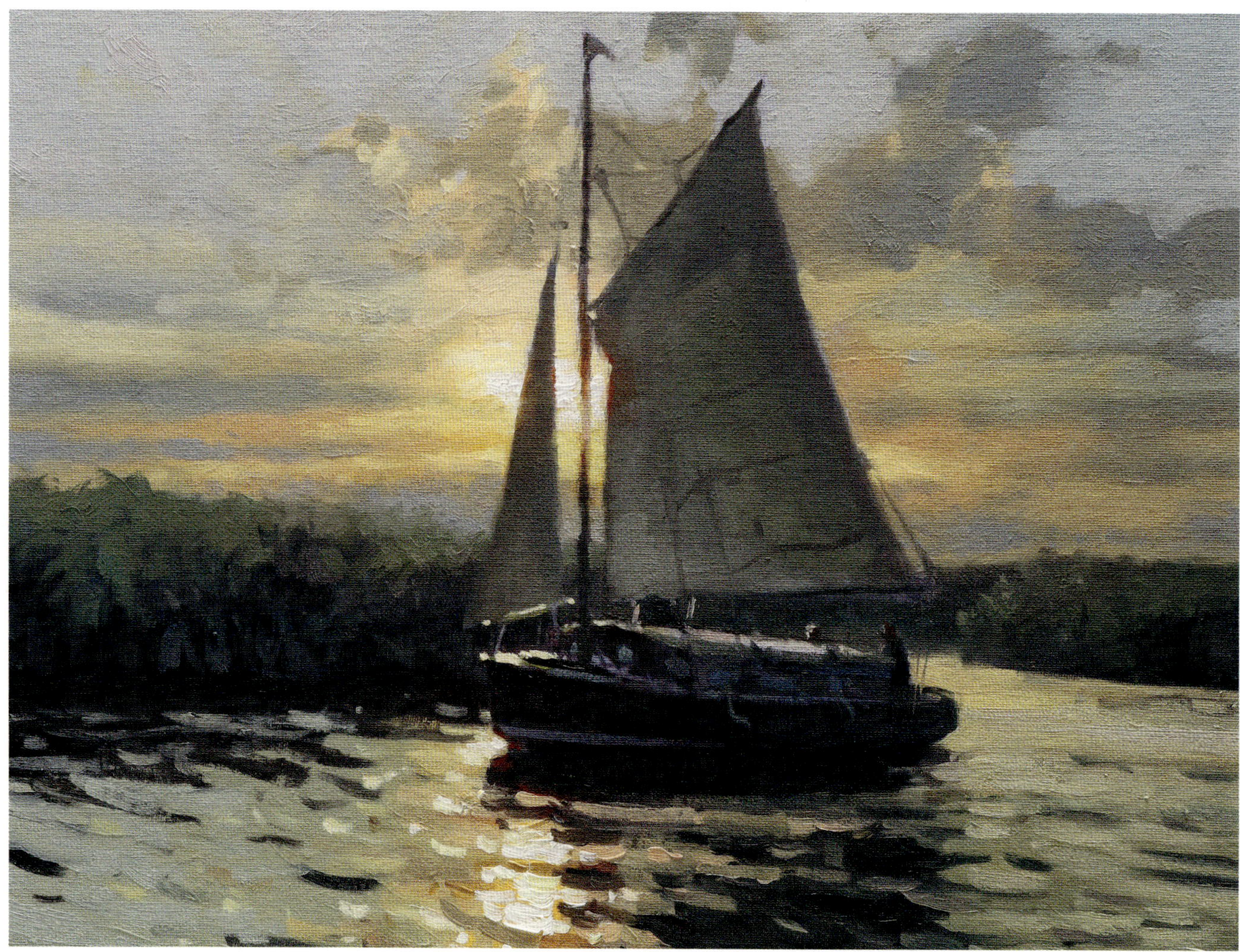

A simple subject, but painting this beautiful Norfolk wherry took a great deal of thought! It's a strong example of getting away with it, composition-wise. The sun and the boat are nearly central – but both are just enough off to either side to avoid the bullseye effect. The water flows from right to left, angling up and behind the boat to a twist in the river on the right; the clouds on the right angle in and down, helping to draw the eye around the scene.

The main sail, placed in with a 12mm (½in) flat, needed careful brushwork. While the contre-jour lighting resulted in this silhouette effect, I needed to repaint the sail twice, to ensure the brushwork suggested the right movement and texture. The loose lines added at the end were necessary in this case, as the sails would look odd without them.

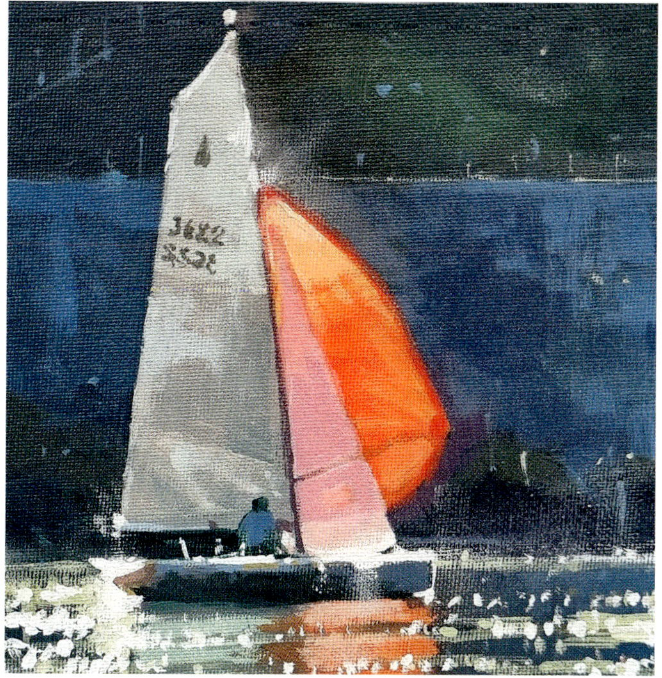

I love it when the sun seems to halo an object, partly because it removes the need for accuracy in detail! The brushwork in the sails here was all important, reflecting the transparency of the jib (foresail) and the shape and vibrance of the full, red spinnaker, glowing in the morning sun. Where the light is strongest, the red of the sail is bleached to light orange. The cool off-white of the jib is warmed to a pink. Sails can be such sparkling, exciting subjects!

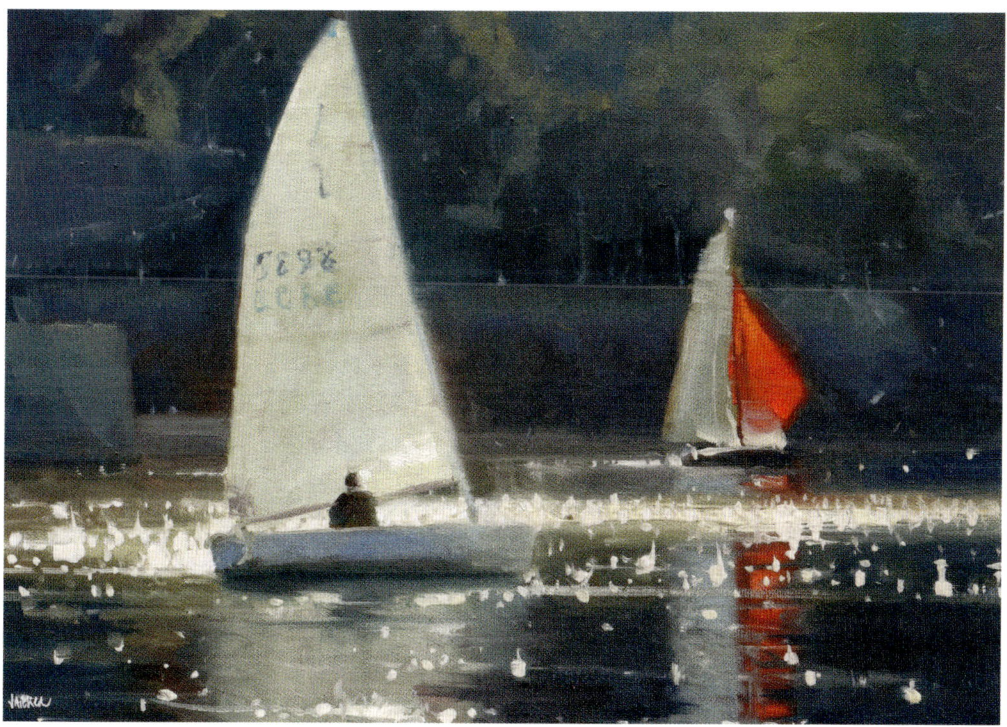

Boats really do have a lot of detail, and believe me, keen sailors are often happy to point out where you might have missed the odd cleat! For this particular painting, I stuck with basic shapes, angles and suggestion. Boating experts can happily use their imaginations to fill in the gaps, and the painting retains atmospheric light at its heart. It's win–win!

BRUSH LANGUAGE

'To see, we must forget the name of the things we are looking at.' **Claude Monet**

Birds are in a constant state of motion, always hyper-aware of their surroundings. Shore birds seem even more active to me, their legs almost comically blurry as they run along the tideline. I love painting these beautiful little creatures, and never want them to appear static on the canvas, so often treat them more loosely than my other work. Try drawing a bird without a reference. Compared to a horse, or a car (if you don't usually draw them!) a bird shape is relatively simple. As we know, however, this 'knowing what a thing looks like' is not always helpful! As soon as we lose concentration, it is easy to start drawing on perception rather than observation. It is all about getting those shapes and angles right, so you can be loose in every other way.

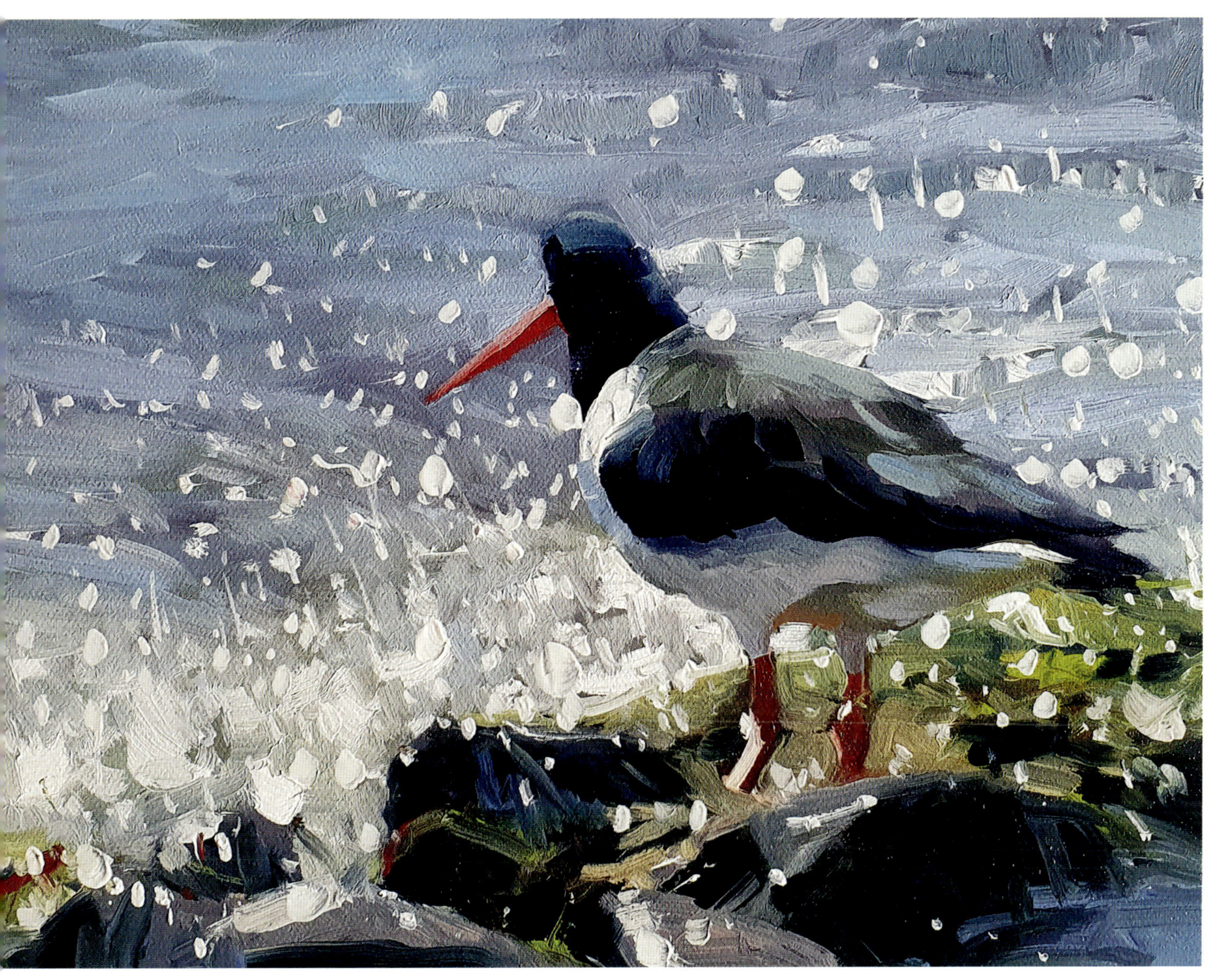

Splashy Oystercatcher

40 × 30cm (15¾ × 11¾in)

The direction of the brushstrokes tells us about the three-dimensional shape of the oystercatcher, while soft edges show movement. Here, I wanted a strong sense of a split-second moment: every aspect of the scene is energetic. The sea and rocks are almost abstract shapes, just as they appear at a quick glance in reality. I kept the brushwork on the bird minimal, but applied relatively heavy amounts of paint with each considered stroke. The springy shape of the 12mm (½in) flat brush helped to create pointed feathers.

LOST EDGES

I remember hearing the phrase 'lost and found edges' when I was at the beginning of my painting journey. It is an invaluable way of thinking about your painting. For those who haven't heard this saying, its basic meaning is to blur some areas – these are the lost edges – for better atmosphere and compositional flow. It helps focus the eye exactly where you want it.

In the painting below, the point of focus is the third bird on the right. You can see the feathers are detailed and developed, his beak bright and he is watching us. He could occupy that off-centre space on his own and the painting would still work. The other birds are compositional aids, bringing atmosphere and energy to the story. They're a backdrop for the main player. The right-hand bird is made from a few simple shapes, and part of his leg is lost. We don't need him to be more than this, as he is in our peripheral vision when we look at the main bird.

The way to do this is quite simple, in theory: establish the focal point, then regularly step back and consider your painting as you go. Don't aimlessly colour in or fill every 'messy' gap. Put neatness right out of your mind! That mess could be a revealed layer, adding contrast and life.

It can take quite a bit of self-control to leave a subject broken and unfinished. Hang on to the knowledge that it will bring life to your work! If you find yourself at the end of a painting with no strong focus, you can always 'lose' a few areas at the end with big brushwork, a knife, or a wipe.

Beachcombing   50 × 20cm (19¾ × 8in)

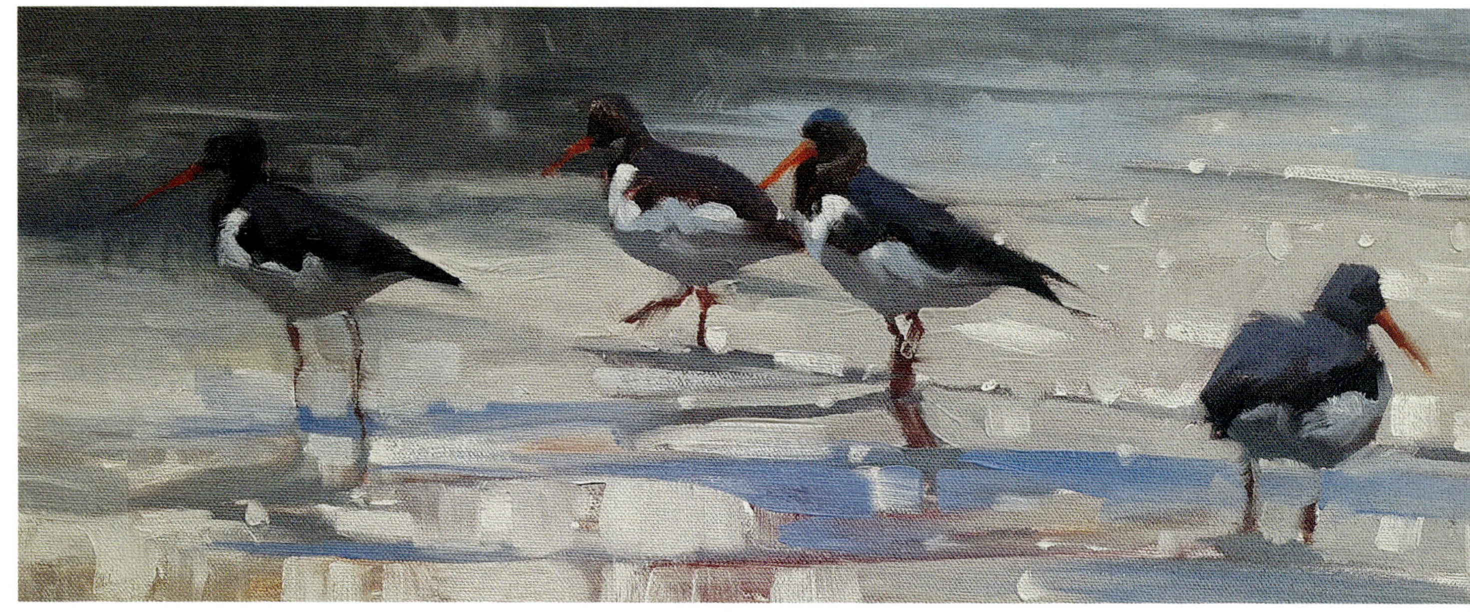

MAGIC STROKES

Simplicity of brushwork brings movement and life. With the right colours, a brushstroke in the right place will evoke a bird. A better brushstroke will describe both the physical nature of the creature and lighting. An excellent brushstroke will do all of this in a seemingly loose way, without fuss, bringing that essential sense of life and movement.

As mentioned at the beginning of this book, magic is only achieved by method, and looseness through discipline. My brushwork is never guided by emotive response – it is designed to look that way. Lighting and subject remain authentic, with the apparent freedom of brushwork representing atmosphere, movement and joyful life.

For me, birds are where economy of brushwork and awareness of shape really come to the fore. I stick to large flat brushes and a light touch, both for the birds and the negative space around them. Towards the end, I will use a rigger or small round for detail, but only as grace notes in the symphony of shape.

When cutting the background strokes into the bird, don't be afraid to break in a little. As long as the bird is convincing, this is the time to mess things up a touch and make those strokes look even more carefree than they were! A smudge here, a broken line there.

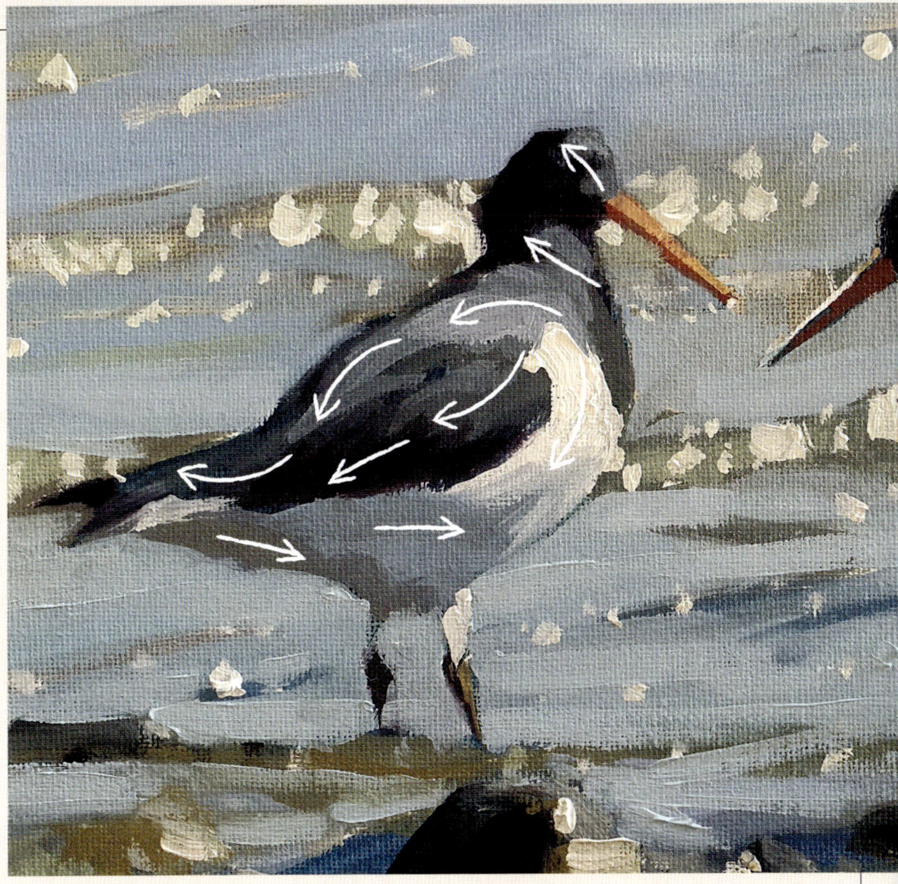

1. Reduce the bird to two-dimensional shapes. Study each part of the anatomy: head, neck, wings, back, tail, belly, breast, legs and beak. Observe where it is placed in the space. For example, viewed from the side, a bird's right shoulder is closer to us than its head.

2. Using a large brush (I used my trusty 12mm (½in) flat) lay bold strokes in the way the feathers appear to lie. Work dark to light and thin to thick.

3. Paint the beak with the shadow colour in the direction it is pointing, and then brush the lighter colour on top with opposing strokes: I use the sharp end of the flat. This gives it a three-dimensional feel.

4. The placement and visible angle of legs is important to the credibility of the bird's stance, but they can be relatively undefined. Paint them with a thin shadow colour, larger than they are, then cut the background in to shape them, retaining the general angle.

5. Finally, lay in the highlights.

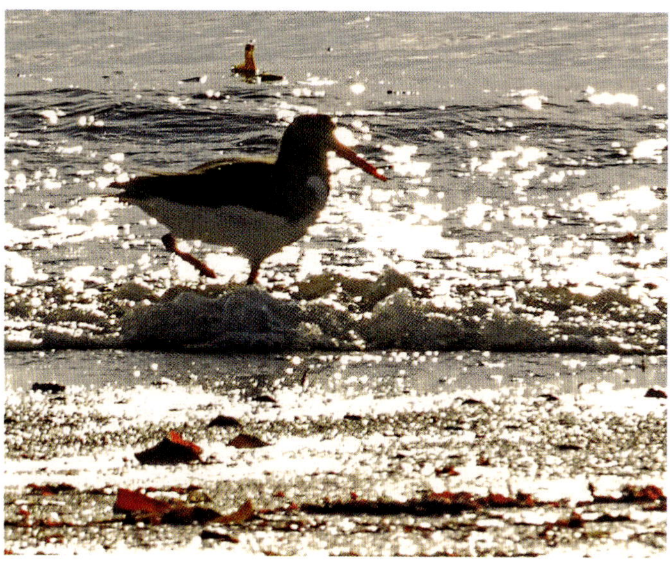

OYSTERCATCHER

Oystercatchers have always been my favourite – their scarlet beaks and legs glowing against the multiple blues, greens and greys of the sea. Their black and white feathers work especially well in *contre-jour* lighting, with enough contrast and definition to stand out against the sun.

This is one of the subjects I like to paint with the reference photograph upside-down through most of the process, as I find the results are always looser and stronger. Perhaps one day I'll be practised enough not to need this in the studio – I will just activate control over my mind's eye and force myself not to deviate! As it is, this is currently my best bet for vibrant, atmospheric bird paintings.

You will need

30 × 24cm (11¾ × 9½in) canvas board

Brushes: two 12mm (½in) flat, 6mm (¼in) round bristle, small rigger

Paints: titanium white, bright yellow lake, scarlet lake, deep purple, sap green, phthalo green, burnt umber

Low-odour solvent

FIRST STAGE

Before you start mixing and painting merrily away, turn the photograph upside down and take a good long look at the shapes of colour on the bird, and the shapes of the negative space around him. There are two important colours at this stage: the dark back and the grey tone of the bird's belly.

· Make a thin mix of burnt umber with phthalo green, with titanium white for the lighter tone. With an eye to the overall triangular shape of the bird (see below left), lay down your first marks with the face of a 12mm (½in) flat brush.

· Once the basic shape is in, use a brush handle to measure the angles. This simply means holding your brush up to the photograph and tilting it until two points are on the same line: the beak and the leg, the tail and the leg, whichever makes sense (see below right).

· Keeping your brush at that same angle, move it to your canvas and check that yours are similar.

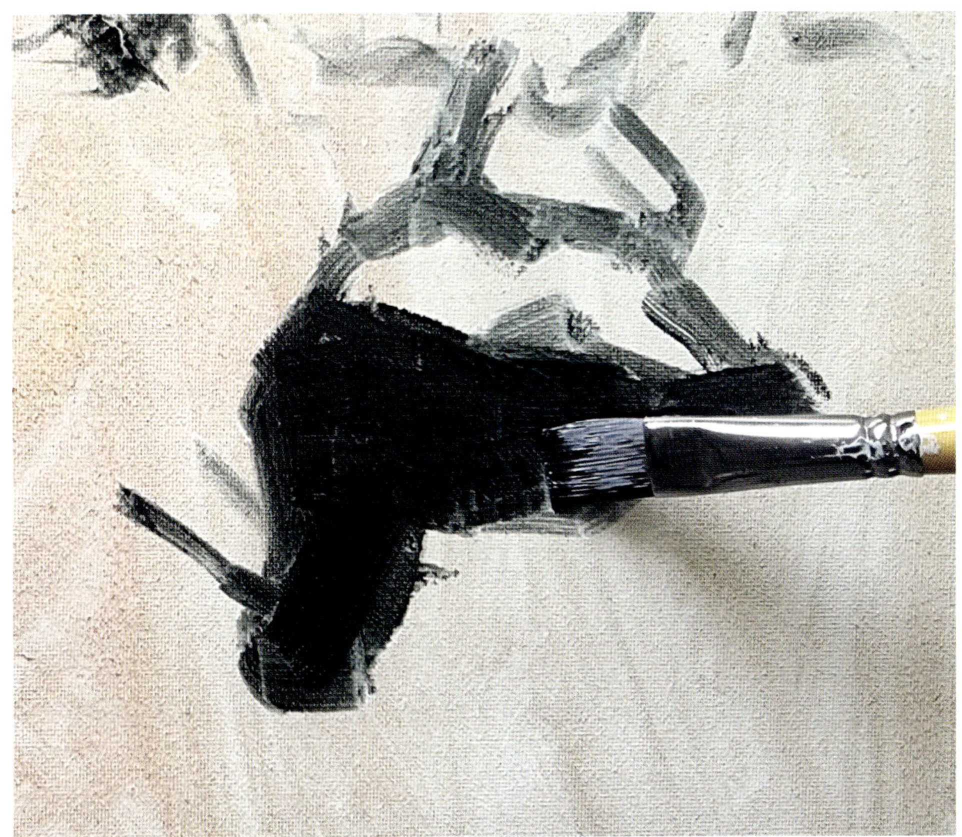

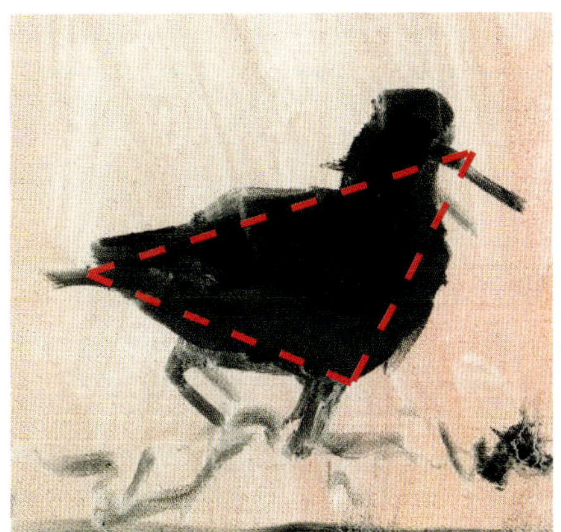

The angles between the head, tail and front leg.

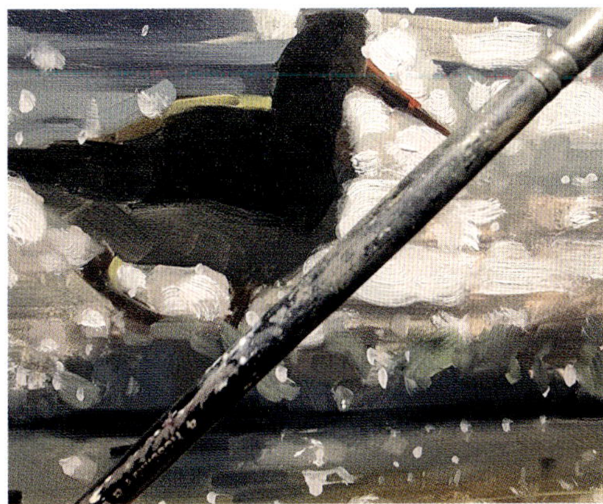

Checking the angle between the tip of the beak and the leg with a long brush.

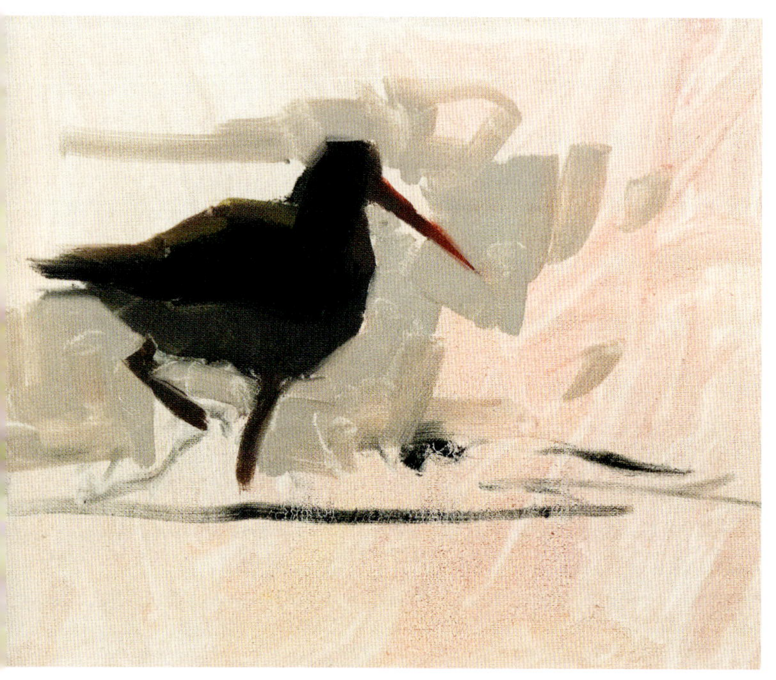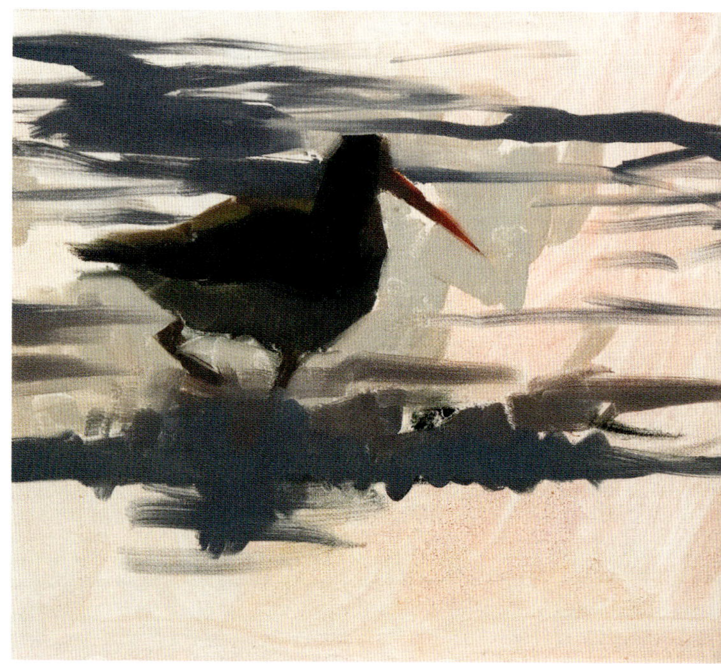

SECOND STAGE

As with painting figures (or indeed any object), I was overly generous with the size to make room for cutting in with the surrounding colour. I wasn't worried about the beak being too big or long, but what I do want to get right is the angle and where it starts from the head.

- Paint the beak with a 12mm (½in) flat brush. Use a scarlet lake, bright yellow lake and deep purple mix for the beak shadow, and a mix of scarlet lake and bright yellow lake for the saturated colour.
- Add some mustardy tones to the edges of the bird and for the legs, using a mix of sap green, scarlet lake, bright yellow lake and titanium white. As with the beak, work slightly oversized, but ensure the angles are correct.
- Once the bird is in place and you are happy with the angles, mix a neutral grey from titanium white, phthalo green and burnt umber and start cutting in. Keep this mix thin, as it is the base for forthcoming highlights.

THIRD STAGE

Here we start to build up the shoreline and sea with dynamic brushwork for an atmospheric setting: unfinished marks, suggestions and looser shapes without tidiness or too much description.

It's very tempting to fill in, join up and neaten as you go, risking turning the painting into bird illustrations – 'nice but dull', to my mind. Avoid the temptation!

- Continuing with the 12mm (½in) flat brush and both canvas and reference image upside down, put in some of the shadows in the water with cool, dark mixes of phthalo green combined with burnt umber and titanium white.
- Scrub in the foaming wavelet with a mind to the way it was moving, adding warmer highlights to the top.

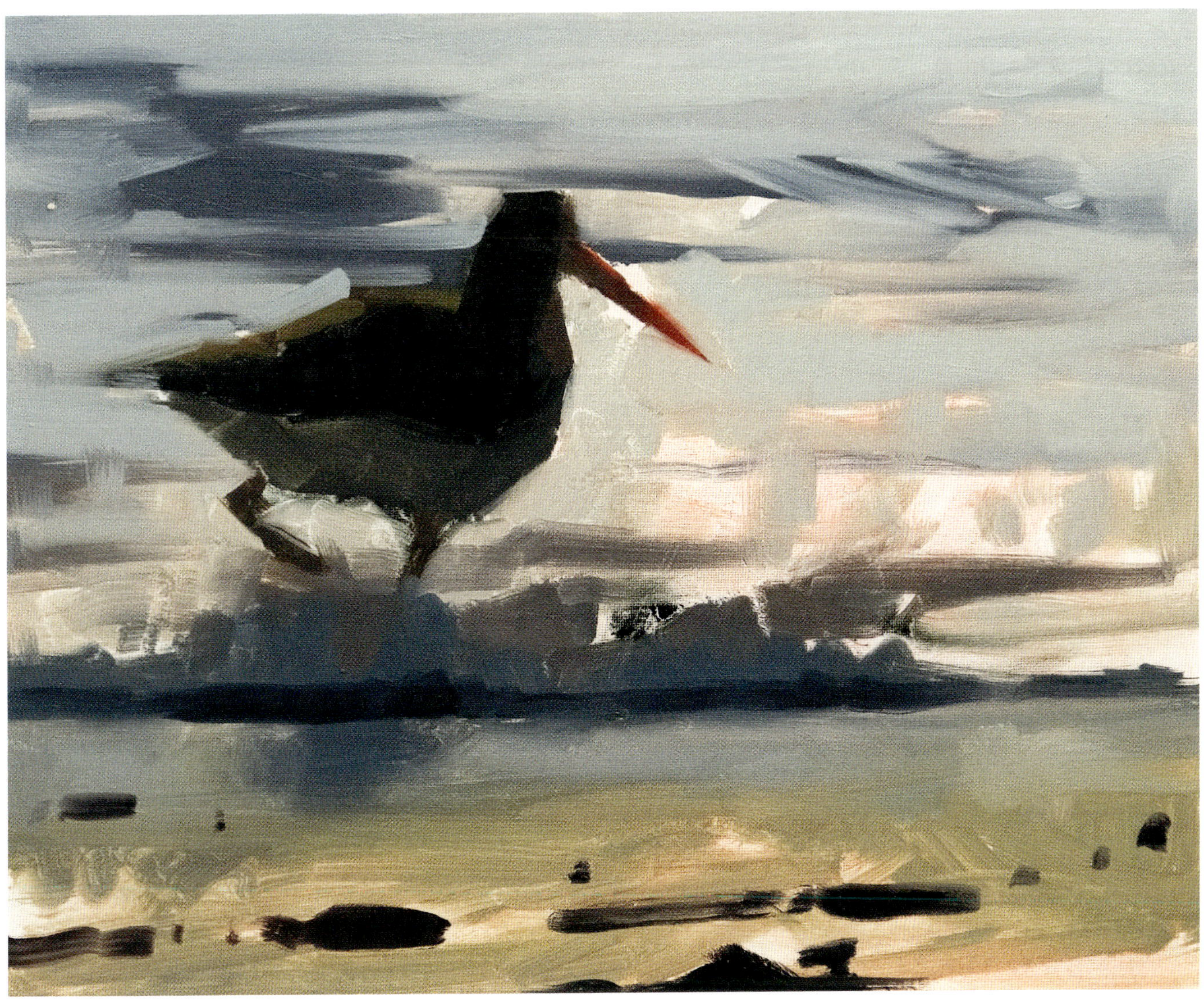

FOURTH STAGE

Here we add the reflective sea, thin but opaque.

The pinky, transparent base formed a lovely contrast with the grey sea surface, which I wanted to retain if at all possible. I just had to curb my desire to fill everything in!

- Still using the 12mm (½in) flat brush, start to add the sea using more of the neutral grey (titanium white with phthalo green and burnt umber).
- Add notes of bright yellow lake in the background, and warm burnt umber on the shore. As ever, check your mixes against the original image, looking to match the temperature and saturation.
- Thicken the darkest notes on the bird and add a few shadows to the foreground and the wave using the mixes on your palette.

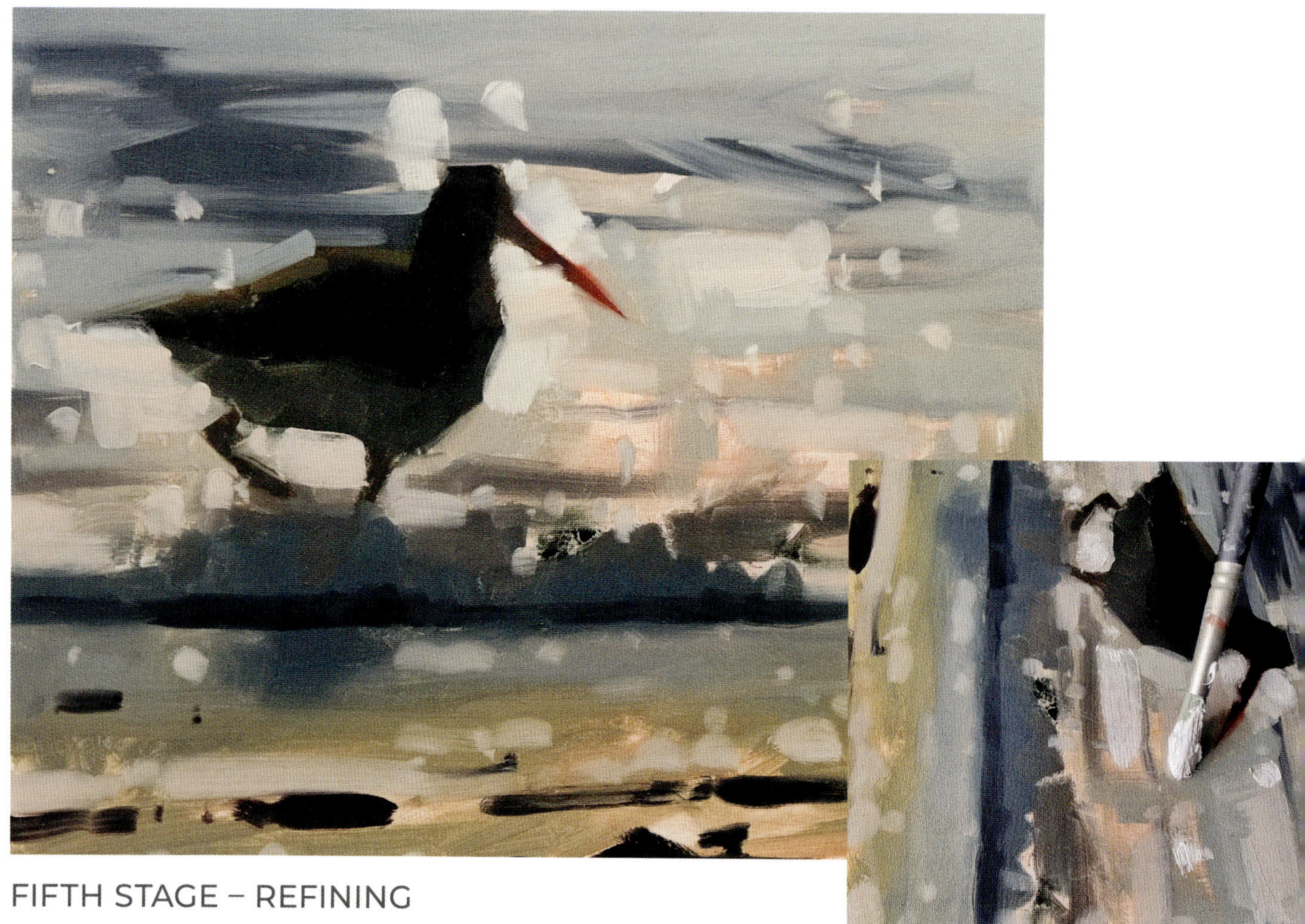

FIFTH STAGE – REFINING

Onto the thicker paint for refining and adding the highlights – and at last, a change of brush! After splodging on the white sparkles everywhere with the bristle brush, we can sit back and judge what is needed to finish off the painting. Often at this point I need to thicken any darks as a contrast to the bright lights, and swap to the rigger.

As soon as this brush comes out, it's tempting to get fiddly, resulting in an unwanted change in style and feel. Here, I ended up needing to re-do the beak as a result of over-fiddling with the rigger. Watch out for the tendency!

· Using a clean 12mm (½in) flat, mix titanium white with scarlet lake, bright yellow lake and a touch of burnt umber to keep the contrast soft. This colour will be the glow around the brightest lights. Cut it in around the bird, adding a few blobs and rectangles around and about. Not too many – just enough.

· Load your 6mm (¼in) round bristle brush with titanium white tinted with scarlet lake. This brush lets paint go beautifully onto the painting, and even if it moves the layer beneath, it will still have the desired effect of light (see detail – note I have turned the painting upside down to help paint this light intuitively, as explained on page 55). Twirl on some round shapes for chunky sparkles.

· I added some colour to the shadows in the foreground, and a little greenish lighting to the wave.

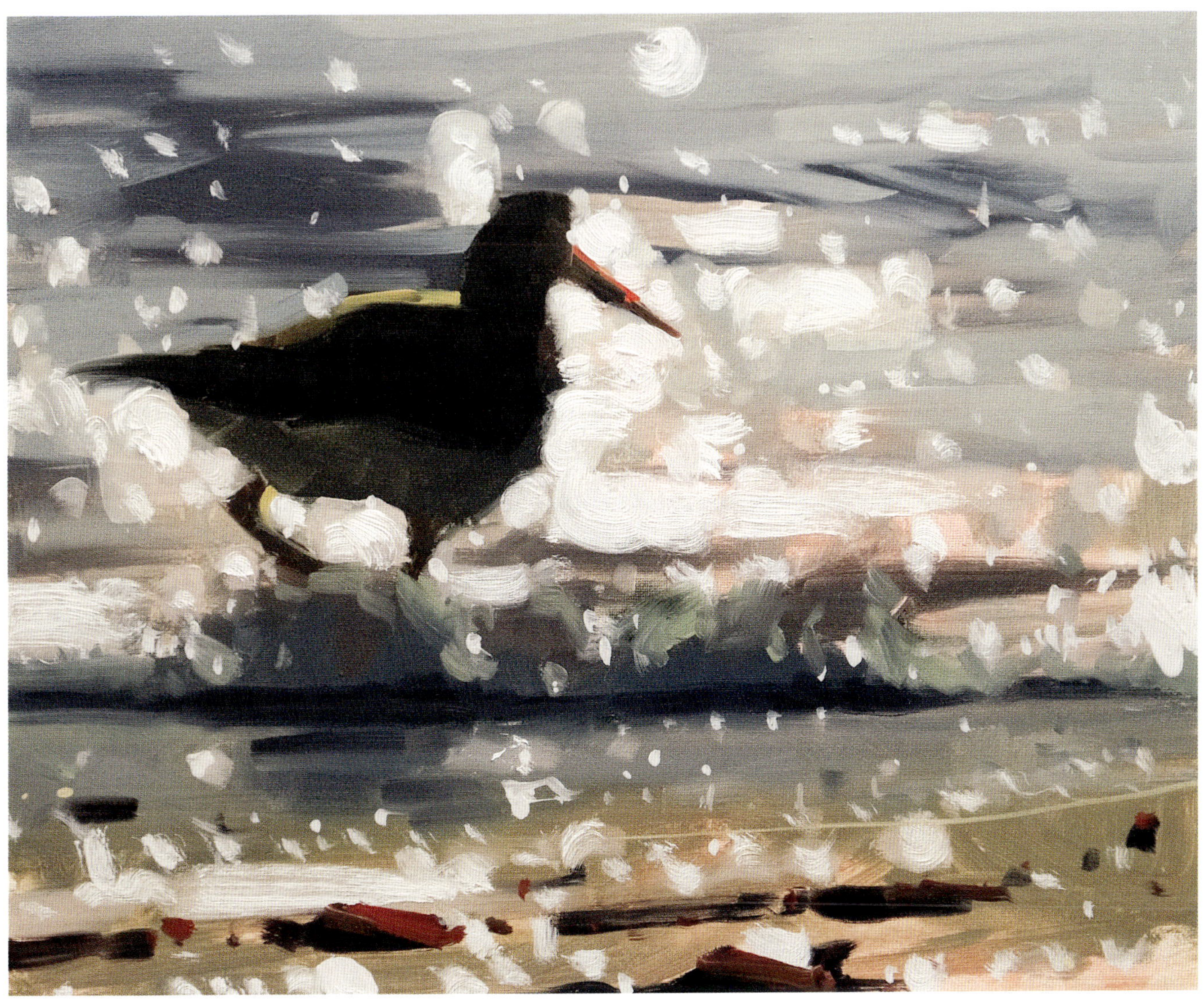

The finished painting

Once you near the end of a painting, slow down, step back, evaluate: what is really needed? I felt the atmosphere was lacking in a few smaller marks, so I got my rigger and added some splashy light. I also used it to lay on some gold highlights on the bird's back and leg.

Within reason, try to keep the same energy flowing through your brushwork – all the way through the painting.

SKIES AND CLOUDS: INSUBSTANTIAL SHAPES

By this point in the book, I hope I've drummed it into you that everything is just colour and shapes. Nowhere is this more true than for clouds – an essential part of almost every subject – although they come with a funny little caveat. Remember our ability to turn shapes into faces? When painting clouds, we need to avoid creating any eye-catching, familiar shapes. Everyone loves spotting animals in the sky – and there have been times that I've painted mighty cumulus skies, only to have my partner point out the sky dolphin dominating the view!

It is the old argument of whether to paint exactly what is in your photograph, or to edit. I would suggest that softening that dolphin shape in the clouds will mean that the intended message of your painting comes through that bit better.

In terms of brushwork, as the nature of clouds is effectively texture-free, using directional strokes and good composition will be key to defining the focal point. Think of it as subtly brushing the eye in towards your focal point. At the risk of sounding like a broken record: don't draw the clouds, paint them. Whatever brush you use, make your paint application sensitive to their nature and movement.

'Some painters transform the sun into a yellow spot, others transform a yellow spot into the sun.'
Pablo Picasso

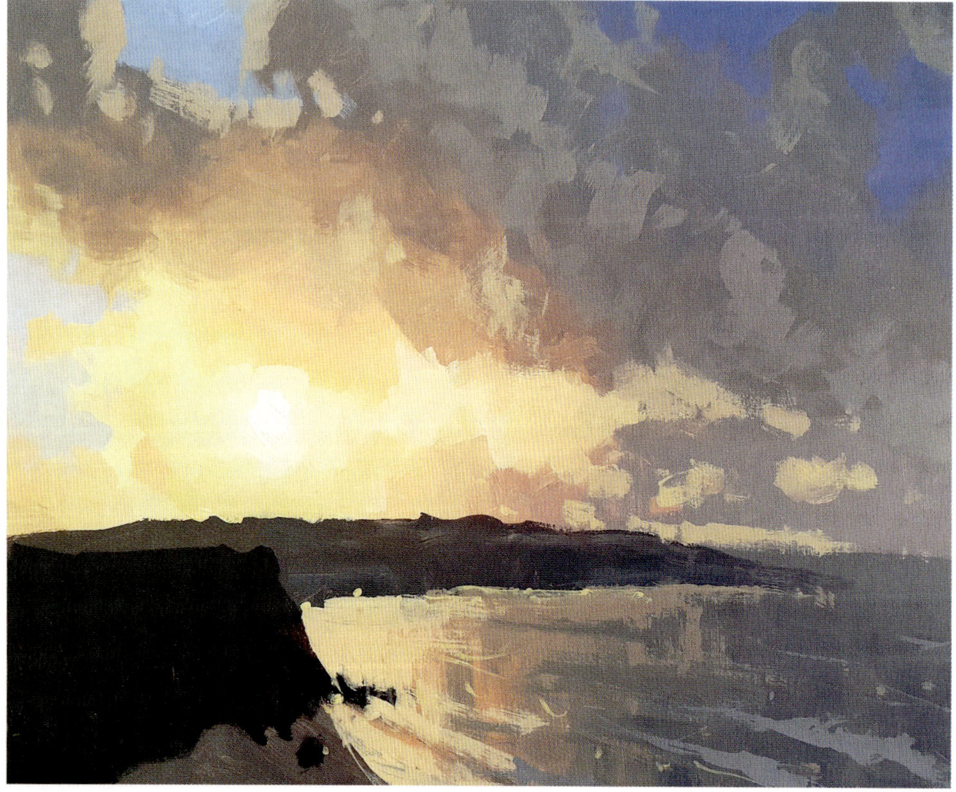

If the point of interest in your clouds scene is a sunset, remember to work outwards from the sun with your colours. Start light and warm near the sun, deepening then desaturating and cooling as you get further out.

The blue sky nearest the sun will not be blue – try to match the colour that is actually there. I find a touch of purple, yellow and white is often the right mix for this area of clear sky.

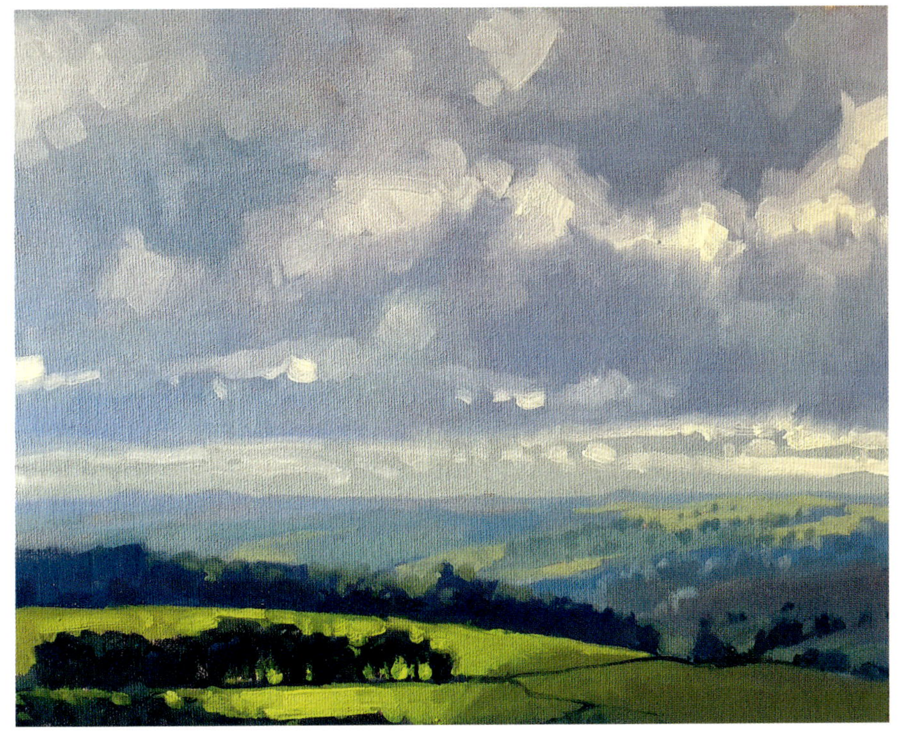

On blustery, cloudy days, that contre-jour light can be at its most dramatic. One of my favourite subjects is the broken light in scudding clouds, patchily illuminating the landscape. When light falls in shafts like this, don't just add white; mix the actual colours you see within the light shaft. Equally, don't paint them with the brush direction of the angle they are falling; this will look like a substance, rather than light. Just softly paint the colours you see in the same way as any of the other clouds.

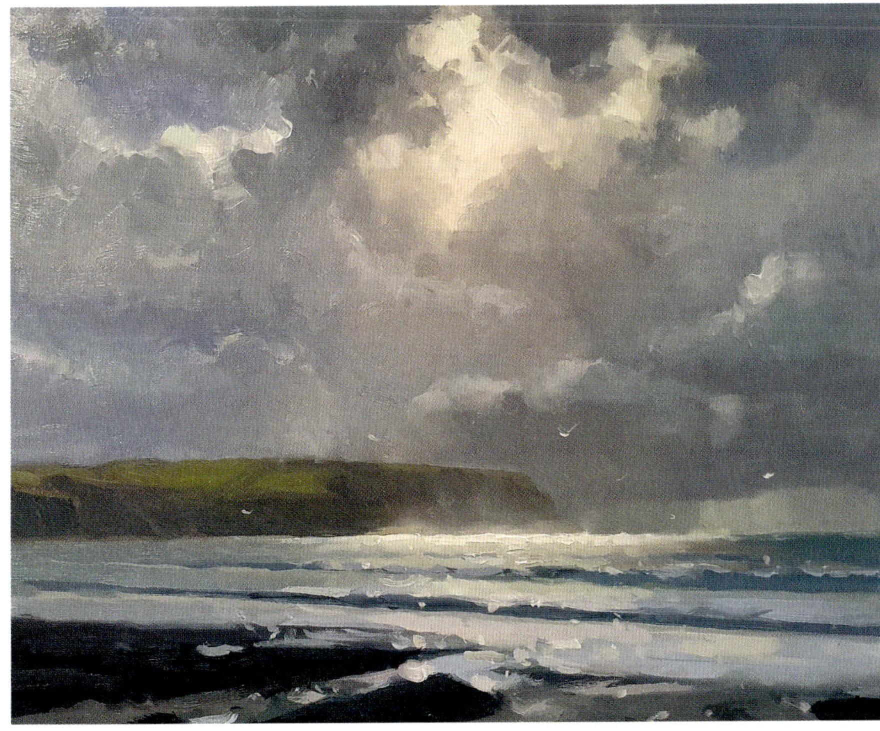

As artists, remember, we can leave reality behind as much as we like. In this view of the emerging sun over the sea, I have used much artistic licence and made the clouds around the sun considerably warmer than they were in real life. I have also increased the contrast in lighting and the saturation levels in order to add impact and a little bit of dream-like fantasy.

AFTERWORD

It has been fascinating to set down my processes here for you, all in one place. At every turn it has prompted the question: why do I do things the way that I do?

Each of my artistic decisions has a reason; every stroke and colour a purpose. The illusion of light requires a symphony of elements working perfectly together. This could be seen as extremely controlling – except that one of those vital balances is between control and chaos!

More important than control in oil painting is *awareness*, and this word is what I would like you to take away most of all. Notice colours. Hunt for contrasts. Watch how things move, grow and fade. Open your eyes – and your mind's eye – to what you are seeing, both on the canvas and, more importantly, in the world around you. Some call this mindfulness; I think of it as having my senses turned up to the maximum in as many moments as possible. Breathe in the landscape, bask in the lighting; soak up every inspiring visual moment that you can. All of it will go into your vast mental library and there is no doubt that this will benefit your painting journey more than any book could hope to do!

After much soul searching, I found the answer to my question above: I strive to communicate the beauty I see, in this brief life, in the hope that you and I will find connection in a shared way of seeing.

Thank you for reading, and happy painting!

Jenny

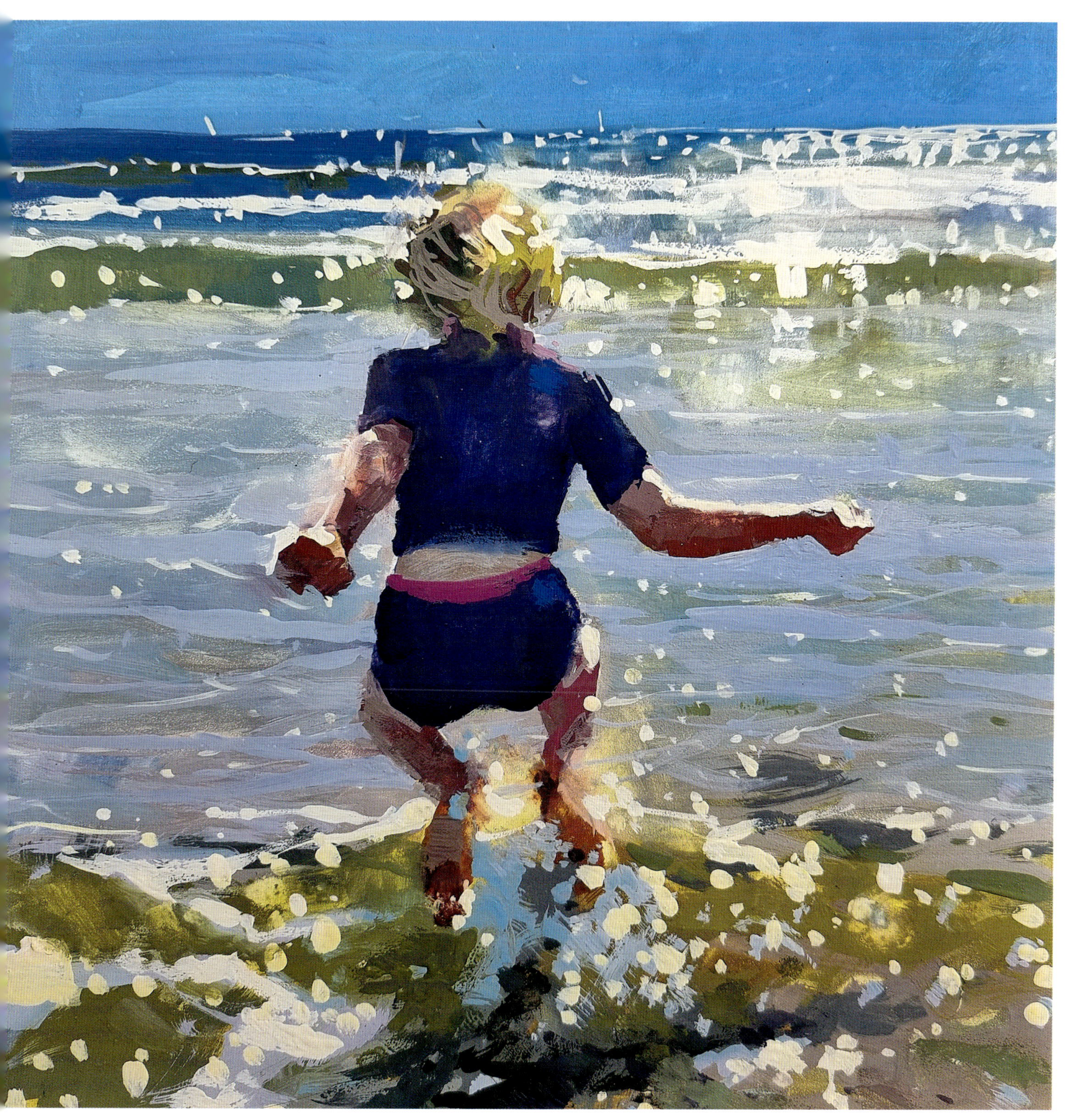

Lola in the Waves

30 × 30cm (11¾ × 11¾in) canvas

INDEX

First published in 2024

Search Press Limited, Wellwood, North Farm Road, Tunbridge Wells, Kent TN2 3DR

Reprinted 2024, 2025

Illustrations and text copyright © Jenny Aitken 2024

Photographs by Jenny Aitken, except for pages 13, 17, 19, 20, and 22–25, by Mark Davison at Search Press studios and on location

Photographs and design copyright © Search Press Ltd 2024

ISBN: 978-1-80092-127-6
ebook ISBN: 978-1-80093-117-6

Publishers' note
The Publishers and author can accept no responsibility for any consequences arising from the information, advice or instructions given in this publication.

No use of the artwork for commercial purposes is permitted without the prior permission of both artist and Publishers. Readers are permitted to reproduce or copy the paintings in this book only for private and personal study/practice.

Suppliers
If you have difficulty in obtaining any of the materials and equipment mentioned in this book, then please visit the Search Press website for details of suppliers: www.searchpress.com

You are invited to visit the author's website at: www.jennyaitken.co.uk

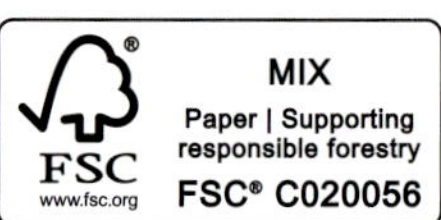